NOTHING BUT
THE BEST

NOTHING BUT THE BEST

Making Day Care Work for You and Your Child

DIANE LUSK and BRUCE McPHERSON

QUILL
WILLIAM MORROW
New York

It is the policy of William Morrow and Company, Inc., and its imprints and affiliates, recognizing the importance of preserving what has been written, to print the books we publish on acid-free paper, and we exert our best efforts to that end.

Library of Congress Cataloging-in-Publication Data

Lusk, Diane.
    Nothing but the best: making day care work for you and your child
        p. cm.
    Includes index.
    ISBN 0-688-09547-X
    1. Day care centers—United States. 2. Child care—United States.
    I. McPherson, Bruce. II. Title.
    HV854.L78   1992
    362.7′12′0973—dc20   92-12887
                                                         CIP

Printed in the United States of America

First Quill Edition

1 2 3 4 5 6 7 8 9 10

BOOK DESIGN BY BERNARD SCHLEIFER

for Dorothy and Ewing Lusk

Acknowledgments

I WANT TO THANK my own parents, Dorothy and Ewing Lusk, first of all. Their generous financial support and consistent encouragement made this book possible.

The parents and staff of Harvard Yard Child Care Center (1975–1988) inspired and informed this book; it is in many ways a summary of what they taught me. I particularly wish to thank some of its exceptionally talented leaders: Ronnie Littenberg, Libby Zimmerman, John Hildebidle, Cathey Cyrus, Ted Scott, and Dianne Perlmutter. These wise and kind people enlightened my directing work and created the faith in cooperative effort which is the heart of this book.

The parents and staff of Meeting House Child Care Center showed me new possibilities for the best in day care, and refreshed me through the long revising process.

Jerome Kagan and Marshall Haith taught me science at its best: enough reverence to understand the difficulty and nature of proof, enough irreverence to keep the process lively and amazing. Their commitment to interdisciplinary study and their appreciation of the role mental development plays in emotional life continues to assist my own understanding.

Some good friends helped get the book written. Nancy Powell gave several chapters a kind and careful editing, and wrote "Yes!" in the margins when I really needed it. Dennis Chinoy provided key insights about tone and structure, and some wonderful general enthusiasm. Janet Seely gave generously of sounding-board time for ideas, and offered her own fresh and useful views of parenting and day care. Katherine Kates contributed the inspiration of her own beautiful writing about children, and many long and heartening conversations about the process of writing. Ronnie Littenberg read through several versions of every chapter, listened to several versions of every idea, and gently helped me find the way through them all; she is a continuing and cherished source of light, sense, and courage.

Both directly and indirectly, the encouragement of Joan Berlin is significantly responsible for this book. Her respect for things human has been a touchstone for me and my work; her faith in me steadied and warmed this writing.

I have the great good fortune to be married to a fine man who was also a day-care teacher and is now director at The Harvard Law School Child Care Center. Gary Yablick supplied perfect examples on demand, helped me see the important parts of ideas which I had despaired of untangling, and inspired new, clearer ideas when I thought I'd never even have an old rusty one again. He also cheered "Go get 'em, tiger!" too many times to count. Thanks, Gar.

Contents

Introduction

THIS IS NOT A BOOK about how to choose day care; it's about how to live with it. This is not a book about how to manage everything perfectly; it is a book of possibilities: what might be true of your child or your day-care teacher, what might be worth trying when you want to make things better. "Nothing but the best" is what we want for our children every single second but too rarely feel sure we can provide. *Nothing but the Best* offers some paths to peace of mind.

Working parents have the same child-raising questions all parents have: Is my child eating right? Sleeping right? Am I encouraging learning the right way? Where is this weird mood coming from? Is this behavior *normal*? Using day care sometimes makes answering these questions easier; sometimes it makes everything more complicated. Using day care raises questions of its own: What do tears at good-byes mean? Why is my child "busy" at pickup time? Those other children—are they good company? What do you do about fighting? Is this teacher doing a good job? What can I say to teachers to make things go better?

Whole chapters here are devoted to most of these questions. "Is it normal?" and "What can I say to teachers?" are discussed regularly in each chapter. Chapter 1, "Arriving," looks at the difficulties of getting to day care in a good mood and talking to teachers in the morning. Chapter 2 explores "separation" as a technique and as an issue in the whole parent-child relationship. Chapter 3, "Bodies," tackles eating, sleeping, and toilet training. Questions about early learning and curriculum in general, and school-readiness in particular, are addressed in Chapter 4. Chapter 5 opens up the world of children's social life at day care, its chemistry, the skills involved; Chapter 6 focuses on fighting issues for "victims" and "villains." Chapter 7 explores some ways adults can understand and help deal with children's feelings. "Picking Up," Chapter 8, discusses getting news from teachers and getting out of the building with minimal grief. Chapter 9, "Changing," explores children's reactions to all kinds of changes and offers ideas for making decisions when you're thinking about changing day-care arrangements. Chapter 10 reviews problem-solving with teachers in general.

Most chapters treat two main topics. For example, "Separating" looks at technique and relationships; "Social Life" looks at chemistry and skills. If you don't find what you're looking for in the first part of a chapter, look farther on. Within each main topic in a chapter, you can find four special-interest sections. (Working parents sometimes have only two minutes to read at a stretch; this book was organized with that problem in mind.) They are:

- *Find the Questions:* descriptions of the different ways other parents have thought and felt about each issue, with ideas for raising the issue with teachers.
- *Developmental Issues:* descriptions of the ways children's interests and understanding at different ages affect their reactions to a situation, with ideas for help geared to each age. There are separate sections for infants, toddlers, and preschoolers.
- *Parent-Teacher Talk:* descriptions of the ways discussions with teachers most often get bogged down, with ideas for getting conversations unstuck.
- *Things to Try:* lists of approaches you can try or suggest to teachers to solve a particular problem or make living with it easier.

These descriptions and ideas come from my own fifteen years of teaching, directing, and consulting work in day care, from eight years of graduate study in child development, and from twelve years of parenting (not in that order and only two at a time). Most of them also come from a special experience that brought light—and voice!—to the parents-and-day-care world.

In the spring of 1971, a small group of parents lobbied Harvard University for space in the basement of its Memorial Church to use as a day-care center. These parents formed a cooperative. Parents worked beside hired teachers as co-teachers, partly to save money and partly to stay close to their children's daytime lives, since academic schedules made that possible.

Parents governed the center in monthly meetings. The questions were different back then. In one early meeting, the main topic was nudity: Why wasn't there *more* of it at the center? (Side 1: Young children shouldn't be taught to be ashamed of their bodies or taught to hide them; they should be Natural as long as possible. Side 2: Maybe . . . but *not* in the middle of Cambridge!) It was a different age.

An old ROTC building fell vacant; parents lobbied for permission to use it. They had to band flyers to trees: "Don't bomb the ROTC building! Our children are there!" Now there was room to grow. Over the next ten years, the center grew from ten to sixty families. Committees and policies and bylaws multiplied. Through it all, parents kept control—making the policies, hiring the staff, coming to each other and teachers with anything that wasn't right. They also slaved, carving from bare khaki walls and an empty drill yard a child's world of bright spaces for play.

Parents struggled to put names to all the pieces of good child care and to figure out how to make them happen. They tackled everything—from whether to add a kindergarten or another infant room and what to look for in new teachers to how to get better news of their children at the end of the day and when the toddlers should eat snacks. Teachers worked in a goldfish bowl, constantly surrounded by parents doing their co-op teaching time, constantly questioned on the who-what-where-when-why of every choice. Everyone complained of the time and energy this system took, all the talk and challenge. New parents and teachers could barely believe all the extra hours required and all the meetings, but soon doing things any other way seemed impossible: How else could parents and teachers make the best world for children?

I joined this group of parents and teachers in 1974 as a graduate-student volunteer, taking a break from the dry stuff to learn what a real, whole child was like. I fell in love and stayed for the next thirteen years: five as a teacher, eight as director. When my daughter arrived, I took my turn learning what it's like to be a working parent using day care.

"You ought to write a book." Every time I put a letter about children in his parent mailbox at the center—which happens often in a co-op—Bruce McPherson stopped by the office, encouraging. He'd published his own books on education; he knew good and bad day care from personal experience; he cared about getting out the word: Day care can be great! Through two years of meetings, we thrashed out the shape of the book and found a publisher. Other duties claimed Bruce's energies; I stopped directing for a while and finished what we had begun.

So the ideas here are not just my ideas but ideas from more than two hundred parents and more than fifty teachers. Co-ops are great places for ideas. Parents learn what the inside of day care is like; they can see what happens when you have to balance one child's needs with group needs. They come up with good, workable ideas for things to try. Teachers learn from parents what the inside of loving one child is like; they come up with more ways to keep each child central and all children well. Working together—in any day-care arrangement—parents and teachers not only get *more* ideas, they get *better* ones.

Eight years of graduate study in child development are also part of what's here for you. Science has a lot to offer parents in some ways: It turns up interesting developments to watch for and enjoy; it protects us from putting too much faith in any one point of view. It shows us we don't *have* to listen to our mothers or our neighbors or the latest study in the newspaper. Almost all the do's and dont's about children others have tried to foist on parents melt into myths under the bright lights of careful study. Experts disagree, for good reasons. As a graduate student, I found this somewhat depressing: Oh no! Children are too complicated! We'll never really understand how they work! As a teacher, director, and parent, I have appreciated the freedom. We need to find out what works in real situations for real children, and we *can* start fresh.

Good science is mainly a *method* of finding things out, and a certain attitude toward the natural world: innocent until proven guilty, mysterious until carefully observed. You figure out what you ought to look at and then *go see*. If you have an idea about what ought to work, you try it and see what happens. You'll find some skepticism here about particular "expert" views of children; you'll also find constant invitations to be your own good scientist: try something, see what happens, and take it from there.

Study and day-care experience alone, however, would have created a different book. It's one thing to read about the "emergence of the individual" in a two-year-old; another thing to sing catchy songs while getting a whole group of two-year-olds ready to go outside—and another thing still to stand by the front door, late again, trying not to yell when your own little emerging individual absolutely won't put that jacket on. I learned why it's so easy to forget to bring boots and so hard to talk calmly about the child you love. Parenting brings up so many loud and wordless things.

Maybe someday the United States will welcome its children with real support for parents backed by real tax dollars, and day-care choices won't be so hard to make, so expensive, so uncertain; but in this country today the burden of getting the best for children falls almost entirely on individual families. The nation as a whole does not support families through funds for child-care centers, through parental-leave policies, or through caregiver-training programs, as many other countries do. More than most other parents in the industrialized world, we're on our own. Many parents in nonindustrialized nations have it easier, too, either because their work is close to home and children can come to the workplace, or because families are larger and stronger: A whole big circle of adults provides help with child-raising, for free.

Day care can make getting the best for your child much easier or much harder. In the "harder" version, day care can mean that other people shape your child's daytime life, and you have to struggle through their personalities and policies to influence it—when you're already tired. In the "easier" version, day care replaces some of what industrialization has cost parents: It gives us back a circle of caring adults, a whole, safe, child-welcoming world. It gives children more buddies and toys and ways of learning things than home could possibly provide. In the "easier" version, day care means your teachers have good ideas when you run out; it means the company of other parents whose ideas, information, understanding, and funny stories can enrich your own. Parenting, and growing up, can still be tough, but it's not so lonely. *Nothing but the Best* was written with the hope of helping you make *your* day-care experience an easier version.

1

Arriving:
3-2-1 Contact

Ben insisted on eggs this morning and then ate only two bites. He goofed around with his cars when he was supposed to be getting out of his PJs; he whined at Laurie the whole time she dressed him; he threw a tantrum about his jacket—"Me do it!"—then wouldn't put it on. She had to carry him kicking to the car. The traffic was terrible.

Stepping into the toddler room, Laurie fights the urge to throw all Ben's stupid bags of stuff onto the rug and flee. She gets a grip and doles out coat, blanket, lunchbox, and extra clothes in their assigned places. When she opens the fridge to unpack his milk bottles, it's crammed full. That's it. She snaps to the nearest teacher, "Why don't you just get a new refrigerator? This one's a joke." When the startled teacher opens her mouth to respond, Laurie plops Ben's bottles onto a table and blurts out, "Will you—please—do something with these?," then swerves away to say good-bye to Ben, who will, of course, throw another tantrum.

WE WANT MORNINGS THAT launch us and our children into our days with some upbeat energy; we want morning contact with teachers to be effective and pleasant. Yet all too often, our mornings leave us in no mood for anything but murder or sleep. This chapter looks at the first challenges of the workday: getting to day care in a decent mood and communicating with teachers. Are there ways to make things easier?

Getting There: Finding the Questions

- "Now we just bring the bagels to the car. The car is gross, but the yelling is over—so who cares?"
- "I used to get her fed and clean and dressed and then get myself ready, bags collected, coat on, keys out, only to find an incredible diaper waiting for me. We'd have to start all over. Now dressing her is the last thing I do."
- "We just said, 'You can't watch *Teenage Mutant Ninja Turtles* until you're dressed,' and now we aren't nagging anymore."
- "I've just discovered making lunches the night before! . . . It only took me two years. Our mornings are *so* much better."

Many parents feel as if they've put in a full workday by the time they get to day care. When they find a change that lightens the load, they're often shocked by the difference it makes, especially at day care: "It's so much easier to leave her now! I hated leaving when we'd fought all morning." Shaking their heads, these parents wonder, "What took me so long?" Coming up with the idea usually wasn't the hard part; many success stories turn on simple ideas. Getting free to *try* a change was the real breakthrough. What keeps us from trying new ideas?

Heavy Downtown Traffic Sometimes the sheer *number* of morning chores and frustrations is mind-numbing. On top of the basic treadmill—"Get 'em up, get 'em dressed, get 'em fed"—there's the fact that small children generally find ten things to do *wrong* in any five-minute period—fight, spill, whine, bump themselves on the head while jumping on the bed when they were supposed to be getting dressed. Changing all of this looks impossible, and changing just one thing—well, wouldn't that be pointless? Parents who've found a change that works would encourage you: One success *can* turn the whole feel of the morning around. "When I finally sat down and really showed her how to get a shirt on by herself, it changed everything. We have this working-together spirit now"; "This sounds dumb, but discovering whole-wheat frozen waffles saved our lives."

Toll Roads Ideas about what Parents Ought to Do sometimes get in parents' way. The bagels-in-the-car mother struggled with breakfast for months. She believed parents ought to feed their children at home in cozy kitchens. The no-food-in-pajamas parent waited ages for patience and firmness about dressing to pay off—she believed parents ought to avoid using food as a reward. Many beliefs about what we *ought* to be doing make sense by themselves; the problem comes in their hidden costs. Sometimes we *can't* have it all; we can't be Cozy Kitchen Feeders *and* Perfectly Patient Parents. We have to choose. If you're stuck in miserable mornings, check out your Ought-to's. Is there one you could live without for a while? What are the real trade-offs?

Rude Drivers Laying out the practical choices frees some parents from another common obstacle to change: the dread of feeling mean. The inventors of the "no TV till you're dressed" rule desperately wanted to avoid anything *like* this kind of rule. They wanted mornings to be a nice, friendly family time; "Do this or else" was out of place. Gradually, however, it became clear: Having a completely friendly morning *and* getting the boy dressed was not in the cards. The real options were be "mean" for ten minutes or nag for an hour.

Roadblocks When there are two parents, there are almost always two opinions, and who has the time or energy to work them all out? Some parents break through disagreement roadblocks by holding short, "results-oriented" planning meetings after children go to bed (ten face-to-face minutes sometimes accomplish what hours of over-the-shoulder comments cannot). Some parents take turns being "in charge" of the mornings, or take turns trying each other's ideas. Disagreements like "Dress her first and get it over with" versus "Feed her first so she's in a better mood" lend themselves to turn-taking; others might need boiling down first. (See "Goal Refining," Chapter 4, page 142.)

New Route/No Map Taking a chance on any idea for a change leaves you open to comments like "I told you it wouldn't help!" and "But you promised!" Discouraging prospects. Setting up a tryout time can free you to backtrack: "Let's just try this for a week and see if we want to keep going." You have a right to experiment, and that includes a right to guess wrong. Children and mornings are just too complicated to tell what will work and what won't ahead of time.

Adjusting the Driver's Seat Is there anything you could do for *yourself*, to protect your patience supply a little? A Danish instead of bran flakes? Promising yourself a cup of coffee and ten minutes with a newspaper *between* day care and work? Your comfort in the driver's seat makes a smoother ride for everyone.

When your mornings get miserable, ask yourself, "What one small change could I try?" Try it, and see what happens. You might set yourself and your child up for easier days without too much strain and without having to ask, "What took me so long?"

Getting There: Developmental Issues
INFANTS

Eeeeeeee! The kettle is screaming in the kitchen, and the mirror screams at Cathy to find a brush, but if she leaves Brian for a minute, *he'll* scream. Lugging him from room to room while she handles hot water and hairbrushes makes them both nervous wrecks. Should she just let him cry? Why is he so insecure?

Babies were originally designed to cling to hairy parents and to live in small forest clearings surrounded by ape aunts and uncles. Having a built-in alarm signal for the condition of "no-adult-nearby" kept them from being eaten for thousands of years. Twentieth-century parents have lost the hair, but twentieth-century babies still have the alarm system—they cry if you get too far away. If another adult cannot hang around with your baby while you run around, you may have to make a lot of decisions about lugging versus crying in the morning. You can cut down on some of this wear and tear by using some

TACTICS FOR THE "STAY PUT!" STAGES

- *The Play Cycle:* Some infants play-eat-sleep, some eat-play-sleep; most tolerate parents' eating and dressing better during the play part of the cycle. If this means dressing yourself *before* feeding your child, take cover—a summer robe you can wear backward?
- *Play Breaks or Snuggles Breaks:* Break up rush-around periods with five minutes of play or snuggling to restore basic calm.
- *A Home Base:* Use one room for dressing yourself and your baby.
- *Baby-movers:* Use backpacks, car seats, or strollers to move your baby with you from room to room.

- *Voice Contact:* Talk steadily to your baby when you have to be out of close range. Soothing or lighthearted tones of voice may not come naturally in the morning rush but usually help the most, and with infants you can *say* any old insane thing you want to.

However you manage your awkward choices around carrying versus crying, at least let yourself off the hook about the alarm signal. Your baby is not too sensitive or insecure, and you don't have to worry about "spoiling." Nature arranged the scene a long time ago; you just have to get through the phase.

TODDLERS

PAUL: "It's *cold* out, honey. You *need* to wear mittens."
BECKY: "No!"
PAUL: "Would you like to put them on yourself?"
BECKY: "No!"
PAUL: "Look. Just till we get to the car and it's warm."
BECKY: "No! No mittens!"
PAUL: "It's too cold not to wear mittens. Your hands will freeze. You *have* to wear them."
Becky hurls herself at her father: "Nooooooooooooooo!"
    O-kay: Time to give up. Balancing thirty pounds of briefcase and day-care baggage on one side and thirty pounds of wobbly toddler on the other, Paul negotiates the snowy steps. Halfway to the car, Becky plops down on the sidewalk and bursts into tears: "Hands! Cold!"

Toddlers put 110 percent of their energy into the Present Moment. When we are playing with them, this bent becomes a talent for extracting the most fun out of everything, and it's wonderful. When we have a job to get through, toddlers' presentness is a pain. We want them to think ahead, move ahead; they can't see a future, and they resent us messing up their present.

When your toddler resists your "interference" or tunes you right out while pushing a piece of cereal around in a little pool of milk, you are fighting the pull of a timeless present. Here are some ways to cope with this:

SOME TODDLER TIME-WARP TACTICS

- *Games:* Invent games that bring the "chores" into a Present Moment game: "I see five things that have to go on for outside; here's One . . . Two . . . What's next? . . . Right! Three . . ."
- *"No" Jokes:* Capitalize on the "no" stage: "This cereal says, 'No! Don't eat me!'" "Oh no! [with a big smile] Don't put that sock on!"
- *The "My-self!" Urge:* Capitalize on "do-it-myself" interests by supporting workable pieces of independence in the morning: learning how to get PJs off or pants and socks on.
- *Song and Dance:* Distract with singing or questions while you dress or feed: "Let's sing ABCs (while I slip these pants on you, ha-ha)," or "What's the biggest thing in this room? (No corrections, get one sock on)," or "What animal do you like the very best? (Other sock!)"
- *Speedy Surrender:* Pick your battles. Ask yourself: Is this issue vital? What would happen if I let it go—is that so bad?—and give up quickly when you can.

Toddlers bring formidable weapons to their conflicts with adults: total commitment to winning, tremendous energy, a genius for quirky demands that stop action every twenty seconds. Adults are too old, tired, fair-minded, and clock-conscious to win more than two or three battles in an hour. When your other tactics fail, and a battle looks probable, make a conscious go–no go decision: Is this one of the Big Three I need to win this hour? Let all the others go with as little time and as few words as possible. Paul probably would have found himself in the exact same spot on the sidewalk with Becky if he had only tried once to get the mittens on, or never even mentioned them. If you *usually* surrender quickly on nonvital issues and hang on mainly when you *have* to, your child can more easily notice a difference. A sharper distinction helps relax everyone in the morning.

PRESCHOOLERS

Q. Why do I have to get dressed now?

A. Because if you don't hurry and get dressed now, we'll be late!

Q. Yes, but why do we have to go? I want to stay home. Can I watch cartoons?

A. No. Today's Thursday; I have to work. You have to go to day care, so *you* have to get dressed. Soon it will be Saturday and we can stay home, but not today.

Q. Why do you have to go to work?

A. I have to work to get money to pay for things—our food, the apartment, clothes. . . .

Q. Why don't you go to the bank and buy more money?

Preschoolers' "why?"s sound like such old, big questions, we almost forget how little they are. We try to explain about lateness, days of the week, money—things they are years away from understanding. Personal explanations like "Because my boss will be mad at me" or "Because lots of people are waiting for me" make a little more sense to preschoolers, but they also make getting ready sound like a personal favor. When we're working partly to make possible their dreams, this doesn't sit right—but what can we tell them—"In fifteen years you'll thank me"?

Preschoolers are not always hunting for the big reasons with their "why"s. Most of them discover that asking "why" drops a nickel in our slots: We always produce a few interesting ideas when asked. "Why?" can be a delaying tactic or a search for bargaining chips. "Let's talk about that on the way to day care" lets you slip past the roadblock without squelching curiosity.

"Why?" probably also reflects a developmental shift toward separate "work" and "play" categories. Infants and toddlers don't divide their experiences into work and play; eating and dressing and playing are *all* play for them. Pre-schoolers see a difference. All along we've been saying "Stop fooling around and get dressed," "Don't play with your food," and now they get it—they don't necessarily *do* it, but they *get* it: Some things are play, others aren't. They don't want to set fun aside for chores. Their morning "why?" is not so much a question as a complaint, like our "*Why* are weekends so short?" Tackling the complaint directly, you can try

HEALING THE WORK-PLAY SPLIT

Turn work back into play with:

- *Friendly challenges, races, bets:* "I bet you can't get dressed before I do" . . . "before I finish making this coffee. . . ." (Parents lose by a hair every time.)
- *Pretend games:* "I wonder if Goldilocks will eat this porridge while I'm out . . . (dressing, shaving, whatever)"
- *Reading or playing music during (and only during) eating or dressing*

Let work have work-style rewards, like:

- *Praise:* "Look at you! You got your shirt *and* your pants on straight—and all by yourself!"
- *Access to interesting company:* "We'll talk to you *after* you're dressed"; "We can play as soon as you're done."
- *Sense of teamwork:* "You pour the juice, I'll spread the butter . . . what a team!"
- *Access to specific rewards, like:* the "dress before breakfast" rules, or nag-free playtime

Give yourself some pure playtime with your child in the morning, even if it's only a few minutes. Inevitably, infants are adorable but messy and clingy; toddlers are fascinating but uncooperative; preschoolers are dear *and* draining. Staying in touch with the wonderful stuff can give you energy for the rest.

Getting There: Parent-Teacher Talk

"Someday," Andy's mother, Janet, tells herself, "he'll love people, and sports, and movies, maybe even his job . . ." but right now Andy's universe *is* small metal cars. He plays with them before bed, at breakfast, in the car on the way to day care. Teachers have banned the cars from the room—they get lost, and Andy is miserable; they start fights, and several children are miserable; when he brings the cars, Andy spends the whole day protecting them. But this morning Andy won't go into day care without his cars. Janet and Andy sit in the parking lot awhile, stonewalling each other. Time is running out. Janet cannot face dragging the cars out of Andy's hands and dragging him screaming into day care. She decides the teachers will just have to deal with the cars today.

Breaking the Rules If you made this decision, what would your teacher do? Would you get a glare and a lecture? Would your child get the lecture? Would your teacher smile and say, "One of those mornings, huh?" and strike some creative deal with your child? The "Things to Try" section lists some possible "deals"; this section looks at the attitude issues breaking rules raises.

Many teachers find it incredible that parents bring children in with can't-dirty clothes or can't-share toys. Why on earth would we sabotage a whole day, make a day *more* difficult? They see themselves working hard to create an interesting and varied world of play with as few no's and don't's in it as possible; fancy clothes wreck this. Now they're supposed to keep your child from playing freely? They're supposed to add watching for dirt to all their other watches? Teachers see themselves working hard at teaching children to share toys and materials at day care, and exposing them to a variety of experiences in a day; home toys can wreck this. Most children under five don't share home toys easily; home toys require constant reminders or complex sharing rules, and crowd out other pleasures. Why don't parents just say no?

Teachers who are parents themselves often do understand why we arrive with the wrong stuff; they know we've already said "no" about ninety *other* things, or didn't understand, or didn't have a real choice that particular morning. Being parents, they know about our mornings in their bones.

Teachers who don't have children of their own have to imagine our reasons for sabotage. They wonder, Do we let our children wear the impossible clothes or bring the impossible toys because we just don't take teachers very seriously? (More work for teachers, less work for parents, that's fine; Teachers are only Hired Help.) Some wonder if we have Problems with Authority, if we think of teachers as mean and rigid, and we're just acting out: the heck with the rules! Who *do* we think they are? The hot issue becomes what the rule-breaking says about our attitudes toward the teachers.

If your teacher tends to react fiercely when you break the rules, you might try offering reassurance about your attitude. Sometimes painting a vivid picture of your morning will settle all doubts. Sometimes a neighborhood kind of politeness packs a powerful message. If you spilled coffee on a neighbor's couch or showed up late when you were counted on, you'd apologize, explain how it happened, and offer to help fix things—even if you weren't at fault in any way. You can treat your tricky arrivals the same way. When you have to bring in a child dripping white lace or metal cars or without the boots or the permission forms—whatever your teachers consider sabotage—saying spilled-coffee kinds of things is worth a try. By handling the problem the way friendly adults would—not inferiors or superiors—you answer attitude questions very clearly.

With parents of toddlers or preschoolers, teachers also worry about the attitude message children receive. What did we say when we decided to break the rule? "Your teacher won't like this but. . . ?" But what? But it's a stupid rule anyway? But I can't cope with you today? Children who get either message tend to have many more battles with teachers than they usually do; teachers and children get a miserable day, and we get very cranky children at pickup time.

Unfortunately, "I can't cope" or "It's a stupid rule" may reflect our thoughts precisely. What can you say? Putting the teacher in the picture at home offers some ways out of this bind.

PUTTING THE TEACHER IN THE PICTURE

- *Remind your child that the teachers* care *about the decision and raise the question* What will happen?: "I don't mind if you bring it, but what will Dave say?" "Joan says this makes too many fights. . . . What can we tell her?"
- *Refer to the teacher as a problem-solving resource:* "Well, I'm sure tired of fighting about those shoes, let's see if Dave can help us out. . . ." "I don't see why you can't bring it either; let's ask Joan. Maybe she can explain it."
- *Reserve final decision-making power for the teacher:* "Okay, we can bring it, but if Dave says it can't come in, I'll have to take it with me." "Let's explain how you feel to Joan and see what she says. If she says no, it's no."

When they lock horns with us over toys or clothes, young children often forget that teachers even exist. Just remembering teachers may inspire rethinking. At the very least, putting the teacher in the picture gets *you* out of having to back up a rule you don't want to defend right now *without* making you set up extra conflicts at day care.

Toddlers and preschoolers are very interested in how adults handle awkward moments and differences in rules. At home they set parents up, until we learn to say things like, "Did you *already ask* Daddy/Mommy about those cookies?" Annoying on the surface, down deep their interest in our differences is lovable and wise. What could be more important to study? How else, where else, should they learn? When you can put some energy into handling differences around teacher rules with care, you not only make arriving at day care easier and get more of your teacher's best, but you offer your child reassuring and useful ideas about solving problems with people.

Getting There: Things to Try

"Things to Try" sections list possibilities for you to choose from. Maybe only one idea will make sense. Sometimes contradictory ideas will be listed—like feeding your baby next to a musical mobile and feeding your baby in a quieter than usual place—simply because either one might work. Ideas described in the "Developmental Issues" sections are included in outline form.

INFANTS

SOME TACTICS FOR THE "STAY PUT!" STAGES (page 23):

- The play cycle
- Play breaks or snuggle breaks
- A home base
- Baby-movers
- Voice contact

DRESSING:

- Bag up and store, hide, or throw out all outfits that cannot be installed and removed in under thirty seconds.
- Pick out your clothes and/or your baby's the night before.
- Dress baby last of all, just before you leave the house.

FEEDING:

- If you've been warming everything perfectly, try cold or lukewarm milk and food. Some infants don't really care about temperature.
- Try solid foods before bottles, after a short sip.

- Tie a zillion washable toys to the high chair.
- Hang a musical mobile near eating place.
- Try cutting down distractions during eating.

TODDLERS

TODDLER TIME-WARP TACTICS (page 25) USE:

- Games
- "No" jokes
- "Do it my-self" interests
- Song-and-dance distraction; questions good, too
- Speedy surrender on nonvital issues

Also:

- Give choices *within* your own plan: "Should we put on the shirt or the pants first?"

DRESSING:

- Bag up and store, hide, or throw out all toddler clothes that cause fights or have "interesting" fasteners. Look for elastic, Velcro, or "spray-on" clothing.
- Invest teaching time and praise in the getting-dressed job, taking it one step and one item at a time. Weekend mornings might be best for teaching, or
- Use a timer: Let your child dress alone until timer rings, then you finish. The first 3 times you use a timer will still involve fights, but the next 103 times should be easier.

FEEDING:

- Look for fast and easy: whole-wheat frozen waffles
- Breakfast in bed
- Same breakfast every day for months on end
- Breakfast on the way
- Help with the sitting-still problem: story tapes or adult reading aloud

PRESCHOOLERS

HEAL THE WORK-PLAY SPLIT (page 27):

- Friendly challenges
- Pretend games
- Reading or playing music while child dresses or eats
- Praise
- Access to good company
- Sense of teamwork
- Access to specific rewards

"DEALS" FOR "I HAVE TO BRING IT! / I HAVE TO WEAR IT!" PROBLEMS:

At home:

- Find something *else* special to bring or wear—a special T-shirt, belt, hair clip, a game several children could play.
- Find a pocket-sized version: small piece of blanket, a key chain with a tiny car attached.
- Allow "it" just on the *way* to day care: "It can come with us, but then it has to stay in the car," or "in your bag" or "in your cubby," or "Bring clothes to change into."

At day care:

See if teachers can be comfortable with letting your child have it/wear it:

- For a short period of time at first, or at nap, or outdoors. . . .
- As long as you don't care if it gets lost or dirty.

Getting-to-day-care troubles have all the key ingredients of every other day-care issue. "Heavy Downtown Traffic" kinds of change-blockers will meet you everywhere: Will changing only one thing make a difference? What can you do if working on one goal compromises another? When other adults disagree with you? When you're not sure you're right?

Raising children brings snuggles and giggles and miracles of growth; it seldom brings nice, simple problems we can tidy up without conflict or doubt. Getting free to *try something,* despite all the uncertainties, will often play a big part in getting more of "the best" for yourself and your child.

Parents and teachers have trouble seeing each other's perspective on problem toys or clothes; the different experiences involved in parenting and teaching create misunderstandings on other issues as well. We expect teachers to understand things about parenting life that they just *don't;* they expect us to understand things about the teaching life that we don't. The fact that we both know so much about our children confuses everyone. We need to find ways of turning the frustration into education.

Morning Talk: Finding the Questions

"No! Robin!" Jake yells, bolting up in bed from a bad dream. Robin is the new boy at day care; Pat resolves to find out about him in the morning. At day care in the morning, however, Jake spends five minutes at his cubby, admiring the fine rocks he is stowing there; then he insists that Pat play trains with him in the room—another five minutes. In the middle of train play, Pat looks around for a teacher to check in with. Pat's favorite teacher, Marcie, is sandbagged with children in the book corner. The other teacher, Audrey, sees Pat looking around and comes over; she scolds Pat for forgetting Jake's boots again. Now what? If Pat doesn't leave in the next five minutes, she'll be late for work. Jake looks fine now. Should she ask Audrey about Robin, run over and interrupt Marcie, or just leave?

Many day-care books, including this one, urge parents to *talk* to teachers. Easy to say, harder to do. By the time we unwrap our children and settle them in at day care, time to talk is already running out. Teachers are busy, or not quite as lovable as we'd like; more delicate topics get lost among the reminders about boots. How much should we struggle against all this? What's the point?

Morning talk with teachers is both a small, simple thing and *everything*. On the one hand, it's just today's newsflash: "Justin woke up really early today . . . he might collapse before naptime"; "Julie's teething—I left extra gum stuff in the fridge"; "Jake had a nightmare about Robin last night—I guess he had a fight with him." On the other hand, those five to ten minutes in the morning make up about half the total time you have to influence your child's days and get the best from your day care. Depending on how those short talks usually go, you can feel in touch with teachers, safe about leaving your child, informed about what's typical for an age group, and comfortable about bringing up issues—or none of the above. Your quick sketch of your child and your concerns form part of a whole wall mural of day-care life. It doesn't have to be great art—there's room for a little graffiti—but you want a generally pleasing effect.

Choosing the Colors The short, simple news matters. Teachers, like parents, look at a moody, aggressive, or uncooperative child and say, "What's up? Is it me? Is it him? Is he sick? Tired? Hungry? Is something bothering him? Maybe he just doesn't understand that we're *serious* about this rule. . . ." Your news guides teachers to a best-guess diagnosis. If you've said, "His brother came home from school with laryngitis yesterday," teachers are more likely to reach for a thermometer than read the riot act to your child; if you've said, "Our dog got lost last night," they're more likely to offer a lap than a lecture at a critical moment. Your newsflash provides a Guide to My Child Today that makes it possible for teachers to give intelligent care.

What's a good Guide to My Child like? What counts as news? Any information that might help teachers interpret your child's behavior is worth mentioning: any sleeping or eating or health news; anything new going on in your house—a visiting grandmother, a kitchen under repair; little things that might be mysterious for your child—garbage-truck roars, sick fish, an older sister's tears, dreams. You don't have to be *sure* something has affected your child to mention it to teachers. You might expect a big reaction when you move your child from crib to bed and see nothing; you might hear about the agony of one skinned knee for months. It's hard to tell what will stay with a child. The more teachers know about the possibilities, the more sensitive their care can be. Your news about little things also sets you up to get more specific news in return. If you remembered to tell teachers about the dentist visit or the lost bear, you can find out if they noticed any effects. The "Things to Try" section includes a reminder list of useful news items.

Morning Light Morning is often the best time to bring up what worries you. It's not really a *good* time. No one planning "a good time to talk" would arrange for parents and teachers to confer right before a work deadline in the middle of a roomful of interrupting children. What are the options? Pickup time works out better for some people, but many find that parent, teacher, and child are all very cranky by then. Special conferences can be arranged, but not very often. Even when the morning is a terrible time to talk, it might still be the *best* one.

Painting Yourself into a Corner If you let the morning scene discourage you from bringing up problems too often, you run a risk. Suppose Pat, for example, trying not to be a "nervous pest," decides not to say anything about Robin. One of several things might happen:

- *The issue disappears*. Jake never has another dream with Robin in it; Robin never lays a hand on Jake or vice versa; Jake never comes home and says Robin called him a dummy.
- *The issue builds up*. All of the above things *do* happen, one

by one over time, none of them compelling alone. At the end of six weeks, Pat blows up: "I expect you to take better care of Jake! This is unacceptable!," or Pat icily demands Robin's removal from the group. Unprepared for the strength of her feelings, the staff reacts poorly.

• *The issue becomes another brick in a wall of disappointment.* Jake's worry about Robin joins a list of medium-sized problems that don't get taken care of. Pat begins to feel vaguely depressed and discouraged about the whole place, but can't really put her finger on what's wrong.

You don't want to paint yourself into a corner by having very narrow criteria for what's worth talking about. Bringing up small issues as they pop up buys you extra room to move in the future, as well as helping out today.

Too Much Gray But what about Pat's worry? If you bring up absolutely everything with teachers, won't they begin to see you as a Nervous Pest? The difference between parents seen as "nervous" or "demanding" and parents "who keep teachers informed" is mainly a matter of *percentages*. Whether you talk a lot or a little, if 99 percent of your talk revolves around worries, criticisms, and requests for special efforts, any teacher will be hard-pressed to greet you with a smile and an open mind. On the other hand, you can bring up a hundred problems a month and still retain star status if you *also* tell many cute stories about your child and say some appreciative things about a teacher's work.

The Gallery Good teachers *want* to talk to you. They may have some personal shyness to get past, some mornings they may have too many busy children to give you full attention, but good teachers know you have news and ideas that will help them work better with your child. They are also deeply interested in the children they care for; they *enjoy* swapping stories. Sometimes you have to tell a story to get one:

PARENT: Kevin told me last night that I'm only going to have one baby, but *he's* going to have a *hundred*.

TEACHER: Yesterday he told me, "I have a small penis. Do you have a big penis? Do you have bbbbbbrrrrreastsss?"!

(Old Kevin is clearly working on his "sex-role identity" issues: how do you love yourself and love both your parents when they come with different equipment? Good luck, Kevin.)

Good teachers actually like problems, too, when parents bring them up as questions. Solving problems with children is their area of expertise; they enjoy strutting their stuff, using their talents, as much as any of us do.

Put Adults in the Picture If you want to talk to teachers and they want to talk to you, but it still never seems to happen, you might want to talk *about* talking first. With all the competing demands on both of you in the morning, it's easy for parents' and teachers' signals to cross. Many parents find it relaxing to give teachers a Guide to My Style: "I'm just a rush-around type, but . . ." or "I could talk about Chris for *hours*, you'll just have to tell me when you need to stop." Getting a guide from teachers about interrupting might make things easier as well.

You are your child's bridge from the world of home to the day-care world. When you stay and play a few minutes in the morning, your child can walk gently from you to day care instead of "beaming aboard" too fast or alone. Helping your child make that walk has to be your first priority; talking to teachers should be a strong second. Morning talk gives you a chance to:

- Improve teacher strategies with your child that day
- Set up good watching or thinking for later information
- Unload some worries

- Develop a background of family and day-care facts for future help
- Pick brains about your problems
- Hear some interesting storiese about your child
- Build a reputation for being easy to talk to, which should keep you informed, entertained, and powerful

When your child is tugging on your arm, your work is tugging on your brain, and the teacher is talking boots to you, you might want to take a raincheck on chatting. Maybe tomorrow will be better. You just want to give yourself plenty of time in the sun and make sure tomorrow comes.

Morning Talk—Developmental Issues

INFANTS

PARENT 1: "She had a bottle at six and some cereal around seven-thirty and a little nap on the way here, so, I don't know, she'll probably be ready for another bottle in an hour, and she might really nap then, too, I don't know. . . . She slept pretty good, but she cried on and off in the middle of the night—it could be teething, but we couldn't feel anything in her mouth; it might be gas from the cereal, she's not that crazy about it, but she doesn't seem all that hungry these day in general, just milk."

PARENT 2: "I think we're all fine this morning—a little tired and cranky but nothing serious. How are you?"

How much information does your infant teacher *need*? It depends on your baby's biological style—is it easy to read? Some babies are born with strong, clear *rhythms* around eating and sleeping. Their lucky parents can sound so organized; they can hear a cry and say, "Oh! It must be six o'clock—he's hungry" or "It's seven-thirty—she'll sleep now"—while the rest of us would be trying to decide whether to check the diaper again or keep singing. Some babies come with very clear *signals*. Even if the schedule of hungry-tired isn't regular, their cues for each need speak plainly. These lucky parents get to say things like, "That's her 'hungry' cry," or "He always does that when he's tired." If your baby's needs are easy to read in either of these ways, your teacher probably doesn't need much detail from you in the morning. You can just give an update on what's new—a new food, a new tooth, a change in schedule.

For all other kinds of babies, you may want to offer a lot of detail about eating and sleeping. These details make rhythm-discovering and rhythm-building possible. Helping babies build clear body rhythms—so they don't spend all their time half-hungry, half-tired, and half-miserable—is one of the most important things adults do for infants in the first year of life.

Giving lots of information also frees you from the *instruction* problem. You may feel certain that your baby will be ready for a nap in one hour, but if you *say,* "Put him down in an hour," you might 1) Be wrong—day care can wake up sleepy babies *or* tire them out faster than home life, and 2) Annoy your teacher—good care requires sensitivity to on-the-spot signals, not hours-old instructions, and, if your teacher has seen ten infants to toddlerhood successfully while you're still on number one, the whole idea's a bit insulting. Leaving detailed information makes an intelligent decision possible without risk.

The first year of life is full of amazing changes. Those little useless waving, nose-bopping fists come under control, open, grasp things, pass toys from hand to hand, build towers, place puzzle pieces. The quavering voice once raised only in distress slowly shapes itself to squeaks and murmurs, syllables and singing, conversational babble, and freshly invented words. Infants' preferences change. You may notice changes in what kinds of pictures your child likes to look at—big and simple? small and complicated? lifelike?—or what colors, sizes, and textures of objects interest your baby most. Tell this kind of news in the morning, too, and ask teachers what they notice. This "have you noticed?" news gives teachers a new way to tune in to and appreciate your baby; their news might work the same way for you.

In short, good infant news includes:

- What's new? news—about food, sleep, teeth, family uproar
- Timing news—for unstable patterns in eating and sleeping
- Have you noticed? news—about developmental delights

TODDLERS

Didi rides into the toddler room on her father's leg, peers around it, then tears off to the loft yelling "Boing! Boing!" —the latest toddler signal for "Booggie down!" Her father smiles, shakes his head, and offers a morning report: "On a scale of one to ten, I'd give her a seven or eight this morning. Last night she was a minus twenty, I think. It was bed or the garbage bin, I'm telling you. Did anything happen here yesterday, or is she just a mess everywhere now?"

When infants wake up and stay "cranky," we suspect sickness, gas, or teeth. Toddlers can *actually* "wake up on the wrong side of the bed." It still might be sickness, gas, or teeth, but with toddlers—who knows? Teachers can't always change this mood weather, but your forecast makes a difference.

Good teachers handle toddlers in good and bad moods differently. A good-mood toddler might still blow up at a frustrating toy, throw it on the floor, and kick it around, yelling. A good teacher treats this as a "teaching opportunity." Here's a chance to teach, with questions and directions, what *else* to do when frustrated, what happens at day care after children throw things on the floor, how to get that toy to work. The basically good-mood toddler clears the air with the fit of frustration and stands ready for new thoughts; the coaching pays off. Try this with a miserable-mood toddler, and the small fit turns into a full-blown tantrum. Better to pack up toy and talk, and pack up the toddler to a couch for a snuggle or a book. Teachers need these two approaches but don't want to mix them up too often. They don't want to drive the bad-mood toddler to rage and despair with educational questions, and they don't want to be teaching the good-mood toddler that people snuggle you on couches when you yell and throw things. Your mood reports in the morning help teachers zero in on the sensible approach much faster.

You might want to use morning talk time to decode home moods and things your toddler has said the night before. Toddlers use words in unique ways; they have no concept of time; they are fascinated by the slapstick and opera side of life. "Leni ate my lunch" might mean exactly that, or "Last week Leni took three of my raisins after I ate her cookie," or "Leni ate Juan's lunch, and she *might* eat mine if we don't watch out," or any number of things.

Good toddler news includes:

- Infant-style body and beauty news where needed
- Mood-weather reports
- Toddler tales that need translation

PRESCHOOLERS

PARENT: "But we haven't said anything about moving!"

TEACHER: "Well, I can't think what else could be up with B.J. He's been a wild man this week—he's picking fights with Carlos, and they *never* fight—and he won't do anything for *me* without a struggle either; won't sit down at circle, won't wash his hands, talks at naptime . . . It's like he's saying 'Okay! I've had it with all of you!'—and that's just what kids usually do when they know they're moving away. . . ."

PARENT: "We've been so careful—how could he know? We never talk about it in front of him. . . ."

TEACHER: "You know, you told me Monday, and he was only a few feet away—I just didn't think about it at the time."

"Little pitchers have big ears" was surely invented for preschoolers. They understand much more of what we say, they can fill in many blanks, they mull over many possible meanings. When life is cruising along on steady, their big ears and lively curiosities mainly bring us streams of interesting questions; when big changes are in the works, however, their "overhearing" talents present some dangers. Big family changes are common in the preschool years. Getting the youngest child out of diapers often releases energy for parents; projects like having another child, taking on a tougher work schedule, or reorganizing family housing suddenly seem possible. Since toddlers don't "overhear" very effectively and react to changes mainly when they become visible, we're used to being pretty casual about news. Preschoolers, however, can worry early and long unless we *plan* when and how they hear the news. (See Chapter 9 for ideas.)

Teachers need to know your big news in order to provide sensitive care, but morning drop-off time might no longer be the best place to deliver it. If your preschoolers' ears are getting bigger just when your news is getting bigger or your child's issues are getting more complicated, it may be time to shift methods of communication. You might:

FOR PRESCHOOL PRIVACY NEEDS

- Write your message or questions in a note.
- Arrange a phone call with your teacher during naptime, lunchtime, break-time, or after hours.
- Ask someone else in your center's office to relay the news in a quiet moment.

If you've been talking about some big news or a troubling topic and see your child looking worried, offer the best reassurance you can right away, and plan a good talk when you get home. A light and confident approach often reassures best: "Did you hear me talking? I am just talking about what the best thing to do is. You know me, always looking for our best choices." Emphasizing thinking it over and "choices" lets your child know that there's no instant problem *and* that you are taking charge—two of the best relaxing messages.

Busy drop-off mornings leave little absolute time for updating teachers, asking questions, and telling stories, but you can actually say quite a lot in just thirty seconds (try talking for thirty straight seconds at home just to see). Some parents like to plan what to say; others feel better just letting go with whatever comes to mind and trusting in the everydayness of talk to sort it all out. However you choose to use those morning minutes, remember: "Your news helps make wise decisions possible.

Morning Talk: Parent-Teacher Talk

Dorothy and Alan fought at breakfast in front of their three-year-old son, Max. With the new baby, and Max bugging them or the baby constantly, they are both so worn out it was bound to happen. Alan told Max he was acting like a baby, Dorothy defended Max, Alan accused her of babying Max, she accused Alan of being the third baby in the family; everyone came in for it. Max looked scared at first, then mad; he hit Alan. Should she say something about it to the teachers? Max *might* forget about it now that he's at day care, but he's already been in trouble twice this week for fighting, and now today will probably not be one of his better days. She also doesn't want him mulling over the fight all day without anyone understanding what's on his mind. On the other hand, Dorothy doesn't want to bare her private life or confess to marital difficulties—sometimes teachers take things so hard. A sympathetic look might be more than she could take right now, too.

Giving teachers good guides to our children's moods helps all day long, but it isn't always easy. Sometimes the news is just embarrassing—"Well, we wimped out at bedtime, she's probably exhausted"; sometimes it's painful—"I might have to have an operation; I'm worried about it, and it's showing at home."

The best teachers often react in the "worst" ways to troubling news. Good teachers have a habit of sympathy, developed for our children; we don't always want sympathy. Good teachers also work hard at figuring out a child's behavior; if it has been "off" lately, and our news seems to explain it, we might get "Whew . . . *that's* all it is. . . ." or "Gee, I wish I'd known this earlier," as a first reaction. Good teachers have high standards for themselves; sometimes we see their anxiety about saying the right thing to us.

If you worry that teachers will misinterpret your news, will treat a little thing as a big deal, or will focus on the wrong piece of a problem, try

POINTING TEACHERS IN THE RIGHT DIRECTION

- *Say what you want as a reaction right away.* Be blunt: "I don't really want to talk about this now, and please don't be sympathetic, but I think you should know . . ."
- *Explain what kind of help you'd like:*
  1. Ask for feedback: "Please let me know if he says anything about it today, or seems different to you."
  2. Ask questions you'd like answered: "Do most children this age worry much about family fights?" "What's the best way of reassuring her that I'm okay?"
- *Supply perspective:* "We were both just really tired; a little sleep will fix us up" "I lost my cool last night, but really there's only a five percent chance I'll even need more tests, let alone an operation. Tell Sheila I'm all right."
- *Direct attention to the right part of the problem, or to real future concerns:* "We've just got to get some more sleep and figure out this whole new-baby thing with Max. Maybe we could talk about new babies later. . . ." "If I have to go in for tests, Sheila's aunt will pick her up. They get along fine, Sheila will just need reminding about that before her aunt gets here. I'll know Thursday."

Many times we can't point teachers in the "right" direction; *we* don't know what it is. We don't know what we need from them, we don't have a perspective on a situation, we don't know which part of the problem is worth worrying about. That's why we're talking to them in the first place! That's fine. The chance to reach out to other people who know and love our children, to tap into extra ideas when we're stuck, is one of day care's most important benefits. When you do see a right direction, however, don't be shy. Taking some control over how teachers respond to your news makes it easier to tell the news, and your telling helps them take better care of your child.

When teachers know what to look for, they can sometimes give you reassurance: "Well, he didn't seem different here today. . . ." Children don't always worry about what worries us; sometimes day care just distracts them. Either way, it's nice to know.

Morning Talk: Things to Try

When your child makes it hard to talk:

- Settle your child first with toys or friends, talk with teachers, then go back to say good-bye.
- Hold your child or snuggle while you talk.
- Write notes or plan phone calls.

When you usually can't think of what to say on the spot:

- Plan ahead:
  1. About how to raise your concerns (see Chapter 10)
  2. Some "good" news (funny story, interesting development) and some "bad" news—a concern
- Babble—say whatever comes to mind; trust time to sort it out.
- Think of this Guide to My Child checklist.

GUIDE TO MY CHILD CHECKLIST

1. *Biology:*
   - Short on sleep or food? New foods introduced?
   - Teething? Ear infections? Minor illnesses in family?
   - Cuts, scabs, or bruises that are bothering?
2. *Psychology:*
   - Little things that seemed to matter, a bee on the porch, a power failure, a dead bird, broken toaster, lost hat
   - Day-care worries, anything mentioned about teachers, children, rules, routines
   - Child moods, unknown origin
   - Parent moods, mysterious excitements or crankiness at home? Unusual fights with each other or with child?
3. *Sociology:*
   - New people in the house: sitters, visiting relatives, grandparents, plumbers, wild parties?
   - Any regulars leaving for a while?

WHEN TEACHERS' BUSYNESS OR STYLE MAKES TALKING DIFFICULT, GET A:

GUIDE TO TEACHERS CHECKLIST

Ask:

- How to tell when it's fine to interrupt
- If it matters which teacher you talk to
- If arriving a little earlier or later would help
- If there's any kind of news they're especially looking for

When you're basically satisfied with morning talk but still a little uncomfortable, give teachers a:

GUIDE TO MY STYLE

Tell teachers:

- If you think you might need pulling in or pushing out
- How and when you like to be reminded about boots and forms
- What news you'd like from them in the A.M.

Some situations allow an easy and efficient variety in morning chats: On different days parents find themselves giving five-second newsflashes, having five-minute figure-it-out sessions, trading "cute kid" stories, recommending pizza places, and raising issues for long-term work. The teacher skills, the time, the children's morning needs, work together to make talk easy; parents just have to let themselves go to take advantage of it all. Other situations require focused effort before they can satisfy anyone. If your morning talk doesn't satisfy you, you might pick one small piece of it to change and see what happens. Like getting-to-day-care obstacles, obstacles to good morning talk might be movable by a small step you'd never guess would really help.

Getting to Day-Care Worksheet

Describe what happens between waking up and getting to day care:

_____

_____

_____

Which piece of this would you most like to change?

_____

_____

What could you try in order to change this?

1. _____   3. _____

2. _____   4. _____

Which idea has the most appeal and/or fewest obstacles in the way of trying it? _____

Pick one you can try for 1–2 weeks: _____
Did this help? _____ What's the next most appealing thing
to try? _____

Morning Talk Worksheet

What do you usually talk with teachers about in the morning?

_____

_____

_____

Does this satisfy you? _____

Do you wish talk were: more relaxed? _____ more efficient? _____ more pleasant? _____ more varied? _____ more frequent? _____

What stands in the way? _____

What could you try to get more of what you want?

1. _____   3. _____

2. _____   4. _____

Pick the best or the easiest; try it for two weeks. Does it
help? _____ What makes most sense to try next? ____

_____

Have you talked with your teacher about what you'd
like? _____

If you teacher sees your first goal as the impossible dream,
is there a different one you could have both work on?

_____

_____

_____

2

Separation: Oh Baby, One Last Kiss!

CHILD: "Stay! Don't go!"
TEACHER: "Go! It'll be fine once you're gone."
PARENT: "Aaaaarrgghh."

WE NEED VIDEOTAPES of how fine it is after we've gone. We need a big Hand of Employer to reach into day care and haul us out, so we don't have to do it ourselves and feel like such traitors when we leave. We need work to be more fun, more worth it. Sometimes saying good-bye in the morning challenges every decision we've made; sometimes good-byes just hurt—we're attached to our children.

There are many, many reasons for sad separations—chief among them is the basic fact that leaving someone you love *is* sad. This chapter will explore other, not-so-inevitable reasons for sad separations and ways to ease their strains.

"Separation" has many meanings. It is often used to cover the whole process of getting used to day care; if your child is just beginning day care, see Chapter 9 for ideas about initial separation issues. Here, we'll look at separation first as technique—how can you say good-bye and leave your child in the best possible shape?—and then as parent-child relationship—how can you stay steady through all your child's changes in clinginess and rebellion?

Separation as Technique: Finding the Questions

> Georgia looks down at Matt, who has buried his head in her skirts and is crying. She has tried to leave twice, but Matt won't let her go. She has said everything she can think of to say; the teacher has told her, again, that Matt is really fine after she leaves. Waiting for Matt to calm down, Georgia sees Mary sail in with her son Alex. Mary peels off to talk with the teacher; Alex charges right over to the truck shelves. Two minutes later, Mary joins Alex, hugs him, gets a kiss, and takes off. As Mary leaves, Alex yells one more "'Bye, Mom!" over his head, but that's it. Georgia wonders, How come she gets off so easy?

No Special Message Difficult good-bye scenes make parents wonder: What's wrong? Is it day care in general? This place? Me? My child? Don't use good-byes to answer your big questions. Children who are quite happy most of the day still cry at good-byes; they just hate the moment of leaving. If you see other parents "get off easy," take it as reassurance about the place, not a sign that something's wrong with them or you. Often good-byes are just good-byes—hard to pull off gracefully but no more than that—not a symbol of other problems. Many parents who change their good-bye technique find that nothing else, after all, needs fixing.

The Medium Is the Message Treating "good-bye" as a technique might seem crass. Good-byes stir up strong emotions; is it wrong to *manage* such feelings? The Alexes, however, show us important truths: The whole power of the parent-child bond does not *have* to be played out each morning. Simple good-byes can leave happy children.

How can you say good-bye simply when your child won't let you go? Teachers usually stress speed and simplicity: "Just do it." When you read the story above, did you think, Lucky Mary, she can say good-bye to Alex in ten seconds because Alex is so relaxed? Teachers might say "Alex is so relaxed because Mary says good-bye in ten seconds." When teachers take this point of view, they are actually passing on the fruits of former parents' efforts. Experienced teachers have seen parents force themselves into quick and cheerful exits and work miracles: Children who *had* to have five more minutes and then five more minutes and then five more began to accept a two-minute good-bye, *and* these children looked relieved, not abandoned. How does this work?

Sign Language Even as infants, children look to adults to interpret events for them. When they hear a sudden noise, take a medium-hard fall, see a strange face, their eyes fly to parents' faces: Are things okay? When we look relaxed, they relax, too; if we look tense or worried, they are much more likely to burst into tears. A natural sign language of faces, voices, and movements seems to be wired in. We often use this language consciously with our children. We look calm and croon when we want to soothe them; we look fierce and bark orders when we need to stop or warn them. Our sign language keeps going even when we aren't consciously using it. What do children see on our faces on day-care mornings? Do we look worried? Like we're doing something terrible? If children receive such a message, why *shouldn't* they worry and cry? A calm face sends an "I'm okay—you're okay" message that makes the moment of leaving much easier.

Body Language Parents' *actions* send unplanned signals, too. Suppose you say, "I have to go"; your child protests, and you stay a little longer—maybe a few times before you *abso-*

lutely have to go. What's the message? We'd like children to read this flexibility as "I care about you," but most children are tuned in to more immediate, practical matters. They're more likely to get the message "You can stop me from leaving," or even "You *should* stop me from leaving." When we finally do leave, they feel they've really failed.

Address Correction If you really are worried about your child at day care, in general or just on a particular day, of course you should take action. With a "just today" doubt, you might call day care later to see how things are going, or make doubly sure your teacher knows how to reach you during the day. With a more general concern, you might look in other chapters for ideas. If you plan a different action to address your concern, you can keep your face clear and reassuring for your child until you decide what to do next.

Editing Work You can't see your own face, and it's always hard to know how children are interpreting things. You can ask teachers for opinions about your good-byes or watch other parents' techniques for ideas. You can also answer "What message am I sending?" by trying something new for a week or two and seeing what happens. Think up one simple thing you'd like to say at good-bye and try saying that with face, voice, timing—everything you've got.

Separation as Technique: Developmental Issues

INFANTS

Ray bursts into the baby room with eight-month-old Ginna in his arms, talking 90 mph about the horrible traffic, about the cute thing Ginna did last night, about what she ate for breakfast and when she'll be hungry next. He puts Ginna on the floor, grabs a few toys, and shakes them in front of her—"Look!"—then turns back to stash bottles and talks about the last movie they rented and the date of the next parent potluck. Ray picks Ginna back up and lifts her over his head. Cooing and smacking, he swoops her in for kisses, punctuating them with orders to be good and have fun. He flies her back down to the floor and heads for the door. Ginna bursts into tears. Ray turns back to her. The teacher motions him to stop. Ray wants a happier good-bye, and this entry *was* too wild for Ginna . . . but will a few more minutes of Ray in this mood really help Ginna now?

Short, sweet, and upbeat is generally great as a good-bye style, but you have to guard against being wild with infants. An overstimulating style crowds out the sights and sounds of day care that make it feel familiar and safe. Adults who haven't seen each other for a long time often take a minute to connect: "Hey! Don't I know you?" Infants, whose mental machinery grinds a bit slowly at first, need some quiet minutes to re-connect with day-care memories. Quality of time is more important than quantity—think molasses. You can support your infant's reconnecting at day care in several ways:

HELPING YOUR BABY CONNECT

- *Lump of Home:* Sit down with your baby and be still. Don't talk, hand toys, or point things out; just be there. Let your baby case the joint and make contact with people and things, in his or her own time and fashion. When your baby has made some contacts, give the teacher the news quietly, tell your baby good-bye, kiss, and go.
- *Tour Guide:* Sit holding your baby, pointing out favorite people and things: "Look! Here's Esther, and Michael, here's the soft bear and the red train. . . ." Actively but gently remind your infant of familiar pleasures at day care. Then pull back and wait a bit, or hand your baby to a teacher, kiss, and go.
- *Delivery Service:* (For speed-emergency days and for easy phases) Stop at the door and take a deep breath. Go into slow

motion for just a few minutes. Hold your child while you unpack and give the teacher the news, then hand your baby to your teacher, kiss, and go. Your teacher's arms should be full of warm touch and smell memories strong enough to evoke quickly the sense of a safe, familiar place. As long as you hand your child over in slow motion and leave looking confident, fast good-byes with familiar people can work fine.

Routine also makes the "I know you!" connection easier. If your good-byes seem rocky, and you haven't had much routine so far, you might try leaving your child at the same time, in the same spot, and in the same style every day for a week or two.

TODDLERS

Arms out, Neal flies down the hall, whips off his jacket, and zooms his bird body into the toddler room—he likes it there. His father, Bill, usually lopes in a minute behind Neal. Smiling, Bill reports pajama wars and breakfast battles headlined "Neal Wins Again"—yet here they are, dressed, at day care. Now comes the battle nobody wins. Every day when Bill tells Neal he has to go to work, Neal tackles his knees and bursts into tears.

Teachers suggest that Bill try getting Neal to push him out the door. Feeling foolish but thinking anything's better than the tears, Bill tries: "Hey, buddy. I gotta go now—wanna push me out the door?" Bill spins around to present his best pushing place; Neal takes the bait. Both arms stiff, he shoves Bill to the door yelling "Good-*bye!*" Bill leaves the room and waits outside for several minutes for a late-breaking storm. No cries. Bill shakes his head and takes off for work—can it really be this simple?

Toddlers like Neal are good candidates for the push-you-out-the-door technique. Comfortable with day care, comfortable with their parents, their real hate is the moment of "being left," the helplessness. Put them in charge of the separation and they're much, much happier. Of course, you can't really put toddlers in charge of saying good-bye or anything else that *has* to happen, but you can find some area of choice: "I have to go now. I can walk or you can push me," or "I'm leaving now—you want a kiss or a hug or both?" Since your lovely, clever toddler will eventually discover the trick of making you wait forever for the decision, you need a backup plan, like, "If you can't decide now, I'll just kiss you and go." Routines seem to change toddlers' feelings of being left, too; somehow they make departures feel more inevitable, not so much a parent's private decision, more a magic action that just leads to leaving.

Even ten-second good-bye routines can make a great difference to toddlers. Rituals speak to them. They are just beginning to think in symbols, and to use word symbols; they are wide open to symbol power almost anywhere. They can see monster bees lurking in the lowliest ant and an army of protectors in the teddy-bear lineup at the end of the crib. Toddlers are also just beginning to master sequences—this comes, *then* that, this leads to that; familiar sequences anchor life for them, especially during changes. Toddlers have an acute sense of doing things *right*—parents find themselves standing in a certain place on the rug to get the last "good night" accepted or singing "good night" individually to every object in the room; good-bye routines seem to make leaving right. All this sensitivity to magic elements drives us nuts sometimes, but at good-byes, you can make magic work for you. (There are some ideas for rituals in the "Things to Try" section.)

Magic objects—a blanket, bear, pacifier, frog, dog, truck, dinosaur, or old undershirt—whatever your toddler drags around everywhere—ease good-byes as well. Are you really replaceable by an old rag or a couple of Godzillas? No, but the familiarity comforts, and the rubbing, twisting, and sucking of these things seems to bring on a soothing trance.

(If these objects are forbidden at day care, see Chapter 1, page 28 for some possible compromises with teachers.)

The toddler love of ritual doesn't mean that yours won't still test your will to leave or get stuck in the process of saying good-bye. Toddlers can turn one rock over and over and over, find a million uses in one stick, fill and pour a water bucket forever. One object or action can capture all their attention, emotional drive, and inventive intensity in a timeless present. When the moment of a parent's leaving captures them this way, they need parents to lead them out of the moment, to free them.

A stuck, stormy, desperate toddler screaming at your knees makes it very tough to be a good leader. You have to be able to believe that the storm is really a Moment-of-Leaving problem, that your child really will be fine if you can only get past it. If your teachers say, "She's fine ten minutes after you go" and you trust them, hold on to that. If you need extra certainty, leave and listen outside the door. Unless you are just starting day care or you've had a very long buildup to your good-bye, your toddler should recover and plunge into day-care life pretty quickly—ten minutes is about right. Here are some ways parents have found for

LEADING OUT OF THE GOOD-BYE MOMENT

- *State the facts:* "You're really sad [or angry]. I'm sorry you feel bad, but I have to go now. I'll see you tonight."
- *Add comforts:* "Here's your . . ." (teacher, bottle, blanket, pacifier, bear, favorite book, cozy couch, whatever).
- *Keep moving.* Don't stop moving once you've said "I have to go." Get the comforts, say "I love you . . . I'll see you" again, hug or pat or kiss, and make your feet go out the door.

After a painful good-bye, you might want to call the day-care center later and ask how your child is doing; if your child has bounced back quickly, a phone call will save you a tough day.

PRESCHOOLERS

Charlotte is swinging back and forth on her mother's arm, thudding into her stomach on the backswing. Charlotte's mother, Liz, goes on talking with the teacher. Charlotte is an old hand at day care; she should be off pretty soon. After the third thud, Liz asks, "Honey, why don't you go play?" Charlotte twists herself behind Liz like a rolling gear wheel and begins winding her mother's skirt around her fist. Finally, Charlotte's friend Christy skips through the door and grabs her hand. Charlotte vanishes; Liz staggers from the sudden release.

For easy separations at any age, day care must exert some magnetic pull of its own. With infants and toddlers, teachers are usually the main magnets; with preschoolers, friends take first place. When friendships aren't working out, morning good-byes may turn difficult. You might invite a would-be buddy to your house on a weekend; more private play often helps get a relationship past an awkward phase. You might also check with teachers about the timing of the morning social scene: When do key friends arrive? When do cliques close rank? Would coming a little later or earlier help?

You can also try increasing the pull from other possible magnets: Steer your child toward an activity and join it for a short while, or ask teachers for a bigger, more personal welcome. Preschool teachers get so used to rowdiness and independence from their group, they sometimes forget the value of a big teacher hello or a personal introduction to an activity.

You might also try asking your child at home, "What would make it easier to say good-bye at day care?" This age group has the memory resources to plan a good-bye with you. A normally wily preschooler may suggest some unacceptable bribes; sensitive souls may dread the whole idea—if they make a plan, will they have to act happier? Feel free to reject impossible ideas, and help your child feel free to try a plan and *see* if it makes a difference. Putting a personal plan for good-byes into effect usually helps a preschooler feel smart and in charge—a good way to start a day.

FINDING PRESCHOOL MAGNETS

- Encourage friendships, showing interest and approval about friends; invite a would-be friend over on a weekend.
- Encourage the pull of activities:
  1. Help your child find attractive activities in the room.
  2. Update your teacher on favorite home activities; ask if some of these can be available in the morning.
  3. Bring in some favorite home activities.
- Ask for a bigger, more personal welcome from teachers.
- Make a plan with your preschooler: "What would help?"
- Check on arrival time for best time in terms of friends and activities and teacher availability.

Sheer routine helps with children of all ages and is probably the single biggest secret to easy good-byes. No good-bye routine you set up will last forever. Children's needs change as they grow, and colds, trips, or family changes will of course wreck any organization you achieve on a regular basis. When you need to change a routine, either on a long-term or a one-day basis, avoid confusion by giving advance notice—"I want to try a new way of saying good-bye this week. How about . . . ?" or "I really have to rush this morning, so . . .". With younger children, using visible signals helps—take off your coat if you usually keep it on, sit down if you usually stand, say good-bye in a different part of the room.

When things get tough in the morning, remember:

- Tomorrow is a new day; you can always try something different.

- You can never fit everything you want to say or do into those good-bye minutes.
- You have the whole rest of your life together to say everything you want to say.

Your morning goal is freeing your child to enjoy a different life for a while. Staying simple about good-byes is hard but frees you fastest.

Separation as Technique: Parent-Teacher Talk

Annie is trying to smash a puzzle piece into place; Pete, her dad, searches for a piece that *would* fit. Annie's teacher, Fran, slides into the chair next to Pete, and leans over to Annie: "Your dad needs to go, honey. Why don't you say good-bye now. *I'll* help you find that piece." Annie grabs Pete's arm and yells, "No! Don't go!" Pete pats her and tells Fran, "It's okay. I have a little more time." A few minutes later, Pete hands Annie the last piece in the puzzle. She seems pretty settled now; time to go. He gives her a quick hug, rises, and heads for the door. Annie leaps up and runs over to him, crying. Pete explains, "I have to go to work now, honey. . . ." Annie grabs his jacket. Pete looks up for Fran—she's turning away, lifting a child onto the changing table.

When your child isn't bouncing off to play at day care, you often need a teacher's help to leave. This requires some coordination. Think basketball: If you plan to dribble down the court and pass off to the free player, that player has to get there, get free, and be alert for your move. Chatter on the court is essential.

Why don't teachers just keep an eye on you and your child, notice when you're ready to leave, and step in at the right moment? Sometimes teachers can do this; it's great.

Why not every morning? Three things stand in the way: 1) Other tasks: In group care, teachers have other parents and children to help; you can have top priority for a time but usually just a short time, and even then, other people's needs might have to come first at a particular moment. 2) Uncertainty: Teachers can't always read your signals. They don't want to intrude at the wrong time or play the heavy if you don't really want help. 3) Frustration: When teachers believe that you won't really work with them—won't negotiate a good moment to leave or won't actually go once they come to help—they give up.

If you're not getting help when you need it, you might try one of these ways of

SETTING UP THE SEPARATION

- *Plan the plays:* In a note, phone call, or conference, describe:
  1. What seems to be happening when you start to leave
  2. What you'd like to have happen, and ask if this sounds reasonable, doable. If not, what would?
- *Chatter on the court:* Say, "Will you be free in a minute? I'm just about ready to go," and wait, or when you're almost ready, ask teachers to come over as soon as they can.
- *Move to the teacher, not the door, when you're ready to leave:* Wait for the teacher's free moment, say good-bye, and go.
- *Signal the teacher:* Teachers can come to wherever you are settling your child at your signal if:
  1. You've discussed this plan and signal ahead of time.
  2. You really go after the teacher arrives.

Don't be embarrassed to bring up the details of leaving. There's nothing obvious about picking a good time or way to leave. When separations aren't smooth, they become complicated, powerful, and awful for everyone. Moving out of that pattern requires planning and solid support.

Separation as Technique: Things to Try
INFANTS

- Help Your Baby Connect, some styles (page 55):
  1. Lump of Home
  2. Tour Guide
  3. Delivery Service
- Slow down, move and talk in "molasses" mode.
- Cheer up, try leaving with confident face and voice.
- Use a routine time, place, style.
- Bring familiar blankets, toys, things from home.
- Try an earlier arrival time so room is uncrowded.

TODDLERS

- All of the above
- Lead Out of the Good-bye Moment (page 58):
  1. State the facts.
  2. Add comforts.
  3. Keep moving.
- Invent routines: Play push-me-out-the-door, read one book together, feed the group pet, give two big kisses and one giant hug, a big waggle in the air and a swooping handoff to a teacher, set your child up near a window to wave as you pass by.
- Give limited choices: "I'm leaving now. Do you want to push me out or give me a kiss here?" Or: "I have to go. Do you want to kiss me, or shall I kiss you?"

PRESCHOOLERS

FIND PRESCHOOL MAGNETS (page 60):

- in friends
- in teachers' greetings
- in activities
- in personalized plans

Separation as Relationship: Finding the Questions

> Kathy and her daughter, Lila, have been at the center for two years. Lila enjoys day care, and Kathy feels comfortable, too, but their good-byes have rarely been easy. When they hit yet another rough patch, Kathy wonders out loud to the director, "Maybe it's me. Sometimes I think there isn't anything she could do that would be right. If she cries and makes a fuss, I feel guilty—that I'm abandoning her when she needs me. If she bounces off to play like I'm hardly even there, *I* feel abandoned. Now we're having trouble again, and I just don't know. Am I doing something wrong? Am I not letting her go?"

Tell It to the Judge "Not letting go"—yet another possible parenting crime. "It's not so easy!" we plead to the judge. Yes, these little folks are graying our hair, but look at those eyes, feel those cheeks, see that smile! How can we just leave and not feel anything!? We also have to turn our backs on a whole world and our place in it. We turn away from a timeless world of play and milk and cookies to a world of paper and machines. In our children's eyes, we are the center of the universe, the sun, the earth, the air; when we leave, we become . . . just us again. Even when it's a relief, it's a letdown.

Guilty, Guilty, Guilty Sadness isn't the only problem. Do we feel guilty? Let us count the ways. . . . We feel guilty because we wonder if children have a right or a need for our relentless presence and we're cheating them of it; because we actually like our work and want to go; because we want a perfect place for our children and have to leave them in not-so-perfect places; because we find our children exhausting and we're a little glad to be away for a while (oh sin!); because if we were only more organized/energetic/patient, we would be rich/smart/loving enough to arrange perfect parent-and-child happiness all the time.

Sadness makes us drag our feet at good-byes, or flee quickly. Guilt, too, makes it hard to pace leaving around children's needs. We're used to treating guilt as a stop signal—Don't eat that fattening stuff! Don't waste that water! Stop being a jerk to this nice person—so we slow down or rush through things.

Criminal or Victim? One reason we ask ourselves "Is it me?" about separation difficulties is the natural confusion deep attachments bring. Who's feeling what? Our children open all our gates. We hurt when they hurt, smile when they smile; we try to see the world through their eyes a little. They, too, respond quickly to our moods—basking in our sunshine, thundering in our rain. Parent and child can get very mixed up with each other. When we're feeling sad or guilty on and off all day, it's very hard to believe that our children are playing away, having a fine old time at day care, feeling completely different. We're also saddled with the adult model of love relationships: Where there's real love, don't both partners miss each other during separations? With children and short separations, the answer is no. Children's minds belong to immediate moments for the most part. When they feel at home some place, they can set us aside for batches of time and still love us totally.

Conflict of Interest If you asked most parents, "Do you *really want* your child to be happy at day care?," their first answer would be "Yes! Of course!," but actually most people have conflicting wishes. For one thing, if "happy" means not missing us at all, well, we want to be missed at least sometimes. Then there's the fear: What if our children like teachers *better*, or have more fun at day care than at home? "Happy" shouldn't mean we come out second best. Even questions of "taste" get involved: If *we* aren't that crazy about the other children, or the teacher, or the activities, *should* our children really be satisfied with them? We do, and don't, want our children to be happy without us. The conflict makes it harder to believe they're really okay.

Motive, Means, and Opportunity So, leaving time is rife with possibilities that good-bye scenes are our fault. Our faces, bodies, tones of voice, timing, could all quite easily be radiating messages like "This is sad. . . . I'm doing something awful. . . . Don't enjoy your day *too* much!" And our children could be playing that back to us.

Collecting Evidence How can you sort this all out? How do you know when it's you? The previous pages described one way of sorting out separation trouble: Change your technique. Go for calm, confident, and short, and see what happens after a week or two.

Another time-honored sorter-outer is waiting outside the door. Say good-bye and go wait in an out-of-sight spot where you can still hear. If your child cries a long time, you want to work for change. If your child cries briefly, then turns to play with some gusto, isn't that exactly right? You are wonderful and important; your departure merits some sadness. If your child has just started day care or you've had a big buildup to getting out the door, longer crying is to be expected, but on a regular day, something between two and ten minutes is about right. Listening-to-crying time always feels fifty times longer than it really is. Watch a clock.

Reach out to other parents and friends. You could ask another parent at day care who usually leaves after you do how long your child seems sad after you go. Or you could make a deal with another parent and collect this information for each other, taking turns leaving late. Or ask a friend just to listen to you talk about leaving, no opinions, please; the chance to hear yourself think often clears things up.

Hating to leave your child is not a crime. Feeling guilty and conflicted and confused about it is not a crime. We want to give our children's needs center-stage attention in the morning, so we have to set our own feelings aside during leaving. Hang 'em on the coat hook with your child's jacket when you get to day care; help your child connect, and say good-bye with confidence. You always can, and maybe always will, pick up those old hard feelings on the way out. You've done the best you can.

Separation as Relationship: Developmental Issues

INFANTS

> As twelve-month-old Ollie and his mother, Clare, step into the infant room, he clutches her neck and hides his head in her hair. Clare is shocked: Ollie usually wriggles right down at day care. She decides to stay a bit. Ollie hangs on to her, finally relaxing, but every time another child arrives, and every time she starts to move, he clutches again. This is ridiculous! Clare thinks. "He knows these people! He likes them!" She has to get to work, and her staying doesn't seem to help. She shrugs to the teacher. "What should I do?" "It's all right," the teacher says, "Ollie's just in one of those glue-you-to-the-floor phases. . . . I'll let him glue *me* to the floor for a while; you can go."

Most scientists who write about "separation anxiety" use for facts the records of what happens when you leave babies in strange laboratory rooms they've never been in before, all alone or with people they don't know. This is *not* what you are doing at day care. You don't have to worry about those studies. They should long ago have been titled "Babies in Labs Need Parents," not "Separation Anxiety Studies."

Nature designed babies very wisely: If they find themselves alone in a strange place with a large, unfamiliar animal, they cry for help. Just what you'd want—good survival planning. We accept our infants' clinging when something unfamiliar is happening—but with familiar people in familiar places? What's going on?

What infants want in the way of relationships changes dramatically in the first year of life. At first they mainly want familiarity, plain and simple. Later they recognize some differences in style among familiar people. (An older infant can greet a rowdy big brother with noisy arm-waving and parents with a quieter, beaming hello; infants may prefer a brother when feeling rowdy themselves but reject him when sleepy.) Finally, infants hit an "owning" phase: one person at a time is selected as Absolutely Necessary, and everyone else can just go hang. This often creates a painful time not only at day-care good-byes but at home—one parent may suffer terrible rejections if the other is in the room.

What's this "owning" about? We can guess something from *when* it typically peaks—around twelve months. About then, infants start to "get" the amazing idea of language. Gestures and noises start as automatic reactions and become food for private goofings-around; now they come under conscious control, start to be *used*, on purpose, to "talk" to people. Breakthrough! On the outside, this looks like just pointing and "Da!," but it is a magnificent leap. Because different adults often understand an infant's "da!"s in different ways, sticking with one adult at a time probably cuts down on frustrations. Walking also starts to take off around twelve months. Perhaps the powerful drive to stay close to one adult at this time is Nature's way of providing a safety balance for the walk-around drive. Wherever it comes from, older infants' demand for one adult to *stay put* is quite a phenomenon.

When a clingy phase hits at home, your options are: Stay glued to the floor, carry your infant everywhere, or listen to the protests. (See some Tactics for "Stay Put" Stages, Chapter 1, page 23.) You'll probably have to do a little of everything. That's fine. If you don't mind putting on hose or shaving with baby arms around your neck, great. Do it. One less fussy minute. If this drives you crazy, don't do it. (Some of us think close confinement with a clingy child would be the perfect way to wring confessions from spies and criminals.) Keep a soothing line of talk rolling so your baby can feel connected to you, finish your task, and go for a snuggle.

At day care, a hand-over directly to a teacher's arms is your best bet. Infants usually don't wander off happily during "owning" phases and ordinarily won't go to a teacher until you leave. Once you've left, a teacher can serve as the one-person anchor.

Your teacher might need help seeing this phase for what it is—a short, intense need to center around one adult at a time. Not all teachers are prepared for it. Like the "other" parent or Grandma at home, teachers may feel hurt, rejected, even betrayed, when your infant clings to you this new way. Teachers may resent the new "Stay put!" demands on them, especially if they felt rejected earlier. If you think the teacher-infant relationship can use your support, you might try

SMOOTHING OUT OLDER INFANT SEPARATIONS

- Tell your teacher it's a phase; you're not doubting the care: "I've read that this is just an especially clingy age. I'm not worried about it. We'll all get through."
- Tell your teacher if you see it at home: "I'm sure she's still crazy about you—she does the same thing to Bob when I'm in the room at home."
- Ask if your baby wants a lot of carrying, etc., during the day and thank your teacher for the extra effort that takes.
- Hand your baby directly to the teacher when you go, and go confidently.

TODDLERS

Ken is sitting on the snack table, staring down at his hands and his daughter, Cindy. Cindy has thrown herself down on the floor at his feet and is screaming. He's stuck. He can't see walking out on her when she's like this, but he's already tried calming her down, reading a book, explaining why he has to go to work, everything. She relaxes when he does these things, but then she gets furious and miserable all over again the moment he makes a move to leave. He wants to be such a great father to her—he loves her so much!—but he just can't stay all day.

Ken has heard that the toddler years are all about "separation," about a child becoming a "real" person, separate from parents, that toddlers have lots of "separation issues"—whatever that means. He doesn't want to blow any of this, but if this hopeless struggle is what everyone's talking about, brother—you can have it!

"Separation," as a special toddler issue, is a funny kind of concept. If you want to think of separation scientifically, you're pretty much up a creek. Studies of orphans, war victims, and hospitalized children have been used to explore "separation" effects, but that's quite different from a day-care separation—as are laboratory studies with strangers in unfamiliar places. And two is the least studied of all childhood ages, for good reason. With a little savvy and a parent nearby, researchers can interest infants in all kinds of things, and they can reason with and direct preschoolers, but *toddlers*? Toddlers don't make good subjects for experiments; they're as uncooperative in laboratories as they are everywhere else. We're all guessing.

If you want to think of separation romantically, you might imagine first a parent-and-child-soup sort of consciousness for infancy. Our hands extend our infants' reach; our strength adds strength to their wobbly feet; they call us and we come.

We become the extension of their wishes. Infants move with us, too. When we need to go, we pick them up and they just come; we show them things and they look; when we want to play, they're almost always ready for us. What we want and what they want flows back and forth so often and so smoothly, we barely notice it happening. Then, boom! Our babies become toddlers. They become mobile and strong and full of ideas. Two sea-monster heads rise out of the infancy soup; the heads say "No!" to each other. For a parent, the "No!" protects basic life—not all toddler ideas are good ones. For toddlers, the "No!" holds the secret of independent identity: "I'm not you, I want different things, I have different plans and opinions, and you have to respect that!" It's a natural, even noble, effort—most of us are still working on it with our own parents.

In terms of what we can *see*, people use "separation" to cover two especially dramatic aspects of the twos: 1) Toddlers object to parent departures more strenuously than other age groups, and 2) More than other age groups, toddlers tend to be desperate and inflexible about getting their own way: If we give in a little, they want still more; if we give in completely, half the time they change their minds and want the opposite thing—just as passionately and right away. It feels as if they are *trying* to drive us crazy, trying to find a boundary line between wills. How do these facts belong together? Is "separation" the best word to apply?

Here's another model to apply: Development drives infants to discover their hands, to practice and explore the uses of hands. The first discoveries are funny: You can almost see on their faces "What the heck! I can move this thing myself!" They practice moving hands in and out of their field of vision; they practice making other things move by batting them with fists they can barely open; they practice using both hands together, opening and closing hands, and so on. They work very hard at this practice, sometimes getting quite frustrated, but they keep coming back to it. Maybe toddlers are doing this sort of thing with "planning power." They discover they have ideas about what they want; they work and work and work at all the pieces of putting ideas into action. When their ideas require cooperation from other people, they work at that.

Poor toddlers! So many things stand in their way. Their brains cook up some complicated ideas, but their hands are still all thumbs in many ways. They can't reach half the world; they don't have the words to say half of what they want. Imagine trying to get through a day with fifty words or less! Then other people have their own plans, or don't get it and won't help! No wonder we see some intense rages.

When we try to leave at day care, we are frustrating their planning power in both general and specific ways. From infancy, and from the morning just left at home, we have been a general, all-purpose part of making their wishes come true. Now they have to regroup: They'll have to work on teachers and other children to get wishes coming true. *Plus*, they like having us around—our departure frustrates that wish in particular.

If the word "separation" haunts you, and morning scenes feel Very Big, you might think about your departure mainly as a colossal frustration. Think about what else drives your toddler crazy and how you handle that. What happens, for instance, when you try to *make* your child wear boots? What happens when you say that all nine little cars *can't* come to the grocery store? Of course, you are more important than these things, and of course toddlers are learning about dependence and independence, love and power, too, but the good-bye minute doesn't have to be *the* crucial event in your teaching or your relationship. You have all the rest of your time together to perfect those things. You can see "I have to go now" as another version of "You have to wear those boots" and apply the same skills. (See also Leading Out of the Good-bye Moment, page 58.)

Since frustration mounts the longer and more totally a toddler focuses on an impossible thing (like your staying forever), it often helps to

FIND ANOTHER FOCUS

For example:

- Focus on an activity together for a while, and then on a leaving routine.
- Settle near some children or activities that interest your child; lie low, let your child's interest shift from you to day care.
- Focus on a teacher. Talk to the teacher yourself, hope that your child will reconnect with the teacher while you talk, ask the teacher to help the child find a new focus as you leave.

PRESCHOOLERS

> "My leg hurts," Danielle tells her mother, Paula, at breakfast. "Well, let's have a look at it. . . ." Paula examines the leg for bruises, scratches, and knotty muscles, getting an "Ouch!" once or twice from her prodding. "I don't see anything, honey. . . . Maybe you're just growing. . . ." The leg is latest on a list of mysterious pains Danielle reports nearly every morning these days. "I don't think I can go to day care," Danielle ventures, a half-worried, half-sorrowful look on her face. "Sweetheart, you know I can only stay home for fevers. We'll tell the teacher you can't run around too much." While she's dressing, Paula hears Danielle singing loudly on and off, and in the car Danielle recounts every word she said to her friend Janie and every word Janie said back when they played Wedding yesterday. Paula relaxes—the leg pain is, at the least, forgettable. But as they head up the hall to the Older Group Room, Danielle begins to limp.

Too old to throw a tantrum and too young to identify everything that troubles them, preschoolers sometimes develop all the aches and pains of people twenty times their age. You have to check out every pain that lasts beyond a few minutes and ask teachers to keep on the lookout for you during the day—you'll kick yourself if you shrug off something you shouldn't. Pains that come and go, mainly in the morning, probably say more about a wish to be especially taken care of, to be nursed and "babied," than about physical distress.

Most people like to be babied now and then. When children ask for this, all kinds of things might be up: plain tiredness, low-level infections, being on the outs with friends, new worries. Your preschooler might just need a mental-health day, as lots of us do from time to time. If you can, scrounge a day off or plan some no-errands, no-TV weekend time. Your child may catch up on some sleep, use the intimacy of a special time to let you know about a worry, or just soak up the taking things slow for a bit. When life is too rushed for special time, think about other special-care treats—breakfast in bed, long bubble baths with stories read aloud—whatever helps your child feel fabulously taken care of.

Preschoolers also have a keen interest in basic categories: boy/girl; good guy/bad guy; dead/alive; baby/grown-up. We see them work on this last interest in fantasy play: They like playing Most Powerful Being in the Universe *and* Tiny Cute Baby Puppy. They seem aware of "babies" as a group that gets bossed around but taken care of and "grown-ups" as a group with power but heavy duties and little help. The "kids" category isn't so clear. They know they're not babies anymore. Sometimes they worry that they're losing their charm and their claim to special care. They feel themselves growing up—how grown up do they have to be? Getting some special nursing care may reassure them: Grown-ups still take care of you, even though you're not a baby anymore.

If your child seems to be sending you lots of "I'm pretty little—you have to take care of me" messages, consider offering general reassurances about growing up. Since preschoolers don't have a handle on "kid" status, they fear they'll have to choose between being a no-power baby and a gets-no-help grown-up. You can work against this scary idea:

OFFER GROWING-UP INSURANCE

- *Read comforting stories.* In many traditional fairy tales, child or adult characters get help from animals and other magic sources—it's a solution to the helpless baby versus help–less grown-up dilemma. And a nice message: Even heroes get help.
- *Be a historian for your child.* Tell "I remember when . . ." stories about smart things they did when they were even younger; you might emphasize smart ways they got help when they needed it.
- *Use pretend play.* When your child's baby play gets on your nerves, go ahead and set the limit—"I need to see Big Nat at the table now, not Baby Nat, please"—but join in when it's not. Be a Giant Grown-up to your child's Baby: Carry, rock, coo, chuck under chin, burp—the whole bit. Saying yes to a "baby-me" wish now and then keeps it simple.
- *Try some serious talk.* Talk directly about how things change and stay the same between parents and children as children grow. "I will always take care of you. The ways I need to take care of you just change when you get bigger. When you couldn't walk, I carried you. When you couldn't talk, I talked for you. Now you can walk and talk, but I still take care of getting food and clothes, and I keep you safe. I like how grown up you can be; I'm proud of you. I like taking care of you, too, and I'll always take care of you in different ways. I'll always love you, too. Even when you get *enormous*."

Some children keep a "grown-up" self at day care and keep all their "baby-me" feelings for home, even with relatively undemanding teachers. This is bound to make going to day care more difficult, especially on low-energy days. You might want to work on

KNITTING TOGETHER HOME AND DAY-CARE SELVES

- Check in with teachers about opportunities for getting "babied":
  1. Is there time for Puppy, Baby, and Hospital play?
  2. Do teachers still snuggle children?
- Talk more about day-care people and events at home for a while.
- Display day-care projects, borrow day-care books or ideas.
- Exchange notes. You can stash notes to your child in pockets or lunchboxes; ask teachers to offer to write down notes for you from your child when a mood is low.

Development does not march along in steady progress toward greater independence from parents. Independence and dependence continually trade places in young children. Staying steady as a parent through all the changes is tough. You just get used to your infant cruising around without you, and bang!—"Carry me" comes again. The often-impossible but urgent toddler drive to "do it myself!" makes toddlers need you and reject you at the same time. Just when you pack up the diapers and the car seat, your too-big-for-my-britches preschooler takes to baby talk all day long.

Such changing demands confuse parents who stay home, too. They also wonder, "Am I doing the right thing? Am I providing the right stuff?" They have the extra burden of trying to provide everything alone. We have the extra burden of not knowing completely what others are providing, and of having the daily good-bye force us to wonder about that again and again. Ideally, day care balances these extra burdens with extra resources. Teachers who have seen many children through many stages can help you figure out what's a stage and what helps with it; other parents' experience can help sort out what's the place or the age, what to worry about, and how to enjoy the rest.

Separation as Relationship: Parent-Teacher Talk

Dave peers over his paper, watching the "women" in his house drive each other crazy. Marjorie is trying to leave for an evening meeting; three-year-old Nadja is pattering after her, trying to show her a scratch, asking why she has to leave, demanding more dessert. Marjorie keeps doing one more thing to try to leave Nadja in a happy mood—it's pointless. Nadja always acts as though she's being thrown to the wolves when Dad's in charge. After Marjorie leaves, they always have a fine time together. Really, it's two-faced, but she's just a kid. What's galling is that Marjorie acts as if she buys it. Does she actually believe that leaving their daughter with him is some kind of major problem? He considers saying, "Would you just get out of here! We'll be fine, for heaven's sake" . . . but maybe the two of them just have to work this out their own way.

Should Dave tell Marjorie to relax and leave? Should he be following Nadja around, trying to get her to read a story with him or something before Marjorie leaves? Or *do* the "women" just have to work this out on their own?

Many teachers face similar dilemmas. There isn't a universal "should" to apply to Dave and Marjorie at home or parents at day care. The first section of this chapter emphasized finding a way to depart that reassures your child. Inside this priority, many departure styles still work. Some parents want active teacher help, some don't; the best way will depend on what works for individual children. Planning it out with teachers and trying different things should help turn up that best way.

It's not always easy for two parents, let alone parents and teachers, to discuss what happens at departures. An insult factor intrudes. Suppose Nadja's behavior does make Marjorie wonder a little—maybe David just keeps reading the paper after she goes? That's not going to be easy to ask him about. If Dave finds Marjorie's efforts to please Nadja a little insulting, if what he thinks of saying is "Who do you think you're leaving her with—Attilla the Hun?," he might not start the conversation either. Settling some of these questions would make everyone happier, but at home there's enough love and trust between adults to tolerate a silence. At day care, you might want to be more aggressive about answering:

RELATIONSHIP QUESTIONS IN SEPARATIONS

- *Reassure yourself.* How could you feel surer of your teacher's relationship with your child?
  1. *Remember.* What evidence do you already have tucked away? Does your teacher's regular talk with you show affection, thought, enjoyment?
  2. *Ask for good news.* Try asking "What went right today?" for a while, or arranging a general conference about how your child is doing. Listen for affection, thought, and delight in your child.
  3. *Visiting.* Your own child will focus on you when you visit, but you can see teachers' relationships with other children and judge from that. What's the general tone?
- *Reassure your teacher.* Say, for example, "I believe that Nadja is fine here after I go. I know it's not you. She just does this, and . . ." "It's okay with me," or—"I'd like your help making it easier."

Separation as Relationship: Things to Try

SORT OUT THE PARENT PART:

- Change your good-bye technique to calm, confident, and short for two weeks. See what happens.
- Wait out of sight at day care after you leave. Does your child recover quickly?

- Ask another parent to notice how soon your child feels better after you go.
- Ask a friend to listen to you talk about morning separations.

INFANTS

SMOOTH OUT OLDER INFANT SEPARATIONS (page 69):

- Tell teachers about the owning phase.
- Report what you see of it at home.
- Check about "stay-put!" demands after you leave; support teachers' efforts with thanks.
- Hand your baby directly to your teacher when you go.

TODDLERS

FIND ANOTHER FOCUS (page 73):

- An activity, then a good-bye routine
- Other children
- A teacher

PRESCHOOLERS

OFFER GROWING-UP INSURANCE (page 75):

- Read fairy tales where heroes get help.
- Tell "smart you" stories from your child's past.
- Join "Baby" play.
- Have a serious talk about growing up.

Separation as Technique Worksheet

Describe your current good-bye. What do you usually do? What happens?

_____

_____

_____

How do you look and sound when you say good-bye?

_____

_____

What message do you think your child might be getting in your good-bye?

_____

Do you want to change that message? What could you try?

1. _____   3. _____

2. _____   4. _____

Does your teacher provide the help you need to say good-bye? _____

What kind of help would you like?

_____

What signals with teachers would make good-byes go more smoothly?

_____

_____

Separation as Relationship Worksheet

How do you feel when you leave day care?

_____

_____

Do you feel safe setting your own feelings aside when you
say good-bye? _____ Would it help to check some
things out about the day-care situation? _____

What do you need to check out?

_____

How could you find out about this?

1. _____   3. _____

2. _____   4. _____

What does your teacher think about your good-bye style?

_____

Would your teacher welcome some reassurance about your
trust or being asked for ideas about good-byes? _____

What big messages do you wish you could get across to your
child when you have to leave?

_____

_____

How could you communicate those messages at home?

_____

_____

3

Bodies: Eating, Sleeping, and Toilet Training

> "Two more bites of chicken. *Then* you can have dessert. . . . No, *two*."
>
> "Okay. But this is the *last* story. Then bed. I'm not kidding."
>
> "I won't flush now, but really, it's all right. It's just a noise."

WE WERE GOING TO BE SO cool. *Other* parents would fret about food, have three-hour bedtime routines and children waking them up at all hours; *other* parents would hold long, boring conversations in bathrooms about inelegant topics. *Our* children would eat, sleep, and use toilets simply, naturally, happily. What's all the fuss about—you just have to be organized, don't you?

Basic body issues take many parents by surprise—it's all so much more complicated and desperate than we expected! Working out answers for home use proves challenging enough; then day-care teachers turn out to have their own ways and schedules. We leave notes: "No bottle before lunch," "Wake her up at two," "Take him to the bathroom at nine and ten," but it doesn't always work. Hundreds of child-rearing books offer many ideas for things to try at home. This chapter looks at how day care affects eating, sleeping, and toilet training, and how to resolve conflicts with teachers over the unexpected complications.

Eating: Finding the Questions

Larry's mom says, "Make sure he eats the noodles first."

(Larry's mom thinks)

If he eats the applesauce first, he won't eat the noodles at all. The noodles have the cheese, the protein that can put some strength in that little body. He needs it; I need it; I've used all my sick days already. If he'd eat better, maybe he'd go longer between meals, too; I won't have to spend my whole life offering food. And if he can stock up on solid food, maybe he'd sleep through the night instead of waking for a bottle, then waking up again soaking wet. . . . She thinks I'm overdoing it; she doesn't understand!

(Larry's teacher thinks)

Of course I'll try the noodles first. Does she think I'm an idiot? But if it's no go, I'm handing out the applesauce—I can't have a hungry, fussy child here. And I have to be the judge of "no go." If she needs to be in charge of details like this, maybe she isn't ready for day care. I only have seventy-five other things to keep track of at lunchtime. Larry is perfectly healthy—this obsession with food is crazy. She needs to relax and let me do my job.

At lunchtime, Larry thinks, Noodles are boring. Where's that applesauce?

Hands-on Training Parents almost always have plans for and fears about their children's eating. They worry that their children are too thin or too fat, not eating enough of the right stuff at the right times. Early infancy sets up the problems. Parents count the number of minutes on each breast, the number of ounces taken from bottles, the amount of time between feedings; parents have to plan which week to start cereal and fruit and how to offer milk, cereal, and fruit so the right amounts of each go down. They study relationships: food and gas, food and sleep, food and diapers, food and mood. The early doctor visits are powerful: If the weight gain is right, you're a success! If not, you are robbed of pleasure and confidence in yourself as a parent.

When parents start using day care, they suddenly lose control of eating; they try shifting to indirect control. They ask teachers, "What did she eat? How much? When? Did you offer the noodles first?" The instructions often fall flat; teachers don't always know *exactly* what was eaten when. Now parents wonder, "Why aren't teachers paying more attention to eating? How can I get them going on this?"

Hands-off Training Teachers usually don't pay a lot of attention to one child's eating because 1) It's very hard to do when you are opening containers, sopping up spills, preventing theft and choking, and refilling milks for many children at once, and 2) It doesn't strike them as necessary or even healthy. Most children seem to do fine with a relaxed approach; not having an adult hanging on their every bite gives them peace and freedom with food. Good teachers will work hard with parents around eating problems, but they need to know that there *is* a real problem before they can join in with a clear conscience.

Handshake If you're feeling stuck on an eating issue with your child's teacher, you might ask yourself: Why am I concerned? Where am I getting my ideas about what my child should eat? Theories about eating in magazines and books assault parents; "theories" from their own pasts operate on automatic pilot. Ask, "What would it take for me to feel safe about eating? What are the *facts* that count for me—weight gain? family medical history? allergies?"—and ask teachers to help you gather the facts you need.

Eating: Developmental Issues

INFANTS

"He's always starving when we get home . . . I know you feed him . . . I just don't understand it."

"She hardly eats anything at home . . . do you think she's too tired to eat? Maybe you could skip the last snack. . . ."

"But I left plenty of breast milk!"

Infants' appetites come in all sizes, timings, consistencies, and parent-torture factors; they vary from day to day on their own and with colds, teething, learning to grasp things, sit, or cruise. Spare yourself worry: Don't count calories day by day. If you need to do some counting, give everyone weeks to make progress.

Day care can add other twists to appetite mysteries. All the action and distraction inspires some babies to eat and distracts others. Some infants fall into a regular stocking-up pattern: They eat a lot at day care and less at home, or vice versa. If you think the distractions at day care are interfering with good weight gain, tell your teacher and ask if a more boring eating arrangement can be managed. Sometimes just facing the highchair in a different direction makes a difference. Many infants do fine with these catch-up eating patterns, however; if your baby seems reasonably healthy, you don't need to change anything.

Stretching feeding times is trickier at day care than at home. How do you stretch feedings at home? Most parents drop everything and try to distract their baby: sing, dance, offer new toys. Teachers can do this sometimes but not always; sometimes just when one starts seriously fussing for food, other infants need changing, feeding, rocking, or rescuing. More important, infants need the sights and sounds of day care to be associated with *good* feelings, not with being hungry. Teachers have to juggle several goals while they work on stretching out feeding times. If you or your teachers feel discouraged about a stretching effort, try keeping records of times or amounts over several days or weeks. You might see more progress than you've sensed or find a pattern you can plan around. Aiming for small but steady changes keeps spirits up.

Experienced or observant infant teachers usually know more good feeding tricks and have a clearer sense of how to work with infant eating styles than anyone else you could talk to, so:

TAP INTO YOUR TEACHERS' EXPERTISE

You might want to ask:
- *About Past Experiences:* For example, "Have you ever had a baby who hated every single kind of cereal? What did you do?"
- *For Specific Opinions:* "Do you think the kind of spoon makes a difference? Do I have to try all forty different kinds . . . ?"
- *About Development:* "How long does it take before they get more down their mouths than their necks?"
- *For Experience with Your Own Child:* "*How* did you get Susie to eat those noodles?"

Offer your own expertise, too—specific stories help most. Your infant teacher is one of the few people on earth who is *genuinely* interested in what happened when you tried the carrots last night, and sharing these tales makes the work in both places more fun.

TODDLERS

Nicholas's dad drops by the center on a day when his work travels bring him close at lunchtime. He leaves astounded. "I can't believe what I just saw!" he says. "At home, Nicky *never* sits down to eat. We have raisins and nuts and old carrot ends all over the house. And he never eats more than three bites of anything at one time. But there he was, sitting, eating real lunch!"

Sitting still long enough to eat goes against the grain for many toddlers. Two special mental quirks also complicate eating. Toddlers don't divide up features of the world like adults do, so they confuse parts and wholes. Adults know, for example, that the taste of oatmeal stays the same no matter what bowl it's in. A toddler won't be sure. For a toddler, oatmeal-in-the-green-bowl may be one whole, taste-producing experience; oatmeal-in-the-pink-bowl is *not* oatmeal. Toddlers are also "ritualistic"—they have a passionate feel for the "right way" some things must be seen and done. Between two and a half and three especially, many toddlers commit themselves to one book, to one way of dressing and arranging the bed, to one or two things they'll eat. They treat any change in these arrangements as a threat, as though the order and safety of the world truly depended on particular objects and actions. If your toddler is being fussy enough about food at home to require a full-time adult slave, it's hard to believe teachers are managing at day care. How do teachers do it? Some common approaches:

TODDLER-TEACHER EATING TRICKS

- Sympathize with toddler reactions to "bad" food—"You don't really like *that* stuff"—and help them recognize other choices.
- Make small special arrangements when it will make a big difference: "Okay. Look. I'll move the tuna over here."
- Then back off and stick to some simple rules: "I've helped you sit down three times; that's telling me you're not interested in eating. I guess you're done. Let's clean up!" or "Five

more minutes, honey. Eat if you're hungry; we have to stop soon."

Simple rules that declare an *end* to eating time usually work very well with toddlers. Many parents might never discover this; limiting access to food at home seems harsh when it's all right there staring at everyone. At day care, however, such rules are essential. Running around, falling off chairs for fun, and singing while eating have to be heavily discouraged because choking presents a more serious danger in a busy group, and food cannot be available all the time. The general success of teachers' rules about eating suggests that they meet some toddler need. Perhaps the rules reassure: "I'm not worried about this! The safety of the world does *not* depend on food arrangements *or* on your eating," and that's just what they need to hear. Ending rules also create a genuine choice: Eat or don't eat. Toddlers often don't know how to finish up with things—think of all the times they dump a box of toys when they're "done" playing. Flexibility about ending eating at home may keep toddlers at the eating chore when the real answer is "I'm not hungry now."

You may not want to have simple, cut-and-dried rules for eating at home at all. Some happy, grubby, open-kitchen chaos around food may strike you as just the kind of coziness that family life's about. In any case, you can think of daycare rules as giving you the results of an experiment. If your toddlers' eating habits at home are driving you crazy, check in with your toddler teachers. If they are having more luck, you can borrow some ideas to try. You may not want to do the same things, but at least you'll know what's possible.

PRESCHOOLERS

"I had to sit next to Jason and I *hate* him!"

"I wanted to sit next to Deborah, but Sarah and Charlene got there first, and they wouldn't move over!"

"Danny has Gummy Goofballs in *his* lunch . . . why can't I have some?"

"*Everybody* gets cookies but *me*! It's *not fair!*"

"We had chicken for lunch today, and I *hate* chicken!"

Sometimes preschoolers find life to be one outrageous insult after another. Nothing is fair. Great new mental machinery for comparisons and relationships and for imagining more perfect worlds makes these complaints possible. Can you think of them as achievements?

If you're deluged with complaints, you might ask teachers about seating or food rules, so you can take a stab at explaining how teachers are *trying* to be fair or brainstorm other possible rules. When you talk with teachers, be prepared for an earful about how "those two never eat if they're together," or "but *she* didn't want to sit next to *her*," or how foods that spell Poison for some parents spell Love for others. Few things are simple with groups. Sometimes parents can come up with compromise rules at group meetings. You might also try pure sympathy with your preschooler—"Oh, that sounds tough" or "What a pain!" Preschoolers often care much more about moral support than they do about practical arrangements.

By the preschool years, eating-to-live worries parents less, but children's manners begin to grate. Relatives are less forgiving about burps and fingers at Thanksgiving dinner; and parents are often getting a little tired of grossness at dinner themselves. Mealtimes become nag sessions. On weekdays parents spend such a huge percentage of their total-time-with-child at meals that the nagging job can poison the week. Most parents find that even fifty thousand repetitions of "Sit still," "Don't talk with your mouth full," "Use your fork," "Don't play with your food," "Say 'excuse me' when you burp," just don't seem to *take* on their preschoolers. You might try picking one day as Manners Day, or one rule to work on for a while, or putting it all on hold temporarily. Check in at day care, too. Most teachers have a set of routines about Acceptable Things to Do with Milk, Sitting Without Kicking, and Saying Please. If you recycle those routines at home, some nice habits might come faster.

KEEPING FOOD PEACE WITH PRESCHOOLERS

- Sympathize with complaints:
  1. Keep explaining or fixing on hold until sure it's wanted.
  2. Show interest in the *thinking* behind objections.
- Protect mealtime enjoyment for yourself and your child.
  1. Keep expectations pretty low until four and a half or five.
  2. Pick just one or two rules or one day (reinvent Sunday dinner?) to work on manners, and just don't look the rest of the time.
  3. Ask teachers about their behavior-at-the-table rules; use similar reminders at home.

By the end of the day-care years, many parents are telling themselves, "Well, I guess children *can* live on milk and two green beans a day," "She'll stop looking chubby as soon as the next growth spurt plugs in," "The purple dinosaur vitamins will have to do until spinach looks good," and "Actually, there's a lot of nutrition in ice cream." You will find your own balance of concern and optimism about food as you go along. Using day care's steady beat of food offerings as background and teachers' many-child experiences as a tour book can make finding a balance easier.

Eating: Parent-Teacher Talk

When she reads LILY—NO PEANUT BUTTER on the blackboard this morning, Donna blows up: "This is ridiculous!" Every morning it's something new: NO APPLES FOR LILY, NO REGULAR CRACKERS TODAY—RICE CRACKERS IN CUBBY, NO OR-

ANGES. Never an explanation: just the order. The unpredict-able notes leave her with the choice of rearranging the whole group's snack, which she makes early in order to be free for children, or giving Lily a separate snack—which Lily hates. When she handed her the rice cracker yesterday, Lily just Frisbeed it across the room. Donna has been so annoyed about the notes, she's barely talked to Lily's parents in weeks. She resolves to capture them the next day. They tell her: Both of them have many allergies; Lily has had several mysterious rashes and low fevers; they were trying to see if she had allergies, too. Donna explains: That's fine! She just needs to know the day before.

When you want to get teachers on your eating team, ex-plain why you think adults need to get involved. Explain at least three times. Reasons don't always have to be ironclad. All of these approaches have worked:

GETTING TEACHERS BEHIND YOUR GOAL

- Make it official: "Our pediatrician said she should have gained several pounds by now, and she's only gained one."
- Make it vivid: "Not eating solids means he wakes up hungry for a bottle at one, then he wakes up soaking and hungry again at three and at five. We're falling-on-our-faces tired. . . ."
- Make it part of a process: "We don't know if he's really aller-gic, but we have to try this to see," "We don't know if more solids will cure the sleeping problem, but we need to try it first," "Maybe she *is* getting enough different kinds of food, just on different days. Could you keep notes for a few days? Maybe that would help us stop worrying."

What if you can't *find* any good reasons? Your child seems fine, but you're still worried. It happens. No one is perfectly rational about everything, and overworked, sleep-deprived, child-adoring parents deserve more slack about this than most people. Most parents also come from families where certain ways of eating or feeding were quite mixed up with "being good" or with loving itself. When eating worries draw power from such big issues, they're very tough to shake. What can you do?

NO GOOD REASON

- *Please:* Throw yourself on the mercy of your teacher. It's not fair to *expect* extra effort where no good reason exists, but *favors* might be possible.
- *Pleas:* Use teachers' success with let-them-alone eating to talk to your Worrier Within: "See?! Nobody's counting bites, and she's *still fine*. So hush up!"
- *Pleased:* Could you be content with the amount of control you have at home? Let weekdays work out however they do, and work on your goals during home time.

Eating: Things to Try

INFANTS

WITH TOO-BUSY-TO-EAT-AT-DAY-CARE BABIES:

- Bring distraction level down:
  1. Turn high chair away from the scene of action.
  2. Arrange a soft lights-and-music eating nook.
  3. Schedule this child's lunch during others' naps.
- Bring distraction to the eating scene:
  1. Use finger food early.
  2. Make toys to chew and handle part of being fed.

STRETCHING:

- Keep records.
- Look for special interest (toys, books, tapes?) to use for distracting at home and bring in for day-care try.

TAP INTO YOUR TEACHERS' EXPERTISE (page 86):

- Relevant past experiences
- Particular opinions
- Developmental knowledge
- Personal experience with your own child

TODDLERS

- Share information with teachers about food loves, hates, and quirks.
- Cut down number of types of food offered at any one time.
- Double-check food facts about expected weight gains and needed nourishment—it's probably lower and simpler than you think.
- Try Toddler-Teacher Eating Tricks at home, too (page 87):
  1. Sympathize about "bad" food.
  2. Make small adjustments.
  3. Consider ending eating rules.

PRESCHOOLERS

When social part of eating overwhelms food intake, teachers can:

- Read or tell stories at lunch and snack.
- Play guessing games during eating times: "I'm thinking of something in this room, big, and red . . ." "How many people have something orange in their lunch?"
- Let preschoolers "own" eating times as much as possible.

Preschoolers can

- Set food out themselves (lunchbox food they made at home if possible).
- Arrange tables and clean them up after lunch.
- Write notes (with teachers) about their food wishes.

KEEP FOOD PEACE WITH PRESCHOOLERS (page. 90):

- Accept complaints; explore thinking behind them
- Work on manners one rule at a time or one day in a week; recycle teachers' manner routines at home

Sleep: Finding the Questions

> 8:00   Shana's parents drag her out of bed. Sleepy and irritable, she fights with them about dressing, eating, and leaving.
>
> 9:30:   Shana arrives at day care talking, bouncing, all systems go.
>
> 1:00:   Lights out for older preschoolers, all of whom fall asleep except Shana, who whispers loudly and often, goes to the bathroom two extra times, jumps up and down on her cot, and generally gets in trouble six ways from Sunday.
>
> 2:15:   Older preschoolers begin to wake up; Shana falls asleep.
>
> 3:00:   Shana's parents arrive; they have to wake her. Sleepy and irritable, she fights with them about dressing and leaving.
>
> 10:30:   After two hours of "getting-ready-for-bed" battles, Shana finally falls asleep.
>
> *Parent answer:* Teachers should not let Shana fall asleep.
>
> *Teacher answer:* Parents should wake Shana up earlier in the morning and make her go to sleep earlier at night.

Greenwich Standard Time When our children are too tired and cranky after day care, or too awake for far too long, many parents think nap: Nap is too long, too short, comes at the wrong time. If they ask teachers, "Couldn't she just skip nap?" or "Couldn't you let him sleep a little longer off in a corner?," they often meet resistance—polite descriptions of the difficulties, a baleful glare, or outright laughter. Parents usually don't see what the big deal is. They're operating on home experience, where a missed nap or a snooze on the couch sometimes works fine. Day care is different. If you want to see a teacher's point of view, don't imagine your child alone at home; imagine holding a birthday party for ten when your child has skipped nap or fallen asleep on the couch. How many days in a row would you like to do that?

The need to work with many children's schedules makes day-care naptime pretty inflexible. So, are you stuck? It depends. Working together, parents and teachers can move a child's sleep schedule around gradually. You have to figure out what your child's natural sleep pattern is, and then plan ten-minutes-earlier-every-day wake-ups at home and at day care until you move the whole cycle to a better time. But what, exactly, is a better time?

Daylight Savings Time An earlier sleep schedule doesn't always fit with other family needs. Working parents don't see their children much during the day; an early bedtime comes too fast on the heels of dinner for many parents. They miss their children; they want to play a little. And who needs early mornings?

Changing Time Zones If your child seems tired and cranky all the time, it might be jet lag. Your family could be operating on a sleep schedule that makes it difficult for your child to use the group naptime; some needed sleep hours could be getting lost. What can you do? In theory, at least, you could canvass other families and see if the whole group naptime could be moved toward your family time; in practice, you might have to move home sleep times toward the group schedule if you really want to make more sleep possible. If this shortens a beloved evening time, you have to ask yourself, "What do I want most?" Ask, too, "Do we all still like each other?" Late sleep schedules not only set teachers and children up for nap battles, they may be setting you up for frazzled bedtimes and miserable mornings. What choice protects your child's circle of affection?

Many parents muddle through without making any permanent choices about sleep patterns. When children seem too tired but still won't go to bed, they get organized and consistent for a while about earlier schedules; eventually "life" takes over again, and the whole family just grabs some sleep whenever they can. Sleep issues never go away; you'll always have a chance to try out a new choice and see how it fits with life at the moment.

Sleep: Developmental Issues

INFANTS

> TEACHER: "I'm having a terrible time getting Matt to sleep. He seems too tired to play, almost too tired to eat, everything frustrates him. He wants to be carried all the time. I *know* he's tired. But nothing I've tried works. How do you get him to nap on the weekends?"
>
> PARENT: "Well, actually [cough] we have trouble too. We usually put him in his car seat and just drive around until he falls asleep."

Wouldn't it be great if infants came with Sleeping Instructions like the cleaning-direction tags in clothes? "Feed, rock gently in warm air, let cry for eight minutes." Instructions would vary at least as much as those for silk and cotton do. (It would *also* be nice if someone would please invent an indoor infant seat with vibrating hummer and tapes of traffic noise or whatever it is that's so magic about car rides. Why should parents have to leave their homes for such great help?) Some infants love holding and patting, others like "space"; some like quiet, others do better with noise; some need something to suck, others just twirl hair, pull ears, rub blankets, or collapse. Parents and teachers can help each other out by sharing all the Sleep Instructions they discover.

Some infants can drop off to sleep anywhere (were they born last of twelve children in some former life?). Some infants sleep easily at home but with difficulty at day care, or vice versa. Most infants find a way of sleeping in both places after a while. If "a while" seems too long to you, you might look for ways to make the home and day-care sleeping scenes more similar. Same songs? Same blanket?

Around the first birthday, infants often have trouble sleeping. Lots of things are going on at this age: a shift from two naps to one, a pre-walking drive to move constantly; yet another peak in "separation anxiety." The second nap sometimes goes later and later until it comes very close to pickup time. Some parents love late naps—they make the ride home and the whole evening smoother. Some parents hate late naps: Their bright-eyed babies protest the confining ride home and stay up too late. Teachers can do some juggling for parents' needs, but not if all the parents *and* all the infants want different things. Here are some ways to work on:

LATE-NAP DILEMMAS

- Get out your calculator, plug in all the infants' napping needs, their parents' wishes, the space and personnel limitations, and hunt for a new solution. Seriously. You might find one.
- Rearrange your pickup time or your dinnertime or home playtime.
- Study your baby's whole sleeping schedule. Does it make sense to try delaying morning nap? Moving afternoon nap back and letting the morning nap disappear? Plan small ten-minute-a-day changes with your teacher.
- Hang on and wait for your child to grow out of this pattern.

TODDLERS

"I don't know what happened. We used to rock and hum a little and give her a few final pats-to-sleep on the back; we let a little light in from the hall to help with midnight changing. Now she wants to sleep with all the lights on. She has to have two bottles in her crib, and we have to read three stories, sing two songs, and prop a stuffed animal in each corner of her crib. She has four little quilts that all have to go on in a certain *order*, for heaven's sake. How did we ever get into this mess? And how do you ever get her to sleep here?"

Many toddlers have no trouble napping at day care but do not fall asleep easily at home. Parents wonder why—are they missing some tricks? Is napping ruining nighttime sleep? Does the separation from parents during the day make "good night" too hard?

Many things make naps easier at day care—a consistent daily schedule, regular outdoor exercise, the "stimulation" of other children. Other children and teachers stay in the room at naptime, so loneliness is not an issue. Good teachers rely on rituals as well. They sing the same songs every day before nap; they know how to arrange the covers for each child just so. Some parents report that learning to sing those naptime songs helps sleep at home; you might try it if you're looking for one more trick.

Nap and night sleep are bound up together. When they're off schedule, it's more accurate to say they're ruining each other. The average toddler requires around thirteen hours of total sleep in twenty-four, about two to two and a half hours of it in the daytime. You might look to see what average is for your child and look at nap and night sleep in that light: When are those hours available? A late bedtime can form part of two trouble cycles: late wake-up—late nap—late bedtime—late wake-up; early wake-up—long nap—late bedtime (one whole sleep cycle—sixty minutes or so in young children—gets shifted to daytime sleep).

The daytime separation does work against early bedtimes, especially with toddlers. Without question, it would be simpler for most parents to put a toddler to bed if they'd just spent twelve straight hours together, although it's tough to get toddlers to do anything, and bedtime is no exception. But a work schedule makes just-before bed an unusually precious time with this age group. With infants and preschoolers, we can get some perky and charming time even in the middle of morning and evening routines; toddlers balk more during these rush hours—parents often feel that they're fighting with toddlers every minute. Just before bed, finally there's no rush; parents get to giggle, snuggle, and wrestle with small beings in soft PJs who adore them. Most parents can use this kind of sweet time before they start all over again the next day.

If you're thinking about reorganizing your toddler's sleep schedule, you could use your day-care network to help you see your own situation in a fuller light.

GET TIRED TODDLER TALES

At a parent meeting, or through teachers, find out:

- When other parents start putting their toddlers to bed
- When other toddlers actually fall asleep and wake up
- What sorts of bedtime rituals work for other parents
- Whether other parents see nap as a problem, wish it were later or longer; whether others stick with a naptime on weekends
- What changes of schedule or routine people have tried and how that's worked out

Other parents' facts may be enlightening or reassuring or good for some laughs. Any of the three might be useful.

PRESCHOOLERS

> "Mom! Mom! I had a terrible dream! A big white thing
> . . . like a cloud . . . a big cloud right in my room . . . It
> came in through the window. It was watching me. And you
> came. But we couldn't make it go. . . . I'm not going back
> to sleep. I don't want that dream to come again. You stay."

When your preschooler starts having nightmares, your
first thought may be that something awful has happened at
day care. By all means, check it out. Tell your teachers about
the nightmare in the morning; ask them to think about what
could have inspired it. Worry of one kind or another causes
nightmares; you want to find out what you can. Even something reported by *another* child, like "My dog got run over
last night," can stir up worry in a child. Chapter 7 describes
some of the worries that just come to preschoolers with age
and ways to explore what's wrong when you have vague
signs like nightmares to work with.

Preschoolers' own new powers of representation may be
partially responsible for nightmares. In their own artwork,
they can now look at a squiggly line and "see" a tree, a road,
a rainbow. Perhaps they now "see" more things in their own
mental pictures at night. Images in their minds, or shadows
in their rooms, can now mean more than they did before.
Because this whole way of seeing things is pretty new to
preschoolers, nighttime images must be more startling.
Nightmares mean it's time to talk about *something* that's
worrying your child (during the day). You can look for clues
in the dream, check with teachers for ideas, or just listen
closely to your child's talk for a few days.

Many four-year-olds complain loudly about naps but drop
off to sleep soundly and wake up bouncing. It's Standard
Four-Year-Old Operating Procedure: Don't let the grown-
ups boss you around without a fight, even when they're

right. Other four- and five-year-olds do stop sleeping at day care but use the quiet time very well—they relax and work through things in their minds. Just as infants practice basic syllable sounds and toddlers practice words in private crib talk, preschoolers sometimes practice counting or rhyming, or great heroic speeches, when resting at day care. If your child complains about nap, find out if sleep comes eventually, and if not, how your child uses rest time. If you get a picture of pointless boredom, ask if some quiet activity, like looking at a book, could be allowed.

Just airing their experiences and grievances helps preschoolers more than you'd expect. Many children this age also love storybooks that deal with their concerns—*There's a Nightmare in My Closet* (M. Mayer) gets very popular around age three and a half, for example. With both nightmares and nap troubles, you might ask teachers to:

BRING SLEEP TROUBLES INTO THE LIGHT

- Invite children to talk about their dreams or air nap gripes in a group circle time.
- Make a group book (with personal quotes and pictures) about sleep and how they feel or think about it.
- Read children's books that deal with dreams and sleeping. Suggest or lend any you've found helpful at home.

Bad sleep problems can crop up at any age. One of the worst things about children's sleep problems is that *parents* get too tired to think about them and stay stuck. Parents really need to take a day off from work, go to a friend's empty house or a motel, get some sleep, and *then* think about it. Real change around sleep problems makes an enormous difference in most parents' lives—they recover the will to live, energy for work, affection for their families. Take that day off if you even think you need it.

Sleep: Parent-Teacher Talk

> Caroline's dad hands her teacher a homemade calendar with her new sleep-schedule plans written out across the days. It calls for teachers to wake her up from nap ten minutes earlier every day for a week and then hold steady at two-thirty for another week. The sleep book he's read promises that this, plus the same effort from him at home in the mornings, will solve all their bedtime and morning blues.
>
> The teacher says, "What's this?" and glances over the calendar quickly, with a deepening frown. "You know, I think we really just ought to let her sleep as much as possible. She seems to need it, and it's a long day for her here with all the kids."

Whenever parents' plans involve them, teachers need to be *in* on the problem-solving efforts before the final-solution stage. When parents figure everything out alone and hand over the answer, it's Hired Help treatment: "You don't have to understand anything about this, you just have to do it." Most parents don't intend any insult; they've just been too busy working on the problem to consider a teacher's view. Or they assume teachers already know what the problem is and will see right away how the plan works. If you've been busy, tired, and talking to yourself in the car and the grocery-store line, it's easy to forget what you've said aloud and whom you've convinced already. When you run into a wall with teachers over any special request, try backing up on your problem-solving process.

BACKING UP

Special requests come from a whole chain of thought:

- Identifying a problem
- Inventing ways to solve it
- Picking one way to try
- Asking teachers to do that one

When you're stuck with step 4, back up. One step in the chain may be enough; more may be needed, or easier, or better suited to your particular problem or your particular teacher. Suppose your daughter was staying up too late at night. You try asking teachers to wake her up earlier: "Too hard." You could:

- Back up one step: "We think she is staying up so late partly because of sleeping late here. Could you start her resting earlier or wake her up earlier?"
- Back up two steps: "Her late nap here means she's not falling asleep until almost eleven. Is there any way to shift this sleep schedule to better hours?"
- Back up three steps: "She's not falling asleep until almost eleven. I don't know if her schedule is just off or she's worried about something or we're just not setting clear limits. I do know this schedule is ruining our nights *and* our mornings. Help!"

You might also describe your thinking so far: "The late bedtimes were getting to us, then we read this article, and it said . . ." You can try making your sleep goals vivid or part of a discovery process (see Getting Teachers Behind Your Goal in this chapter, page 91) or using Getting from Goals to Actions (Chapter 4, page 144).

You may not always hear what you want to hear; you may hear some great ideas. You *will* get better attention. When you backtrack and include teachers earlier in your problem-solving process, they become Solvers instead of Hired Help. Solvers are much more likely to volunteer experience, observations, and special efforts.

Sleep: Things to Try

R. Ferber's *Solve Your Child's Sleep Problems* shows how to move sleep schedules, including nap, around gradually—you might show teachers a sample schedule or key paragraph. Many parents have found other ideas in this book very useful as well.

INFANTS, TODDLERS, AND PRESCHOOLERS

- Share sleep instructions with teachers—everything that helps at home—routines, mobiles, hummed melodies—the works.
- Make home and day-care sleep more similar any way you can.
- Keep records of fall-asleep times in both places. Shift the schedule in ten-minute steps (see Ferber).
- Get information about how other parents at your day-care center are balancing time and sleep demands.

OLDER TODDLERS AND PRESCHOOLERS

- Check with teachers about specific and general sources of bad dreams—what happened yesterday to your child in particular and in the group.
- Talk with your child during the day about anxieties you think feed the bad dreams.
- Encourage teachers to read books and have group talks about sleeping and dreaming; try some at home.

Toilet Training: Finding the Questions

When Marie arrives at day care, after a positively painful day at work, she finds a pair of plastic bags stuffed in her son Jamie's cubby. She knows what's inside—gross laundry for her. Arrrgh! She strides into the room, finds Jamie, and demands to know: "Two accidents! What happened?!" Seeing him wilt and shrug, she kicks herself—what a way to say hello. And it's probably the teacher she should be talking to anyway. He hasn't had an accident at home for weeks now. This is important; where was the help when he needed it?

Two-Wheeler Lessons Toilet training is like teaching a child to ride a two-wheeler. It can't be explained in words; they have to get the feel of it themselves—you can only support and encourage them while they figure it out. When they're ready to get the balance on their own, adults have to run along side to catch the worst spills.

Whose fault are accidents at day care? When children have lots of accidents, teachers wonder if parents have started too soon. Maybe success at home was really parents' success: Parents learned to notice little give-away wriggles and rush to the bathroom; the child doesn't have a clue what's going on. Parents wonder why teachers can't see when a child needs to go. How about some reminders to try before it's too late?

Running Alongside Most children have more toilet-training accidents at day care than at home, for many reasons. Real toilet training requires that children 1) be able to tune into small body sensations that signal "time to go!" 2) be able to interrupt even engrossing activities on their own, 3) be willing to get adult help where needed (getting to the bathroom, getting undressed, wiping, etc.), and 4) feel safe in the bathroom. At home everything works to support these developments. Parents working on toilet training often simplify their weekend lives for a while, so nothing distracts too much and potties are always nearby. One adult watches for the little wriggles or watches the clock; parents interrupt activities *for* a child if necessary; parents drop everything and hang out in the bathroom as long as it takes. Day care can't provide so much special support. Good teachers do operate on red alert when children begin toilet training in earnest, but caring for many children with many different agendas means they can't keep an eagle eye on one child constantly, can't keep all activities boring, and can't dash off to bathrooms with one child for long periods. You have to expect more accidents at day care.

Training Wheels Lots of accidents at day care (two or three a day on a regular basis?) probably signal that your child is not really ready to be out of diapers there. What should you do? Returning to diaper use at day care is the simple solution, but many parents and teachers feel very uncomfortable making that decision. They fear the child will feel like a terrible failure or will abandon the effort all too gladly or will become miserably tense about making any mistakes. In theory, any of this might happen. In practice, the effect of returning to diapers depends on the realistic alternatives and on how matter-of-factly it's done.

Holding children to a standard of behavior they really cannot meet is never a kindness. Children who want to give up on toilet training will probably find some way of doing it. Adults who have to scrub up messy bottoms and wash out soiled clothes day after day are bound to get annoyed, or at least less concerned about protecting children from a sense of failure or worries about "mistakes." By insisting (or letting your child insist) on no diapers, you may create the very conditions you want to avoid. Ask yourself and the teachers, How many accidents a day can we really stay cheerful and relaxed about? For how long?

Hanging On to the Trikes Some children just don't seem interested in toilet training even after their day-care friends are strutting around in enviable underwear. Their parents worry: What's the problem? The fourth birthday usually brings the last holdouts into the toilet-trained fold. Before this, you probably don't need to worry. Differences in bladder and sphincter size and sensitivity, differences in distractibility, and different degrees of interest in joining the grown-up world all affect toilet-training age. Who says speedy toilet training marks a great parent? Making room for natural differences can feel much more gentle and loving.

Toilet Training: Developmental Issues

Justin, nearly three and a half and still refusing to use the toilet, drives his parents to despair. "I was relieved to find out they actually make diapers in adult sizes," his mother says. "You know, for hospitals and such. Looks like we're going to need them." Justin refuses to discuss anything to do with the bathroom; questions get no answers. He also hates being changed. In the middle of struggling to change a loudly uncooperative Justin one day, a teacher points out with some feeling that he wouldn't have to *be* changed if he'd only decide to use the toilet. Justin lets loose a stream of sound; the only clear words are "the pipes . . . the pipes!" Did someone explain too much to him once? Is he imagining himself being sucked down the pipes into the river?

Children of toilet-training age generally don't have a clue about what poop and pee are, where they come from and go to, whether these products are really *part* of their own bodies, and why adults are so fired-up about toilet use. The bathroom itself often strikes them as a little weird. Other rooms have soft, covered, quiet furniture; bathroom "furniture" is hard, shiny, and noisy. Worse, things disappear into bathroom furniture. Toothpaste goes down the sink; soapy water goes down the tub; toilet paper goes down the toilet. Can they go down the drain, too? Young children don't have a firm handle on many impossibles.

These uncertainties are part of children's whole mental makeup between two and three; reason is powerless against them. Detailed explanations may help some children but just confuse or worry others. The best antidote for most children lies in making the bathroom a friendly place. Good teachers make time for lots of hanging out in the bathroom, chatting, even reading or telling stories while a whole group gets "done." They allow a fair amount of goofing around with potties and sinks, lots of unnecessary flushing and toilet-paper spinning; they try to keep a perfect balance of praise for potty-users and hope/acceptance for the disinterested. You can contribute to the relaxing power of this scene.

HELPING TEACHERS TRAIN

- Make the home bathroom a place to relax and chat.
- Send your child in clothes that he or she can get on and off with little help.

- Keep yourself ignorant or quiet about which other children in the group are toilet-trained.
- Get bathroom news from teachers at the end of the day and congratulate your child on *any* forward step—with clothes and with being willing to "try," as well as with specific "success."

Toilet-Training: Parent-Teacher Talk

Sarah's already-used-to-day-care, perfectly toilet-trained-over-the-summer, almost-three-year-old son, Carl, starts having accidents at day care. She asks teachers to remind him more frequently. They try, but Carl usually refuses to go except when the group goes at its regular times. The whole point of training is for *him* to decide to go; teachers tell Sarah, "We'll ask him, but that's all we can do."

As Carl's accidents continue, teachers begin to wonder about the psychology—is Carl rebelling this way? Is this all a move to get more Mom attention? Could this be his revenge for her bringing home a baby brother? He's so organized about everything else—the best puzzle-doer in the place—maybe he's trying to keep a bit of babyhood in his life, just for balance?

Carl's next medical exam reveals another possibility. His sphincter has been stretched by a backlog of feces. Stretched sphincters can become quite insensitive; Carl is probably not getting the basic body signals he needs. How did all this start? The doctor is not sure, but viruses can throw off excreting rhythms, she says, and it could all be as simple as that. Taking care of the backlog did take care of the accidents.

Parents and teachers often come up with different first guesses about "why." Most commonly, teachers think something's not right at home, and parents think something's not right at day care. Even within marriages, people tend to look in different places for causes—not only at the other person, but in completely different fields of explanation. You might say, for example, "She's tired . . . it's hot . . . she's getting a cold," while your partner says, "She's spoiled . . . you don't set clear rules . . . you're acting just like your mother."

Children are complicated; "why" is rarely obvious. You usually have to check out lots of possibilities when you really want to know. When different theories stall plans for tackling a problem at day care, you might try:

COLLECTING EVIDENCE

Parents and teacher can:

- List all the whys they can think of that might be part of a problem.
- Pin down what they could *see* or check out in other ways that would provide evidence about those whys.
- Get together and pool the results of their watching or checking before making a new plan.

"What could we *look at* to help us answer 'why?'" is a good question for many day-care issues. With toilet training, you and teachers might decide to spend a few days looking at how easily your child interrupts play for *any* reason, whether he or she seems comfortable asking teachers for help with things, or how often your child actually "uses" diapers or the bathroom—is this little bladder too little? You might look for other signs of preoccupation or worry. Is this brain too busy to work on training right now? Or ask your doctor to check for physical complications. It's too hard to answer "why?" through theory. Turn to the practical world of this child, this month, and see what you can see.

Toilet-Training: Things to Try

- Wait until success at home is steady and strong before trying it at day care.
- Save underpants until success at day care is steady and strong.
- Ask teachers to note *when* accidents happen, to look for timing patterns—maybe only one special reminder is needed.

HELPING TEACHERS TRAIN (page 107):

- Home bathroom homey
- Easy on-and-off clothes
- No comparisons
- Praise for every step

With our children's bodies' workings, it's tough to find a right "distance" to keep. We have to try to keep them healthy and rested and to help them grow up out of diapers. We have to try arranging good conditions—food they might like offered at reasonable intervals, the chance to sleep on a realistic schedule, the chance to take pride in bathroom management. On the other hand, eating, sleeping, and toilet training are the three battles we can't win. We can't *make* our children do any of them. If we let these areas turn into battlegrounds and try to win the war, we succeed mainly in driving ourselves and everyone else crazy.

Most children are pretty willing to eat when hungry, sleep when tired, and use the toilet eventually. By working with conditions and *then* backing off, perhaps we can keep all these body issues just that simple. Our children can say, "Ahhhh, food," "Ahhhh, bed," and "I'm grown up!" *without* fear of self-surrender or of our disappointment and *with* the pleasure we really want for them.

Eating Worksheet

Are you worried about your child's eating at day care? ___
Why? _____

_____

Do your teachers know about your reasons? _____Do your
teachers disagree with your goal? _____
How have you tried to get them behind your goal?

_____

_____

What would count as evidence, for you and teachers, that
"relaxing" about eating would be safe? _____

_____

How could you get this evidence? _____

_____

Do teachers agree with your goal but not the methods?
What do they recommend? How do they think you could
get there? _____

_____

Sleeping Worksheet

Are you too tired even to think about this? _____ When
and where could you get at least one good nap and
one unbroken night's sleep? _____ . Have you
looked at *How to Solve Your Child's Sleep Problems*?

Do teachers think your child seems tired at day care or report trouble at nap? _____ Are other children having trouble, too? _____
What are teachers doing to help with this?

_____

Are you comfortable with that approach? _____

What difficulties would an earlier (or later) sleep schedule
   fix? _____
   create? _____
   Can you see a compromise schedule? _____ Do you
      have to choose? _____

Does your child seem basically on schedule but suddenly worried about sleep? _____ Have you asked your child or teachers what it could be? _____ Would it make sense to give general reassurances (or explanations) about what's going on lately with:
      you? _____
      family life? _____
      what it means to grow up? _____
   What could you say that your child might understand?

_____

Toilet-Training Worksheet

How often does your child use the bathroom at home? _____ How often can your teacher take your child at day care? _____

At day care, does your child:
　　interrupt activities easily? _____
　　ask teachers for help easily? _____
　　seem comfortable hanging out in the bathroom? _____
How many accidents does your child have at home on
　　weekends? _____
How many accidents is your child having at day care on a
　　regular basis? _____
How many accidents are your teachers comfortably handling
　　every day? _____ For how long? _____

4

Curriculum: ABC and TLC

"What do you think you're doing?" That's what Alicia wants to ask the teachers—not in a mean way, but really. There's Will, off in a corner playing with trucks. He's always off in a corner playing with trucks when she comes. He's having a good time—the "Bbbrrrrr-ammms!" sound fierce and happy—but is there any *value* in what he's doing? After all, how much can you get out of trucks after the first thousand crashes?

WHEN WE SIGN on for space in day care we hope to get more than liberty to work. We want our children to be happy, to make a little progress in getting civilized, *and* to learn whatever it is they're supposed to learn during these early years—for its own sake and so that school will be as easy as possible. But what is it that very young children are supposed to be learning? How can we know if a curriculum is adequate? What does it mean to be ready for school? This chapter looks first at early learning in all age groups, then at school-readiness for preschoolers and parents.

Early Learning: Finding the Questions

> While the teacher sings the two youngest to sleep in the next room, Jeff gathers the other infants around a table for a snack. As they pack in Cheerios and bits of oranges, he points to a big green picture: "Turtle!" he says, "Tur-tle." Jeff treats his co-op time as a break from the high seriousness of life.
>
> Emerging from the nap room, the teacher chokes back a laugh and a protest. Picture vocabulary drills!—there is a "developmentally *in*appropriate" activity if there ever was one. The infants at the table still use books for teething, they say "ba!" for everything—blankets, balls, crackers, squirrels. "Tur-tle" indeed! But the infants look pleased with Jeff's show, she sees; everyone is having a good time—and that's what really matters.

Seeds Sometimes parents ask teachers, "What, really, is your curriculum here?" out of a specific worry, but most often parents ask because they want to know in general: "What does my child's mind need?" Especially if truck noises and cereal spills are dominating home life, parents would like a little general inspiration: What's the interesting part of child care?

Most parents know that some toys and some activities are more "developmentally appropriate" than others. They know that children's minds, like plant seeds, have their own pattern for growth, an internal clock that determines when a child will be *ready* to learn various things. What parents don't know—what no one really knows outside of extreme cases—is what kind of difference special attention to this timing makes. No parent wants to be seen as "pushing" a child; on the other hand, parents do want to provide good quality mental care. ABCs on the wall and varying themes like "Space Explorers," "Purple Day," even "Spring," reassure preschoolers' parents, but is this really it? Is it enough? And what about infants and toddlers?

Ph.D.'s in Horticulture Parents who turn to books find disagreeing experts. One batch of experts urges parents to work at making baby smarter, hang "stimulating" things everywhere, buy the right toys for the right month, or teach reading years before first grade. Some of these people might be serious about "tur-tle" drills. Another batch begs parents *not* to work at natural developments, to let childhood be free of pressure and success worry, to trust Nature's hatching out of six-year-olds for reading-readiness. They say, "Don't push the river," and that play is okay because it's how children learn. Parents are invited to feel guilty if they are *not* teaching Latin and violin at a tender age or to feel guilty if they *are*.

City Slickers When parents turn, quite logically, to their local experts, the day-care teachers, they are often surprised to find teachers practically unintelligible on the subject of curriculum. Some teachers suddenly produce distant early-education jargon; some sputter. Maybe it's like asking a farmer, "How do you grow these plants?" For both the General Foods agricultural experts and the small Maine potato producer, it's a city slicker's question, and hard to answer well.

Good day-care teachers have to be good at explaining things to *children* (among many other requirements); not all of them are equally skilled in explaining things to adults. Even teachers who are very articulate, moreover, may be overwhelmed by a general curriculum question. Where would they start? One forty-five-second song like "Three Little Monkeys Jumpin' on the Bed" provides practice in finger control and coordination, exposes children to simple subtraction, demonstrates a logic sequence, and brings the playfulness of song and story to tensions around adult rules. Much of the important work in early learning takes place in talk; in teachers noticing a child's interests and efforts, in making comments and asking good questions. When they say, "Oh, look at that!" and "Well, what do you think . . . ?" instead of "just" keeping everyone clean and safe, teachers give significant support to children's learning. Nothing shows this effort at the end of the day, though, and talk about their own talk to children would sound silly: "I noticed and described a hundred forty-five times today; I asked two hundred fifty-two good questions."

The topic "curriculum" is just too big. A day-care program's curriculum embraces every aspect of child development and care; it involves equipment, schedules, activities, rules, and the ways teachers talk to children; its best products are enthusiasms for self, life, and learning. Even fabulous teachers cannot explain all the connections in a casual chat. Don't worry if your teacher chokes when trying to talk about curriculum; it is not a sign that the teaching is wrong or thoughtless.

Parents looking for general inspiration about mental developments have sometimes found it in books recommended by teachers, directors, or other parents; some have organized workshops by local experts at their center at night. It may also help to let teachers know your interest is general: "I'm just wondering what this age is all about." "I'm looking for ideas for things to do at home." Teachers sometimes react defensively to curriculum questions; they're not sure they are doing everything right, and they've been busy with those truck noises and cereal spills, too. If they know you're more curious than criticizing, they may feel much freer to talk.

If you are more concerned with your day-care program than early development in general, you can probably rely on your own good sense even more than you know.

Signs of Healthy Growth What can you look for as reassurance about curriculum? Not only is much of teachers' most important work invisible, but what young children are busy learning is invisible as well, and hard to measure. One day your child will have spelling words and math dittos to bring home; you will be able to keep track of how things are going more easily—but now? The kind of mental *content* very young children need to acquire includes a zillion very basic and subtle things—like how this culture divides the sound continuum into *its* kind of language sounds; how to navigate in three-dimensional space; how height, width, weight, and volume fit together in objects. We take these achievements for granted, but that doesn't mean they don't require time and energy from children.

Given a basically benevolent environment and average biological luck, young children are little learning machines for all the information they need. They master it with no special thought on anyone's part. And they enjoy it. Infants' "crib talk," for example—the babbling babies do in awake, alone moments—contains a great deal of specialized practice on a few consonants at a time. It sounds as if they are just having a good time—and they are. Nature very sensibly made practicing essential skills interesting to children.

This *interest* is what you can look for in your program's curriculum. Are the children engaged, involved, *busy?* Most parents have a good "gut feel" about *poor* curriculum: nothing to play with, long waits during or between activities, children wandering around. This is exactly right. When children's internal learning plan finds the right material and time, children connect, engage, play, explore, and generally go for it—they "crib-talk." When there's too little opportunity, they sag. Busyness is a good sign that mental needs are being met.

So "Is this a good curriculum?" can be translated as "Is my child busy?" without real loss of meaning, and your teacher should be able to discuss the details of that question much more vividly. You might also ask teachers, How is my child spending the time? What's he loving to do right now? What's she excited about? If teachers are supporting your child's learning with time and materials, they're watching for sparks of special interest.

Roots If other ways of raising curriculum concerns are not satisfying you, you might ask yourself what other questions you have about your child and your child's teachers right now. Parents find themselves wondering about curriculum when a child seems irritable (Is this child bored? Overworked?) or friendless (Might new activities help make new connections with other children?) or sad about saying goodbye (Could exciting activities make separation easier?). Lack of energy and enthusiasm in teachers can make parents wonder, How *could* there be an interesting program here—the *teachers* are bored! You may have the most success asking about irritability, friends, or separation with teachers directly, or mentioning teachers' moods to the director. Whether you see the program of activities as the root of the problem or one of the possible cures, describing first what you see and hear that bothers you may make the issues clearer to teachers.

Sun, Water, Soil Since most children arrive in the world with the plan and the energy for full development, the adults' main job is to *protect* that drive for learning. Hunger, exhaustion, and tension drain time and energy from learning drives; disinterest and criticism sap curiosity. All the work teachers do to make children feel confident with themselves and materials, and safe in all their relationships, frees children to learn—anything and everything they ought to learn. And all the work you do with food and sleep—your dredgings-up of kind remarks for art-projects at the end of the day, your willingness to be audience for their thousand shows—all protect and nourish learning drives. If you're thinking about early learning, count most heavily this whole-life, whole-child support, and give yourself credit for this good curriculum work you do.

Early Learning: Developmental Issues
INFANTS

> Six-month-old Stephanie has been sleeping her way
> through day care. Her teacher Judy has begun to worry: "Ba-
> bies usually know what they need, and she *is* our youngest
> . . . but could she be sort of overwhelmed by the room?
> Maybe it's too much for her all at once, so she tunes out too
> fast to discover the good stuff." Teachers pore over sleeping
> and staffing schedules, finally finding a time when Stephanie
> could play with Judy in relative peace and quiet. Judy starts
> gentle "conversations" with her and introduces one toy into
> their talks every now and then. Gradually, Stephanie be-
> comes more active while she is awake and stays awake a little
> longer, until she is chatting and batting away with the best
> of them.

Infants learn most easily when they have playtime free
of hunger and tiredness, enough variety to cut their mental
teeth on but not too much to chew, and a "responsive" environment—where what they do makes a difference. All three
elements can affect one another.

Many infants tend toward chaos in their eating and sleeping schedules for what feels like forever. If you and your
teachers seem to be spending most of the year trying to create a little order in your baby's life, add educational benefits
to the list of things that encourage this effort. Half-hungry,
half-tired, cranky infants can't bring all their mental energy
into play.

Like physicists just arrived on a strange planet, infants
survey the basic sensations of the world, building a data base
for later work. Sound, color, smell, feel, motion—what kinds
are there here? How do they fit together? The little scientists have to manage unfamilar equipment, too—those eyes,
ears, and hands might as well be newfangled cameras and

radios, awkward mechanical arms for handling minerals in glass cases. They have to practice working these things and (just like adult scientists) have to figure out if what they see and hear is the real thing or just a problem with the equipment. Lots to do.

What kinds of support do they need from us? A reasonable sample of the world's variety, ready to hand and eye. Walking into an infant room should feel like hiking into marshland—suddenly the world is thick from your knees down. They need time, space, quiet, and freedom from interruptions to practice things and test for effects. Infants love producing effects: I move—it moves; I move—it makes a noise. Parents in cultures all over the globe have invented baby rattles for good reason.

The best infant teachers are as much like rattles as they can manage to be: They don't overwhelm a baby with their own talk and activity, but they "answer" when infants "talk"—coo, call, complain, cry, point, reach, stare at something with interest. Being a good baby slave this way, while keeping everyone fed, slept, changed, and clean, takes a wonderfully organized and incredibly flexible person, who can be constantly active while radiating peace and calm. Few parents can manage this perfection themselves, and they count quite deeply on teachers' affection for their babies; most infant parents do not want to sound critical. Yet this is the year when you may need the most reassurance. You can have input to your child's program without sounding critical by

EXPRESSING YOUR VALUES

- *Notice, praise, and thank your teacher for what seems to be going right:* interesting materials, a lengthening play period: "Hey, this is great!"
- *Ask questions that reflect your concerns:* "When she fusses, sometimes I can't tell if she's bored or if things are too crazy for her. . . . How do you tell?" "I'm kind of out of ideas for things to do with him . . . what is he liking to do here?"

- *Tell stories from home that show what's important to you:* "She kept trying to get this one ball out of a bucket . . . I tried to give her a chance to do it herself, and finally she got it. She was so pleased!"

Generally speaking, if your baby enjoys life at home, your teacher enjoys your baby, and your teacher enjoys telling you what your baby enjoys during the day (except on teething days, when we are all excused from enjoying anything), then probably all is well.

TODDLERS

Two-year-old Aaron doesn't like art, water, or sand activities because they are messy; he doesn't like dancing, gym, or yard play because the other kids bump him. His mother, Beth, is disgusted with the program—it seems as if *all* the activities are messy or bumpy. Aaron likes books and doing the ABCs with his dad—why can't they do these things? Beth has spoken with Mike, Aaron's teacher, several times about this: Where are the *educational* activities?

When Beth arrives to pick Aaron up today, he is marching around on a circle of stools with three other toddlers. "Really!" she says to Mike, "this is just what I'm talking about. Isn't this a complete waste of time? It looks like you're just keeping them busy while you sweep up." "Actually"—Mike forces a smile—"this activity helps to develop gross motor coordination and balance." Getting Aaron into the group *and* doing something physical was Mike's coup of the day. "And"—Mike lowers his voice—"Aaron *needs* to work on balance."

Few parents challenge particular activities so directly, but most have at least wondered heartily about the value of some activities they see. (It's natural: The intentions behind teachers' visible work are no more consistently obvious than in many other jobs.) Toddlers start many parents challenging teachers' activities for the first time, partly because group activities are now possible and partly because toddlers tend to be picky about activities, just as they are about everything else.

Children's involvement with activities is usually a sign of good curriculum, but toddlers may refuse involvement because they are busy owning or sulking. The rules about owning at this age—"If I was next to it, it's mine," "If it's not nailed down, it's mine," "If I can pry it out of your fingers, it's mine"—can make for a lot of standing around clutching things. Claiming things and standing up for themselves in conflicts is more important than it looks. Self-consciousness is dawning at this age; they are becoming keenly aware of their own wills, wishes, plans, as distinct from those of others. Real other-consciousness arises at the same time and in the same circumstances: What do other people do when you push up against them? Sulking says, "I don't have to like it!"—a significant claim to independence, or "Now I hate you. What are you going to do about that?"—a critical question in human relations. Even sulking deserves our support.

Should teachers "push" activities or permit a toddler's rejections? You want to allow for some owning, sulking, and simple preferring, but you don't want a lot of unbusy time. Some adult options for:

REACHING AROUND TODDLER REJECTIONS

- Add safety factors to rejected activities:
  1. Parents try them out at home.
  2. Teachers stay close during the activity to provide extra protection or step-by-step help.
- Add time with preferred activities:
  1. With the whole group: Aaron's teachers might try more group reading and listening activities.
  2. For one child: letting Aaron play quietly nearby during gym and finger painting.

- Subtract some adult-dictated tasks or events from the schedule: Children have more patience with unpreferred activities when they don't feel rushed or overdirected in general.
- Add moral support: Teachers might try sympathizing more often and more loudly: "He bumped you! Oh no! Outrageous!"; "Would you like to wash that off Right Now? Then you can play some more."

Are there special toddler activities that ought to be "pushed"? Probably not. The activities that appeal to most toddlers provide some clues about what they're learning now. Opening and shutting doors, climbing and jumping off, filling and dumping water or sand, building towers and knocking them down, all fascinate this age group, long after adults are bored or dying for a *final* product. They're more interested in getting the shoe on *and* off than in getting it on. In pretend play, they "go to work" and come "back!" or go to sleep and "wake up!" over and over and over. It's as though they were engineers, studying the world's reversible operations—in/out, open/shut, up/down, full/empty, hello/good-bye, happy/sad. What can you do and undo? How do the actions and effects fit together? So many different opportunities for these studies occur in everyday life, your toddler is bound to learn what needs learning here. Learning language is the great masterwork of the toddler year, and here, too, food for growth should be simple: some conversation space and a few interested listeners, an occasional word as needed. Telling teachers some stories and asking questions about things your child *says* may inspire extra focus on talking if it seems needed.

PRESCHOOLERS

Francesca hates morning circle time at day care. They have to sit *forever* doing the calendar and letter games and singing dumb songs. There's hardly any time to play. Michael hates the play period. Special-project time is fun and so is "circle," but free play is torture. The boys he wants to play with won't let him play; he's tired of playing alone and tired of trying to find someone else to play with. Joanie misses her dad. He used to play with her all the time. Then he got a new job. Now he just works and reads the paper. One morning all three children say:

"I don't want to go to day care. It's boring."

Boredom sets in for preschoolers, as for adults, when what they care about and what's happening get too far apart. What do they care about? Each child has special interests, but overall, social relationships figure heavily. If infants are the physicists and toddlers the engineers, then preschoolers are the social scientists of early childhood. They work on what it means to be a friend or not be a friend, to be a mommy, a daddy, a kid, or a baby, a boy, a girl, a bad guy and good guy. The rest of a Preschooler's Perfect Course Catalog might read: Sugar, Betrayal, Slimy Things, Monster Attacks, Poop, Penises, and Death. Preschool teachers have to design some publicly acceptable form of curriculum; when they fall back on "Mammals" and "Vegetables," it just doesn't always work.

Programming for preschoolers holds another challenge. The years between three and five have a big bump in the middle. At either end, we find relatively cheerful, cooperative chlidren, interested in the world at large and pretty happy to accept our guided tour. In the middle period, prickly preschoolers insist on narrower agendas—Legos only, thank you, or witches and weddings and Batman all day long. They greet new facts and adventures with "I know

that!" or "Do I *have* to . . . ?" Zooming independence creates half this mood, insecurity the other half. Even infants
set goals for themselves and know what it is to be frustrated,
but a real fear of failure first appears in the middle of the
preschool years.

Preschoolers care about competence, about feeling big
and smart and great at things. Younger children can feel this
way whenever some plan of theirs works out. Preschoolers'
minds leap ahead of their hands too often; their ability to
compare themselves and their work to others' becomes a
curse. Their drive to feel competent can inspire them to
learn fifty dinosaur facts, to spend ages over careful drawings, and build elaborate spaceships, but it can also lead
them to shun facts, paper, and big projects: If they aren't
already good at it, they don't want to know about it. Teachers have to be sly.

Somewhere in the middle of the preschool years, your
Danny may want to be a dinosaur all day, or your Wendy a
Wonder Woman; your smart son may clamp hands over his
ears at the first sound of counting; your darling daughter
may refuse to look at a single letter. Wait, as confidently as
you can, as long as you can. Most children grow out of this
clutching mood and expand again toward five. Waiting also
keeps letters, numbers, and writing from getting poisonously
connected with frustration or with disappointing you.

While the middle preschool years are not necessarily a
great time to work on specific pieces of knowledge like the
ABCs and 1-2-3s, they are a great time to work on more
general parts of the thinking process: putting words to
thoughts, separating and combining ideas, finding information in memory, using information to solve problems, finding
more than one way of tackling things. Preschoolers sometimes shy away from thinking activities, too. Thinking on
purpose or in any organized way, or the whole idea of "looking" within for answers, can be as complicated as algebra at
first. They've certainly expressed themselves and thought

and remembered and solved problems before, but now they're ready to learn how to use their computers, not just look at the printout. Teachers (and parents) can help by

INTRODUCING THE BRAIN TO PRESCHOOLERS

- Give children practice thinking, remembering, and organizing thoughts through questions: "What do you think?" "What happened to you?" "What will happen next in the story?"
- Demonstrate problem-solving. Child: "Can we go outside now?" Adult: "Well, what did we just do? . . . What do we usually do after that? . . . So that means . . . ?"
- Build confidence in their own thinking:
  1. With praise: "What an interesting idea!" and "You remembered all that!"
  2. With leading questions or multiple choice when first attempts to answer a question fail: "What animal do you think this is? . . . Could it be a whale . . . a dolphin . . . a shark? Right!" Pull out the message: "You didn't think you knew it, but you *did*!"
  3. With "what else?" questions when obstacles or conflicts arise: "Okay, right. That won't work for an airplane. What else could you try?"

Preschoolers who emerge from the four-year "bump" believing in themselves ("I'm a good guesser!") and in the power of persistence have a much easier time with new learning tasks.

It's much harder to know if teachers are providing this kind of good curriculum—there's nothing to take home, no collages on the walls. You probably get some sample of your teacher's approach at drop-off and pickup times; your support still makes a difference. Make a point of saying, "I really like the way you talk to the kids . . . the way you get them thinking . . . you ask great questions," when that seems true to you.

Michelangelo is supposed to have said that he didn't *create* his magnificent sculptures, he *freed* figures from the marble. Good day-care teachers take much the same view: Their job is to clear the way for children's own learning drives. They don't have to push the river; it flows by itself. Using the special power of social support in children's learning is their most important work: The silent touch or company that adds distinction to an effort, the smile that encourages or shares a victory. They start with children's own efforts, offering their interest, confidence, and appreciation for the work. You might encourage good curriculum most effectively in the very same way. What learning issues do teachers see themselves working on now? What's an example of that? Is there a good story about it today?

Early Learning: Parent-Teacher Talk

Parent says, "I think Johnny is getting a little bored. Couldn't you use some new puzzles or something?"

(Parent Thoughts)	*(Teacher Thoughts)*
Gee, this place looks boring— same blocks, paints, torn books. Don't they ever do anything different? This stuff's all been here for months; the kids are older now, they're ready for new things. All Johnny does is play "Peter and the Wolf" all day—there's nothing else to do. At least they could get some new puzzles.	What?! Johnny can't do the puzzles we have and wouldn't touch a puzzle with a ten-foot pole now anyway! What makes her think he's bored?! He's having a great time. If she's looking for alphabet drills, she's in the wrong place. Why can't parents leave their kids alone?

Unwrap It "Bored" pushes most teachers' buttons fast and hard. Teachers see themselves working hard to feed, clothe, protect, and cherish children all day; "bored" degrades all that labor in one ugly word. They see children in millions of moods in a single hour—and yes, there may have been a bored mood in there somewhere, but, hey, that's life, and what makes parents think they can even *guess* how much time was boring *or* thrilling—they're away at work! And so on. In later, calmer moments, teachers may be able to see what started it all and what needs exploring or explaining, but "bored" gets in the way at first.

You want teachers to adopt your problem, not hate it on sight. If "bored" gets you angry teachers, don't wrap your meaning in that word. What's inside? What's made you think your child is bored?

Is your child harder to get out of the house these days? You could just describe how getting to the center is going. Did your child say "It's boring?" Unwrap the word for your child. Children's minds don't do mathematical mood averaging—when they say "bored," something in particular is bothering them. It could be almost anything—get all the input you can. You might ask, "What's the most boring part at day care? . . . What's the best part there?" Are *you* bored to death when you look around the room? Good curriculum doesn't always show, of course—a lot of the best learning takes place in conversations, in little problems solved. And materials don't always speak for themselves; blank paper can become hats, airplanes, signs, drawings, and stories—or just a dusty stack. But you might be picking up the smell of dust from teachers' attitudes, or be feeling disconnected from the whole show for some other reasons. Can you put your finger on it?

When you're "unwrapping" a meaning just for yourself, you might want to ask yourself about everything that could be involved—what you saw or heard that started you thinking about it, how that felt, what other things that reminds you of, how it's connected to your goals, hopes, and fears right now—the works. Probably the more you know about what's concerning you, the better your chances of getting satisfaction. When you're mainly concerned with getting teachers thinking, you can use this all-purpose formula:

HOW TO RAISE AN ISSUE

- Describe what you saw (or heard) that disturbed you.
- Ask for teachers' ideas about what it means—"What do you think?" "Where could that come from?"

For example:

- "Every day when I come he's playing 'Peter and the Wolf.' What do you think he gets out of it?"
- "She didn't want to come this morning—she said, 'It's boring there.' What do you think she meant? What's bothering her?"
- "I was thinking about the program here last night, and I realized that *you've* seemed kind of fed up or bored to me when we talk at the end of the day. Are you? Is it just six o'clock blues? Could you use some new toys or something?"
- "At home all he does is play with his trucks. Does he do that most of the time here, too? I don't really know what he does here. . . ."

Your questions may elicit a different, interesting interpretation, put an issue into focus, bring differences of opinion to light, start a thinking process. You can't tell ahead of time, but at least you'll be opening doors instead of shutting them.

Early Learning: Things to Try

RESEARCH YOUR QUESTIONS

General Curiosity: What's a good curriculum?

- *Books, articles:* Ask teachers and the director for ideas about things to read.
- *Workshops:* Find out if there's money and group interest to support a curriculum workshop at day care or if relevant workshops are offered nearby.
- *Take a teacher to breakfast:* "I'd love the chance to talk to

you about what kids this age are learning and how that all works in a group. I know there's no time during regular hours. Could I treat you to breakfast?"
* *Your own child:* Is my child busy, having fun? Ask teachers about:
  1. *Time:* How does your child spend the day-care time? The whole day's too long to ask about; try one piece of it at a time: "What does he usually do during outside time?" "Does she usually do the special projects?"
  2. *Interests:* "What's he enjoying most lately?"
  3. *Activity Rejections:* "She seems to have very definite ideas about what she will and won't do at home . . . does she join in with pretty much everything here?" What activities or time of day doesn't your child like? What do teachers do about that?

REMOVE OBSTACLES TO LEARNING

* Check on sleep and tiredness. Do teachers think your child seems tired even in the morning or after nap? Are sleeps long at day care and short at night? Work with teachers to find a sleep pattern with more good awake playtime.
* Reach around toddler rejections (page 123)
  1. Add safety to rejected activities
     a) Try them at home.
     b) Ask teachers to stay close, cheerlead.
  2. Add time with accepted activities. Ask teachers to:
     a) Plan more of them for whole group
     b) Allow them for your child while group does other things
  3. Ask teachers to encourage more "breaks" for your child.
  4. Ask teachers what the problem seems to be with the activities—too noisy? Messy? Sometimes extra sympathy alone makes a difference at home . . . would that work here?
* See Breaking the Ice (page 140)

ENRICHING THE MATERIAL ENVIRONMENT

* *Extra Help:* "Is there anything you'd like to see more of in the room?" Money or shopping time may be problems. Volunteer to make, bring in, or hunt for some things in rummage sales.

- A *"Wanted" list:* Ask teachers to post a "Wanted" list for materials on a bulletin board, so many parents can contribute.
- *Trial offers:* Offer to lend a toy or equipment for an activity that your child loves at home. Seeing something new in action first makes a buying decision easier.
- *Using what's there:* Are materials available to children, in reach? Some teachers don't let children use what's already there because the cleanup price (children or room or both) seems too steep. You might:
  1. Emphasize that you don't mind a bit of a mess on child or in room—you take it as a sign of a busy, happy day
  2. Find out how cleaning gets done. Does one teacher have to do it all? On unpaid time? Do kids help, could parents help at pickup time? Is there money for a cleaning service?

ENRICHING THE TEACHING ENVIRONMENT

- Express your values (page 121):
  1. Notice and comment on what's going right.
  2. Ask questions that reflect your concerns.
  3. Tell stories from home that show what's important to you.
- Tell teachers what your child enjoys at home.
- Ask regularly about teachers' discoveries or efforts in any direction. The invisibility of their work often discourages teachers; your interest makes it visible.
- Lobby the director or parent group for paid planning time, professional days, financial support for and recognition of early-childhood courses.

School-Readiness: Finding the Questions

"Josh and me were playing" [jump, jump] and then, and then, we found this leaf [jump, jump] and Josh turned it over [jump, jump, tip the chair] and then we saw [jump, tip, chair crashes over] we saw this ant! And Josh was squashing it? And . . ." This child's mother tries to imagine him sitting quietly in a kindergarten class circle, eyes on the teacher, mouth closed. And, can't.

Going Public Many parents look at their lovable but non-stop, long-winded, still-ignorant, smart-mouthed, stubborn basic four-year-olds and wince when they think about school. Surely this child will hate school, and school will hate back. They ask teachers, "Will she be ready for school?" "Do you think he'll *ever* be ready?"

Long-term Projections School readiness is hard to call, impossible to promise; it depends. Most children's representational and categorizing skills, finger control, and hand-eye coordination improve markedly between four and five—will your child's? Most children's bodies and mouths slow down between four and five—will your child's? It's hard to predict when children will grow the next half inch, let alone anything more complicated. Readiness also depends on what they have to be ready *for:* Will they be getting Mr. Rogers or General Patton for a kindergarten teacher? In one sense, the correct answer about readiness is always "I don't know."

In another sense, the correct answer for any child in day care is "Yes!" Day-care children are already used to being away from home, with nonfamily adults and children; they've got routines around their belongings, cleaning up, getting to and from bathrooms and play yards down pat. They've developed some savvy about dealing with teachers and children; they've been exposed to group meetings, drawing, counting, singing, and all the pencil-paper-scissors stuff of school. Should be a piece of cake. Would they be ready this way if we'd stayed at home?

Market Research But what is kindergarten like now? Will "they" expect your child to know certain things? Day-care teachers aren't always sure what local kindergartens expect. You might call your local school department; many towns have a kindergarten parents' brochure that might answer lots of questions very directly. Find out if your school permits parent visits before registration; a look at the real thing might be reassuring. You can bug everyone in your friends-and-neighbors network: What do they know about kindergarten? What's expected? What's hard for most children? What helps?

Public Relations In calm moments, parents may tell themselves, "Well, kindergarten teachers must be used to all kinds of skill levels. My kid won't be the only one who can't . . ."—but they worry about Personal Habits. When four-year-olds seem "impossible," parents all too easily imagine tight-lipped teacher scoldings; they envision their child standing rejected and alone by the schoolyard fence; they can picture themselves squirming in small chairs during a painful parent conference. Parents want to spare themselves and their children these humiliations. Quick! What can be done?

Planning Consultants Day-care teachers should be good resources for any of your prekindergarten Personal-Habits worries. They know how your child behaves in a group, where strengths and weaknesses lie. They've seen how your child handles teachers, other children, new materials and tasks, and demands to sit still or be quiet for a while. Teachers may be working on some of the not-so-hot stuff already, but your questions and interest count. Some balls get dropped as teachers juggle overcrowded agendas; teachers may hesitate to "push" independence, politeness, or emotional restraint without your specific support. You might ask for their ideas first or focus right in on what you see that worries you: "She still has tantrums at home." "He can't sit still for anything but cartoons."

Some parents are not particularly panicked about school or actively distressed about their four-year-olds' behavior; they just have a general sense that it's time to get cracking. The approach of school makes many parents feel that they've been coping and coasting, waiting for phases to pass; time to get organized! If you're feeling this way, you might ask teachers, "How could my child be read*ier* for school?" Every child is ready in some sense, and every child can use extra attention on *some* skill. Teachers may already be working on some goals and be glad to have your home support; your questions may spark new thoughts.

School-Readiness: Developmental Issues

Few children reassure their parents by bursting into reading and writing while still in day care. Parents can, however, draw some reassurance from watching related skills bloom. This section describes some of those skills and looks at the challenge school presents to parent development, too.

READING

Imagine a friend handing you a cube with hundreds of tiny colored squares on each side. Your friend tells you that each color stands for one or two sounds; she demonstrates a few—you hear buzzes, clicks, and groans. "Look," she says, "if you learn these colors—there're only fifty"—you see eight—"and their sounds, you could learn to read this code!" "Well," you say. . . .

Representing There're an awful lot of things "standing for" other things in reading, made doubly difficult because the "standing for" connection isn't a natural one. Why should the squiggle "B" stand for *B* sounds? No reason. That squiggle could just as easily stand for *K* sounds or for Popsicles or elephants or the color purple. You can't tell by looking.

Young preschoolers don't usually "get" artificial signs like this. Signs need to look like what they stand for. Long association might connect, say, a green kitty sticker with "Toby's cubby," but mainly if Toby's a pretty important character and mainly with that specific object, not with Toby or cubbies in general. Toward the end of the preschool years, representing power extends more easily to arbitrary connections. If you're trying to describe a baseball play to a three-year-old and grab a saltshaker, saying, "Okay. This shaker is you, and the ball is coming," you'll be stuck there forever: "That's *me*? What?" A five-year-old could grasp the symbolism much more easily: "Okay, so I'm the salt . . ." When your child begins to be comfortable using some arbitrary signs, like street signs, color, and symbol cards in board games, you know you're getting there.

Dimensionalizing Eventually, your child will learn to see the key differences between *B*, *P*, and *R* and to hear the differences between *B*, *P*, and *V*, but it doesn't come easily to young children. Detail is not the problem. Preschoolers can detect virtually invisible differences between certain toys; many can duplicate engine noises with miraculous accuracy. The abstractness of reading's signs and sounds makes them tough. We don't have *B*-shaped things around the house; no natural law even says *B* is one obviously separate sound—different languages slice the sound pie between *B* and *P* quite differently. The very conversations that point out key differences depend on abstracting ability. Adults will talk about "the round part" or "the straight line" or the "bottom part" and about "the starting sound."

Preschoolers develop the ability to see and use abstract dimensions—like round, straight, starting—somewhat slowly. Give a three-year-old a pile of buttons to sort, and she might well get lost in the beauty of each button; give a five-year-old the same pile, and sorting by size, shape, or darkness becomes possible. Ask three-year-olds to think of words that start with a *P* sound, and give them a sample like "pizza, pear . . ." and you might well get "spaghetti, milk . . ." or "I had pizza last night!" Ask a group of five-year-olds, and you might hear "purple, people, party . . ." plus all the bathroom words you innocently forgot when you started this exercise. When your child seems to notice dimensions—like light/dark, short/tall, squiggly/straight—and starts to enjoy rhyming and word play, you know you're getting there.

Guessing Since the connections of sounds to letters in English are so arbitrary and changeable, sounding out words involves a lot of best-guessing. Good guessing depends on the ability to project a reasonable answer from cues and partial information, and on confidence. As children's abilities to sort information develop power, flexibility, and abstractness between ages three and five, guessing improves. Confidence to risk a guess varies wildly. Sometimes children say, "*I* don't know!" in outraged or pitiful tones when answers seem clear, obvious, and well within their competence; sometimes they say "*I* know *that!*"—disgusted, you-dummy tone here—when no one thought they'd have a clue. When you hear "I know that!" about something that surprises you, drink in the reassurance. It's a good sign that guessing ability is coming along.

The Payoff Think back to the imaginary cube of colors. What would have made struggling with the code worth it? Several things might help—desire to share your friend's enthusiasm, a lighthearted game-playing way of learning the color and sound codes, a personal passion for code-cracking on your part. But if the cube documented the federal regulations for auto emissions . . . ? The payoff makes a difference.

Children who love books can bring much more patience and energy to learning to read.

The love of books can start quite early. Young toddlers often develop passions for particular pictures (usually on some unfindable page in the middle of the book). Later, children come to love *whole* stories, wanting them read through again and again, steadily, remorselessly, until you can recite them in your sleep. Around four, children often become very active listeners. You may find yourself interrupted a thousand times during a story—"Why did he do that? He should have . . ." Older preschoolers care about the fairness or stupidity of the action; they like using their new guessing talents to predict what will happen next. If you were hoping for a quiet, cozy read together, all this involvement with the story can be a pain in the neck, but it is wonderful fuel for the work of reading.

WRITING-RELATED DEVELOPMENTS

Over loud moaning and groaning, Betsy insists that each child in the older preschool group draw a self-portrait on the first day of every month. The children are outraged: Art is play, and teachers shouldn't tell you what to draw! When Betsy hands the collected portraits back in June, however, they are huge with pride. Every child—even one who avoided drawing altogether between those assignments—sees the remarkable changes. Scribbles and lumpy circles with dots for eyes become human figures with arms and legs, mouths, hair, even some eyebrows. "Look what I did!" they say. Betsy, choking up a little, says to her co-teacher, "Yes. Look what they did. They grew up."

Forming letters requires the finger coordination to make a pencil go where you want it to, the eye-hand coordination to correct finger movements based on what you see (to smooth out a line if it starts looking lumpy), the mind-hand coordination to translate a mental picture to hand movements that re-create it on paper, and a kind of child-to-society coordination that accepts conventions in order to communicate (the willingness to write a *B* without so much imagination that others can't recognize it).

Drawing provides excellent practice for all these coordinations and develops quite a lot on its own in the year before school. You might try Betsy's idea and keep one picture a month for a while so you can see how things are coming along.

NUMBERS

Kyle is beginning to whine about waiting. "I bet I'll be done before you can count to twenty!" Kyle's mother, Liza, smiles at her own fast thinking: This'll keep him busy. Kyle announces, "One, two, three, four, six, seven, nine, ten, fourteen, eighteen, nineteen, twenty!" Listening to this, Liza's smile fades. Is Kyle confused about numbers—or cheating?

For many three-year-olds, "one, two, three, four five . . ." seems to be some magical chant that grown-ups say over groups of objects or to fill time in dull moments. Threes sometimes have a handle on the very beginning of the sequence, but the connection between a number word and a number of things vanishes rapidly. Getting this idea—*one* means one thing, *two* means two of that thing, and so on—is really all the math they need to know before school. Kindergarteners also work on seeing size and shape comparisons and on mathematical language—big, bigger, biggest. Let your child count out cookies or chips for the family. You might get some cheating with the cookie counting, but a guilty look can tell you the child is ready for school.

If your child is willing to do some thinking, guessing, looking at books, drawing, counting, and so forth, and teachers see progress with the practical parts of school-readiness—abilities to listen and follow directions, contribute in a group, manage belongings independently, settle conflicts without major collapses, then—hurray! Rejoice and relax. If your child is saying "No way, José" about even making contact with some of these activities, and school is feeling close at hand, you might make a plan with teachers for:

BREAKING THE ICE

Teachers could:

- Make a puzzle of the trouble, try to get your child interested in discovering or naming what's hard: "I wonder what the hard part is for you; do you know some kids think *this* is the hard part?"
- Connect the dreaded activity with a comfortable favorite: work on counting through sports or handing out snacks.
- Offer a "fancy" but still personal reward for work: decorate hands after challenging pencil-and-paper work.
- Insist on a ten-minute, no-failure contact: "I just want you to scribble for ten minutes—you don't have to draw anything. Just scribble." Or "See what you can do with your shoes in ten minutes. I'll come back and help you, but see what you can do."
- Insist on three tries: "I'll help you with opening that lunchbox (or copying that letter) but I want you to try three times first."
- Pour on the praise; cheerlead. "You are so good with Legos, and this writing is just using your fingers, too. I bet you can do it! Let me see you try. You almost got it that time!"

Around four, children's talk and movement shift into high gear: We seem to hear *all* their thoughts out loud; we live in a wash cycle of their restlessness. As children approach five, thought begins to go underground and silent;

the fidgets ease up. The need to confront adults constantly and the hypersensitivity to failure all cool off a bit. Whew. Natural developments in representing, categorizing, guessing, drawing, and counting will take your child a long way toward school readiness over the year. Just attending day care has given your child all kinds of good practice at many pieces of school life. Chances are, your child is readier than you think. Are you?

PARENT DEVELOPMENT

Remember:
- Your first night home from the hospital?
- Your first visit to the emergency room with your child?
- Your first night of unbroken sleep?
- The first time you felt like hitting your child?
- The first day at day care?

From the first moment it dawned on us that this baby counted on us for breath itself, we began to change. Exhausted and amazed, we struggled on, finding reserves of physical and moral strength we never seemed to have before. When each new stage of our children's development demanded new talents from us, we found them. Our children got bigger and smarter; we built muscle and wisdom.

The first days at day care were painful, stretching the millions of mental, emotional, and physical threads that connect us to our children. Tough as that was, sending a child off to school strikes many of us as a harder task, a much bigger separation, the end of an era. Day-care teachers come to know our children's ways—how they fall asleep, the weird things they do with food, the kind of jokes they like. Will a schoolteacher know about that? And what about us? In day care's small world, we could know people and they could know us. We may be glad to leave some people behind, but others cannot be replaced—they've stood by us through an extraordinary time. When our children leave day care, we both lose a world.

Now we must "go public" to a huge place full of children and adults we don't know, who will judge our children and what they seem to be. These new people have no history; they can't say "I remember when . . ." So, *of course* we worry about our local kindergartens, *of course* we want to send a polished-product child "they" will appreciate right away.

Remind yourself (and your child when it's time) that you are good at change. You can do this. You've both made big changes since Day One when you started out together. It hasn't always been easy, but in the end you both learned what you had to learn and survived. Like Betsy's class, look back and say, "Look what we did!" And remember: Your child doesn't have to be "all done" in September. Kindergarten teachers expect to work for a living.

School-Readiness: Parent-Teacher Talk

PARENT: "Do you think he's going to be ready for school?"
TEACHER: "Oh sure. He's doing fine."

P: "You don't seem to do school-oriented activities here—isn't it time to start some of that?"
T: "Well, we work mainly on their self-esteem. Self-esteem is the most important part of school success."

P: "Don't you think they need more structure in the curriculum at this age?"
T: "We try to balance structured and unstructured activities here. After all, the children are here a long time every day."

Goal Refining Life with work and children means precious little time to think. At home parents have to think breakfast, clothes, dinner, bed; at work parents have to think work. Their getting-to-day-care time may be the main time they have a moment to consider anything else; big questions, especially about day care itself, quite naturally pop out when they arrive. But teachers can't answer big questions in the middle of day care. Like "curriculum," "school-readiness" is too big a topic to handle in short, end-of-the-day talks. Parents who try to raise the school-readiness issue then sometimes get discouraged by a low-quality response and give up.

If you are mainly interested in readiness as a concept or in specific facts about your local kindergarten's concept of readiness, you might ask teachers if they know of anything good to read about it, or call your school department for a kindergarten brochure. If you want to set up some useful conversations about your own child, you probably need to schedule at least one long conversation first.

You might think of school-readiness (or any big goal you have for your child) as a tree. The trunk is the big idea; the fruit—specific teaching actions—hangs several branchings away. When you want to develop a working plan with teachers, or see how what they're doing is connected to a main goal, you have to climb the tree together at least once. The range of actions relevant to big goals is too large for short conversations or effective joint effort.

School is not just readin', writin', and 'rithmetic. School is a lifestyle. Children must be able to follow directions, manage possessions by themselves, and get through a day on one twentieth or less of one adult's personal attention. Children must be able to sit quietly and listen on occasion and be willing to speak in a group on request. A basic "comfortableness" with letters, numbers, drawing, writing, and being willing to try things helps; attitude is more important than achievement now. One "apple" in a school-readiness tree might be scribbling in stencils of ball players; another, toe-touching and stretching exercises. You'd plan the stencils for a sports fan who won't touch paper right now, the stretching for a child who refuses to deal with his own shoes because bending over is too hard. But if you just saw a scribbling or bending activity, would you be reassured? Would you plan either of them?

Climbing from "school-readiness" out to teaching actions involves reviewing the possibilities and picking some at every branching:

GETTING FROM GOALS TO ACTIONS

- *Review* the whole package of strengths and weaknesses. It helps to have the problem in perspective and know what's going right, what you've got to work with: "I want to talk about what we can do to help Sammy be in good shape for school. I think it would help me to know how you see him right now, what his strengths and weakness are."
- *Pick* one or two weaknesses to work on, from what strikes you as most important or easiest to get to work on: "It sounds like he could use some help with being organized about his things, and that he's not doing anything with writing or drawing right now."
- *Review* the pieces: Ask, "What's involved in being able to do it?" for any missing skill or balkiness about activities. Every ability and attitude has pieces. You might think about the:
  1. *Physical Actions Involved:* Can your child do them?
  2. *Personal Connections:* Does the activity make sense to your child? Is it connected to your child's own interests, needs, goals? Is it connected to fears?
  3. *Environmental Supports:* Does your child have the time, place, and information needed to practice the skill?
- *Pick* a piece or two for work. Ask teachers, "Where in all this do you think my child is especially stuck? . . . What makes the most sense to work on now?"
- *Review* options for coaching: "How could you teach her that?" "How could we help him with that?" The options depend partly on which piece presents the most trouble: with physical coordination, any activity that exercises the same muscle groups in similar ways might help; with personal connections, you might want to brainstorm with teachers about how to connect the activity with interests or with "safe" activ-

ities; with environmental support issues, you can think together about finding time, space, useful explanations.

- *Pick* some coaching actions that teachers can try at day care
  and some you can try at home. Both groups of adults doing
  something promotes focus and sustains energy—and gives
  you something short and satisfying to check in about at the
  end of the day.

When you work on getting very specific about goals with
teachers, you may feel that you're losing the forest in the
trees. The compensating factor is this: The closer you get to
the trees, the more vivid and practical planning gets, the
more likely it is that ideas get put into action and fit into
daily talk.

School-Readiness: Things to Try

FOR GENERAL INFORMATION:

- Get kindergarten brochure from your school department.
- Arrange a visit to a local kindergarten.
- "Network"—ask your friends and neighbors about their experiences with local kindergartens, what was expected, what
  was hard for their child or for them.
- Ask teachers about things to read, local workshops, whether
  getting a speaker for the whole parent group at day care
  makes sense.

FOR YOUR CHILD:

One long conference to map out areas for focus and action:
At home: Use any natural, comfortable opportunities that
come up to notice, use, or give examples of:

- *Representing:* "Oops! Here's that Stop sign!"
- *Categorizing:* "Do you want round crackers or square ones?"
- *Guessing:* "Can you guess? The dessert I got is cold and soft
  and brown and one of your favorites . . ."
- *Counting:* "I'm going to give you ten grapes, 1 . . . 2 . . ."

- *Writing:* "Let's leave Mom a note: 'We went to get ice cream, Love, Dad and Joey.' Want to draw an ice-cream cone?"

At home:

Read a little every day together.

At day care:

- Keep in touch about goals you've discussed with teachers.
- Notice what's going right: "I saw some stencils in his art cubby . . . you got him doing it! Was it a struggle?"
- Say what you're seeing at home: "We tried playing Candyland this weekend, but she hated it. . . . What else could we try?"

Teachers' basic curriculums work with a reading of "the average child"—of course, it's what anyone working with a group would do. But the "average child" is always a mythical beast, never really there. It's the real children, with their own loves and hates, blazing strengths and innocent confusions, that make teaching exciting, make it real. Many teachers despair of satisfying anyone about "curriculum" and "readiness," so they're wary and reluctant to try; when we wade in with curriculum questions, we feel like pests. You can, however, think of yourself as a gift-giver all around. When you break through the big topic, the big words, and the "average" child to a lively look at your own learner, everyone wins.

Early Learning Worksheet

At drop-off and pickup times (or visits), do other children look engaged in what they're doing? _____

Does your teacher have things to say about your child's current loves, interests, "projects," excitements? _____

Does your teacher sound interested and engaged in supporting your child *in general*? _____

If you have to answer "no" to the above, find out if it's a matter of

philosophy: "Children need to learn to wait" or to "entertain themselves" or "shouldn't get attached to teachers." Regular conversations with teachers that express your own values may work best. What would you like to get across?

_____

_____

_____

lack of resources: insufficient staffing, materials, training, planning time. Lobby the administration or other parents to improve resources. How could you find out if other parents are interested in these changes? or what's involved in bringing them about?

_____

_____

School-Readiness Worksheet

How could you find out what your local kindergarten expects? _____

What could you look for in your child's changing ways that might be reassuring? _____

_____

Plan a long conference with teachers. Aim for a picture of what strengths and weaknesses your child would bring to school if it started tomorrow, what makes sense to work on now, and how adults can help with that. What information will you bring to this conference? _____

_____

_____

What worries? _____

_____

Pick one area you're pretty sure you'll be working on with teachers:

_____

What could you say at drop-off or pickup time that would support work on this? _____

_____

5

Social Life: "And You're Still My Friend, Right?"

With her three-year-old, Laura, Jane surveys the room: Hunan, Billy, and Ned are running around on the music rug yelling, "Score!" and falling down. Stella's bossing Tasha around in the house corner again: "You sit! It's *dinner!*" Benjamin executes a container trade with Myra at the water table—"And you're my friend, right?"

A fit of giggles targets Molly and Sue in the loft; Laura heads over, yelling on her way up: "*I'm* the Mommy!" Such tact! Jane thinks, That'll start the day's power plays off with a bang. At least Laura belongs somewhere in the group now: A few months ago, she was lost. The chemistry just wasn't right. "We're working on social skills," the teachers tried to reassure Jane. A nice way to put it, she'd thought. Good luck!

WITH SITTERS WE GET child care; with day care we get social life. When the social life works, we're delighted, even smug—here's a world of child-to-child entertainment and education that no lone adult could provide. When the social life is *not* working, we wish we had a sitter—or that day care were a private club, admitting just the right children. We don't know whether to look elsewhere for better chemistry or to hang in there hoping for social skills to develop. This chapter explores ways to help with chemistry *and* skills in the wider world of social life.

Chemistry: Finding the Questions

> Nora smiles sadly at Hannah and Jasmine: They are so cute! They have a real love affair. If only my Abby had a friend like that! Abby hangs back in the morning, practically *under* Nora's skirts, not just behind them; at pickup time, she's always reading with a teacher. Nora wonders, Doesn't she have any friends? Doesn't anyone like her? There aren't many girls in the group, and Abby is the youngest; it's probably hard to compete. . . .

Hungers Parents' concerns about the chemistry between a child and the day-care group take many forms. Sometimes they just reflect the Basic Parent Information Problem: You only get to see your child with other children when you're both in the middle of saying good-bye or hello—not the best conditions. Many children need time to warm up in the morning; some must feel it's disloyal to play while parents are there—the minute parents leave, they burst into play. It's always worth asking teachers if what you see is typical of the *whole* day: "It *looks* like he doesn't really have any friends here. . . ."; "Is she like this with kids all day?"

Seeing a nice friendship between other children in the group sometimes makes parents wonder, Why not mine? Is there something wrong? Probably not. Real friendships—in the very attached, play-all-day sense—are fairly rare among young children. Young children can enjoy each other tremendously, acquire the details of others' lives and possessions, act like old cronies when they see each other on the street, and still not really have a "friendship" that's visible more than five minutes a day. For many children, day care is more like having lots of brothers and sisters: You may not be crazy about *any* of them, but still, they're yours and that feels good.

Some parents' "chemistry" questions revolve around the group of children: They look too young, or too old, too boy- or girl-heavy, too loud or too tame. Parents may worry in advance about the lack of friendship potential or even dread friendships, given the possibilities. These parents may lobby directors to enroll more same-age, same-sex children, but this approach can be pretty frustrating. Sometimes the waiting list for enrollment just doesn't *have* such children; sometimes same-age and same-sex children come—but don't appeal to your child anyway.

Other parents worry most about their own child's personality. Day care seems to put a premium on very sociable children: If yours isn't especially "sociable," is he or she just lost in the group all day? Parents who have struggled with shyness or loneliness in their own lives may be counting on day care to protect their children from the same struggle. But how much can little children be expected to understand? How much can teachers do?

All these concerns are legitimate and important. Children should feel very connected to other people when parents are away, not adrift in a neutral sea. Children should feel socially "successful"—appreciated, loved, enjoyed.

Focusing on *enjoyment* may take you further toward these goals than thinking in terms of "friends." "Enjoying each other" includes the more typical experience, respects differences in the kind of contact children want, and still describes the glow of belonging and feeling special children need.

Appetites You might try asking teachers, "What does my child enjoy about other children? What do other children enjoy about mine?" Children have very different social appetites. Some are big eaters—they like just about everybody; they like action all the time. Others prefer private play near company or love to blow off steam with a crowd in between private projects. Some children love watching best of all: Other children give them food for thought. What kinds of contact does your child want with other children?

Chips and Dips Many children mainly enjoy each other's ideas. Infants watch each other play; they crawl over to just-abandoned toys and try out what they've seen. Toddlers copy each other constantly, even try out each other's ways of being brave and brassy. Preschoolers teach each other facts, games, construction solutions. Reserved children study rowdy ones with big eyes: How will other children handle that sassy approach? What will the grown-ups do? Older children suddenly "get it" when they see younger children doing the puzzles, the art project, the jacket flip, wrong.

Teachers don't automatically notice, encourage, or even allow watching. If you suspect that your child really enjoys watching and feels a part of things this way, let teachers know. You might ask them to look at who/when/what your child watches in free moments and what your child's face shows—interest? worry? boredom? pleasure? Let teachers know you think watching is valuable. (It *is*. Not only is it one way children take part in things, but the idea source is uniquely useful: Adult examples—of what to do with a toy, what to draw, what to say—tend to be overcomplicated; other children's ideas lie within reach.) Join your child's watching when you drop off or pick up. A few quiet moments and friendly comments can say, "Yes, these kids are interesting, you're right. And I'm glad you're enjoying it."

Meat and Potatoes Some children love sheer company most. The urge for simple company seems to be quite strong quite young. Infants crawl over to each other even when it's sure to mean trouble; they'll want to play with a ball by themselves *but* in the middle of a crowd, not off where the ball could be safely all theirs. Toddlers often travel in packs from the climbing structure to the water table to the dress-up corner, even though "He bumped me!" and crowding drives them crazy. The company is too attractive. Preschoolers bending intently over their own work still want to *talk:* "Now I'm putting one here. . . ."

Like watchers, children who enjoy sheer company at home may miss out on this comfort at day care if teachers tend to press children into activities. And some children need invitations. If teachers report that your child hangs back a lot, you might ask them to invite your child from time to time: "Would you like to play that over here by us?" Solitary play is important in its own right and refreshing—but it's good to know it's really a *choice.*

Peanut-Butter Sandwiches Versus Junk Food The way your child enjoys others may surprise you. Quiet parents sometimes find themselves with party-animal children; sociable parents may be shocked by their private offspring. Your child's choice of friends can surprise as well. You pray for a friendship with an angel or an athlete—your child falls in love with a devil or a bookworm. So it goes. You have to allow for some differences in taste.

Parents are most likely to be concerned when a very well-behaved child becomes attached to an always-in-trouble child. This Evil-Twin syndrome is fairly common; perhaps the wild "twin" gives "good" children the chance to feel wicked without losing their Solid Citizen status. If this rings a bell, you might ask teachers to help your child find other ways to feel wicked safely—pretend play?

Sometimes the chemistry between children seems poisonous. Toddlers fascinated by rougher children can find themselves constantly in the line of fire, getting hurt physically; preschoolers get hurt when they want "in" with popular children who toy with their affections. Parents often ask teachers, "Please! Just keep them away from each other!"

Separating two children isn't always the answer. Forbidden friendships may become more desirable, and separation can confuse children: This is punishment—what was the crime? It's worth asking teachers," What are they *like* when they're apart?" If teachers aren't sure, you might suggest separating the children, just to get the information—it's a perspective everyone should have, including your child.

When complaints about another child go on and on, many a preschooler's parent has been frustrated: "Why don't you just stay away from her!" Pure sympathy generally works better. It gives a child the chance to feel again how bad things can get and to "own" the problem; this and a parent's quiet support helps them sort out what they really want from a position of strength.

Ice Cream Many children enjoy most the kind of active play adults don't provide: repetitious and rowdy. Adults get bored with simple games quickly; other children can chase back and forth or build-it-and-smash-it twenty times before tiring. Other children come up with the great ideas adults never suggest: falling down, dumping toys, running in circles. Your child might want to *do* this stuff, or just watch it, to follow a leader or be the leader. Is this kind of play appreciated—even allowed—at day care?

Some teachers believe they must keep directing play every minute. They forget that just enjoying each other nourishes children. You might ask, "Do you let them just get really silly?" and describe the kinds of silly play your child enjoys. Let teachers know that you think silly play is important, too—for "bonding," for release, for joy—whatever makes sense to you.

Day care can be a banquet, if adults notice children's tastes when they make up the menu. Teachers get so busy running the program, heading off trouble, tying the shoes . . . they can use your help focusing. They may not have quick answers to how your child enjoys others. That's fine, in fact better. Taking time to notice what makes your child light up, or feel comfy and connected, gives the question the seriousness it deserves.

Chemistry: Developmental Issues

INFANTS

> Big-city Helen has been substitute teaching in the infant room. "Quick!" she gasps. "Say something *mean* to me! I've been in the infant room for four hours—it's like living in La-La Land! It's soooooo slow and sooooo sweet—I can't stand it."

Given the right atmosphere, even four-to-five-month-old infants enjoy other infants heartily. They smile and wiggle all over when they see a "friend"; they watch other infants with wide-open enthusiasm. Older infants crawl over and pat each other, they squawk and coo back and forth; they love rolling around on the ground or on a grown-up together. All the basic baby joys—pounding on things, shaking heads, making blurble noises—get twice the laughs when another infant joins in.

Something like La-La Land seems to be the right atmosphere for most infants, much of the time. Somewhere on every infant's Ten Most Hated Things list is Sudden Loud Noises. Other infants' cries and happy screeches make for lots of Sudden Loud Noises; other infants' crawling and mauling, however innocent or friendly, can be nerve-racking. A La-La Land atmosphere—very slow, calm, and sweet—pads the little jolts of other babies' noise and movement so they are much easier to take in stride.

Of course, La-La Land isn't perfect for all babies all the time. Babies—some more than others—need action, too. They need the variety of rowdy play for itself and to relax them from the mental work they do. Older infants who seem tense in an aggressive way may be helped by periods of rowdier play.

Infants who are quite sensitive to sudden sound and movement may look shy or unsociable when they are mainly overstimulated; infants whose chemistry thrives on action may look antisocial: pounding on another infant is one way of stirring things up. What is your baby's chemistry? When does he or she seem to enjoy other people most? If you have a sense that less action or more action at day care might help, ask your teachers to think about these same questions and let you know what they see. Then together you might work on

ADJUSTING THE ATMOSPHERE

- Down. Teachers might experiment with:
    1. *Sound Levels:* turning music down or off, fixing or removing buzzing lights or fish-tank filters, getting self-conscious about the volume and tone of their own voices
    2. *Movement Levels:* rearranging feeding and diapering places or times to cut down on bustle, creating low-movement, lie-down-on-the-floor playtimes, getting self-conscious about the amount and suddenness of their own movements
- Up. Teachers can try changing:
    1. *Sound Level:* adding music, reading aloud, or upbeat running talk to some periods in the day
    2. *Movement Level:* creating a "let's go!" time with dancing or bounce-you, fly-you, chase-you play

TODDLERS

Block corner takes:

- Someone jostles Nina's tower. One block falls off. She screams, "Stop it!," puts the block back, and goes on building.
- Someone jostles Cal's tower. One block falls off. Cal laughs

and knocks the rest of the tower over himself, then dances on the blocks, kicking them farther apart.
- Someone jostles Gordon's tower. One block falls off. Gordon bursts into tears and sobs on the floor until a teacher comes.

In a group, other toddlers get in your space and in your face; they invade your territory and touch your stuff. It's unavoidable and constant. So a child's typical way of reacting to interruptions and invasions often plays a major role in toddler social life.

To an outsider, "toddler social life" may seem to be a contradiction in terms. After all, toddlers are the people who take "No!" and "Mine!" from the status of Mere Words to the level of Lifestyle. Despite this, toddlers usually enjoy being together a great deal. They like having other toddlers to watch, chase, copy, crash into, bring things to, jump with; they like a big family scene. All dance, all sing, all splash, all glue, all race to the sandbox: groupiness adds value. People who question whether two-year-olds get anything from groups sometimes point out that most toddlers don't "really" play together. What they do is called "parallel play"—playing *next to* more than *with* someone. This is quite true; that's what they do. What critics of this "inferior" form of play miss, however, is that toddlers love it.

Toddlers are often keenly aware of each other's styles. Odd-couple friendships sometimes develop: Slight and quiet Sally studies big, loud Collin, later trying on his role for size; rowdy Jimmy bugs sweet and silent Tommy—what does it take to get a rise? True friendships can begin this year, too. Two or three toddlers may become just as attached to each other as they are to blankets and special bears. They wait for each other to arrive before playing; if one gets upset, another finds the right blanket, gets a teacher, pats and hugs and worries until all is well.

Such friendships are fairly rare; don't worry if your toddler doesn't have a special buddy. More common is a broader family feeling toward many children in the group.

Toddlers often know each other's jackets, lunchboxes, parents, and pet peeves, and take pride in all this information.

Balanced against such pleasures are the inevitable frustrations. Multiply the one-block-knocked-off examples a thousand times a day, and you can imagine the special ways children of different temperaments get into trouble with each other.

If your toddler, like Nina, tends to *move around* interruptions, staying focused on a goal, social life may be a piece of cake. Movers-around frequently lead the fun, letting disruption flow by them. Some movers-around find themselves chronically annoyed with other children or get too bossy—at home and at day care. These toddlers may need help with learning gentler ways to manage other children, with knowing when to relocate a personal project or get adult help, or with relaxing into other children's ideas of fun.

If your toddler, like Cal, tends to *move with* interruptions, he or she may be quite popular, seen as "easygoing" and always ready for play. Some movers-with, however, get fragmented in a group. They respond to too many ideas for play, get going in too many directions, get wild. Without meaning to, they blunder into everyone else's play and become pests. These children need most help learning when and how to slow down, and how to undo the "pest" problem (a little bit of "sorry," putting scattered things back, a hug?) so they don't feel like pests or get treated that way.

For toddlers like Gordon, interruptions are brick walls. The wall drops in front of their train of thought or action, blocking all vision of repair. The rest of the world disappears; only the ruined present exists. They can't move around or with interruptions; they have to stop, recover, and *move again*. Movers-again need the *time* to recover from a collapse, and leadership from adults to go back and try again.

Many parents whose toddlers have a bumpy social life assume that nothing much can be done: toddlers are just prickly, feisty little people—what can you expect? They only pray that outgrowing toddlerhood will happen fast enough for all to be forgiven in future friendships. Other parents worry about their child's social future: They see a bossiness, a wildness, or a special sensitivity that seems likely to remain even when the "terrible twos" part is gone.

"Being two," however, does not mean that the rough edges of social life or social style cannot be smoothed. Good teachers work steadily on teaching toddlers ways to respect themselves *and* other children at the same time, very often with considerable success. Toddlers can use good social strategies. They are natural mimics, and when a strategy meets their needs, they adopt it wholeheartedly.

You can think of the variety of general needs and strategies as ways of

DEVELOPING RESPECT

Teachers and parents can help toddlers develop:

RESPECT FOR SELF:

- Notice and name the part of a social contact a child enjoys or hates: "You *liked* dancing with Gina," or "You wanted a turn *right now*." Putting words to experiences makes them special and manageable for toddlers. The message is: How you feel counts.
- Arrange some activities with this one child in mind and point that out: "I remembered you liked cinnamon crackers, so I got these!" "You liked the clay we had last week, so I thought we'd try this kind too." The message: You have a style all your own; your style counts.
- Take control calmly: "It's just too crowded for you here now; let's go find another place to play." "Your tantrum shows me it's time to take a break. Let's go relax on the couch." The message: So you can't manage everything all the time—that's okay, not the end of everything, not a major failure.

RESPECT FOR OTHERS:

- Notice and name other children. Photos of other children in the group on the wall at day care (or fridge at home) testify to their importance; pointing out who's who from time to time does the same. It helps to greet other children by name; point out what different children are doing in that "Isn't that interesting?" voice adults all use with lunch food. Message: Other people count, too.

- Stick up for other children's rights (and adults'!) in a matter-of-fact way: "Well, it's her turn right now . . . you have to wait or find another toy." "I'm too tired to play Horsey, but I can read to you." Message: Other people have rights, too.

RESPECT FOR PROCESS:

- Help a child get past a tough moment of fury, wild silliness, or sad collapse; let him or her stop, recover, and try again.
- Take time to explain other people's confusing cues or behavior: "I don't think she feels like a hug right now . . . you could ask her." "He's upset right now; maybe later he'd like to play."
- Feed the needed words: "Tell him 'I don't like that!'"
- Call attention to important cues: "Look at James's face—he doesn't look happy about this."

The message for process-oriented action: What happens in conflicts counts. You don't have to give up or tune out; you can wake up or try again.

Respect for self, others, and the work of living well with people—these may sound like lifetime achievements, the keys to world peace, the foundations of a satisfying life—in short, too much to expect of two-year-olds. Yes, but two is a great time to focus on beginning the work. Twos are in the business of exploring you-versus-me encounters; starting them out with "We both count!" makes their present better and future brighter.

PRESCHOOLERS

> - "I want to be Latisha's friend. But she's not my friend. She's Emma's friend." (Adult: "Can't she have *two* friends?" Child: "No.")
> - "Deborah played with Chris today, and Deborah's *my* friend!" Tears.
> - Child to child: "You can't be Superman. I'm Superman." Second child: "If you won't let me be Superman, you can't be my friend!"

"Friend" is a heavy word for many preschoolers. Sometimes they treat it as an absolute, like a parent-child relationship; bestowed by fate, a claim on total loyalty. Any abandonment torpedoes them; they sink. Some preschoolers see it the opposite way: "Friend" is something to be achieved every day. "You're not my friend!" or "You can't come to my birthday party!" become awesome weapons.

Chemistry between people puzzles adults; it positively tortures preschoolers. Their minds are turning to the rules of things, and friendship won't fit. As they move from focusing on the details of things to categories, other children stop being just themselves or a collection of special experiences; they become Friends or Not-Friends, Girls or Boys, nothing in between. Preschoolers are looking beyond specific situations to rules: They don't say "Mine!"; they say, "I got it first!" They want to claim friendship by similar rules; they don't understand that fairness just doesn't apply to friendship; it isn't the point. Friendship as chemistry goes against their grain of growth. Everything else is revealing an order and bending to their own more mature, more coordinated efforts. Why won't friends?

Preschoolers' drive to nail down shifting loyalties may crowd out all other pleasures; they can be lonely in the middle of a crowd. Adults want to shake them: "Lighten up! There are plenty of fish in the sea." Parents and teachers try to shake their ideas about friendship: "Being friends doesn't mean you have to play together every second." "Of course you have more than one friend!" These efforts usually fail. Preschoolers just aren't ready; they want our sympathy, not our opinions.

If your child is struggling with friendships, the sympathy you provide can make the biggest difference. Most of the trouble happens away from you and, to the extent that sheer chemistry is involved, lies outside your control. Serious listening gives dignity to a child's efforts; it restores the feeling of being important that friendship struggles erode.

You might also talk with teachers about ways to keep your child's self-respect strong through this time. Trying to create a friendship can make a preschooler feel helpless, lonely, or unlovable. Adults can help by keeping a child's sense of power, of belonging, and of being lovable as lively as possible.

KEEPING SELF-RESPECT STRONG

Parents and teachers can help preschoolers with their:

- *Sense of Power:* Teachers can help children see choices in sticky play scenes. They might talk about the choice of a whole scene; "Well, you can keep trying to play ball with those guys, or you can help us build this spaceship, or you could slide," or choices *within* a play scene: "Melissa is the mommy right now. . . . Looks like you could be the sister *now* or the mommy *later.*"
- *Sense of Belonging:* Teachers can emphasize the groups a child does belong to: "It's lunchtime for the Stomper Group kids!" or focus on family-as-unit: make special projects around family recipes, family trees, family customs. Parents can underline the sense of group at home. Even little ways can brighten spirits: "This family gets pretty silly sometimes!"
- *Sense of Lovableness:* Both teachers and parents can broad-

cast the message: You are *enjoyable,* by spending a little extra pure playtime with a child in a friend's role, and by spelling it out: "I like being with you!" "I love your laugh!"

Some children seek others from the moment they can "scooch" around on their own; some care only for grown-ups until three or so, then make a radical switch to children; some remain adult-oriented for most of the day-care years. Day care doesn't seem to alter this timing, nor should it. Day care should leave children of all chemistries and timings with the sense that the world of children is a good place to be themselves—whoever they are.

Chemistry: Parent-Teacher Talk

PARENT: "Being with these younger children is making Noah act like a baby. Now he's just copying their bad habits to get attention. I really want him to be with older kids. There's no one in this group who can be good company for him."

TEACHER: (*No* one here is good enough? Really!) "Well . . ."

PARENT: "Jeanette is absolutely torturing Mona! We had tears about her again last night. First she's sweet, then she bosses Mona around and won't let her play. I think she's a scheming brat."

TEACHER: (Jeanette is no saint, but neither is Mona, for heaven's sake—they're four. And Mona's no dummy— why does she keep coming back for more? This isn't that simple. . . .) "Well . . ."

My Child/Those Children When the social scene at day care seems to be ruining their child's life (and their own), parents quite naturally turn to teachers: In a comfortable relationship, complaints pop out. This particular kind of complaint, however, is very awkward for teachers. Good teachers usually feel protective about *all* the children they teach; like parents, they take criticisms of "their" children somewhat personally. And like parents, it doesn't matter if they agree that a child is being awful—no one else is allowed to say it. That's as it should be.

Rarely do parents like all the children in a day-care group. You shouldn't expect yourself to have no negative feelings. Some won't be your style; some may affect your child in ways you don't like. Most of the time, this doesn't have to interfere with problem-solving. If you are concerned, you have been seeing something—immature behavior or sadness—at home and want help. That can always be discussed without criticizing other children. You can:

STAND BY YOU

- *Describe what* you *see.* "She's started asking for a bottle again," "He's throwing tantrums again. . . ." "She looked sad and worn out; I asked her about it, and she said no one would play with her."
- *Describe how* you *feel:* "I'm really upset about the bottle business—I thought we were through with all that!" "When she said no one would play with her, my heart just sank."
- *Describe what* you *need:* "I need to know how long you think this will last/if it's okay to forbid bottles at home when it's allowed at day care/that you help her feel good about the ways she's older, more grown up"; "I need to know if she really doesn't have friends to play with/how you're handling this/what to say to help her when she's talking about this."

When you describe problems this way, teachers' minds can go directly to the main issues. They don't get sidetracked defending other children out loud to you, or silently to themselves.

Parents are sometimes shocked by the intensity of their own bad feelings about other children in the group: How can they harbor such hatred for the "big bullies" when "big" is two feet tall? How can they think such snide thoughts about that popular four-year-old girl? Well, parenting is protecting, and everyone carries some painful social memories around. Especially when parents are tired, old memories of what it was like to be alone on the playground or bullied by other children may muddy their window on their child's life. Plain information sometimes helps sort things out again. If you think you could use a clearer view, you might ask teachers for more detailed descriptions of what happens—what starts the problem, how does your child react, what kind of grown-up help is available? We can't spare our children all the tough situations we faced, but we can make sure they get better help.

Chemistry: Things to Try

If your child just doesn't seem to be getting much out of the group, you might ask teachers to (watch for a while and) tell you:

ALL AGES

- *How* your child most enjoys other children right now: Watching? Plain company? Silly fun? Play that involves negotiating? Express your support for this style; ask teachers for theirs. Teacher "support" could take several forms:
  1. *Allowing it:* with watching, not insisting on more physical participation all the time; with silly fun, putting up with the noise and chaos, or making sure there's a time and place for it
  2. *Commenting on it:* "You're watching Ned . . . he's making those cars move right up that ramp. . . ." "You like building your blocks right there, next to the sand table—come on over!" "It's fun to be noisy together!"
  3. *Checking in with a child:* "Did you want to play that, or do you like *watching*?" "Would you like to bring that over here closer to us?" "Do you need some more room? It's kind of crowded here."

- What *kinds* of situations your child enjoys: Quiet play next to other children? One-to-one play? Small-group play? Large-group play? Teacher-organized play (in large or small groups)? Express your support for this style and ask teachers, is there much time for your child's favorite situation? Could teachers arrange more time for it, just for two weeks, to see if that made a difference?

Find out if children spend the whole day in a large group. Is it possible to split up from time to time? Smaller groups work better for many children who don't feel at home in a mob. Teachers could try splitting the group:

- Along age lines
- By activity preferences
- Any way at all. Smaller is often much better just by itself.

INFANTS (AND OLDER CHILDREN IN DIFFERENT WAYS)

Parents and teachers can try to:

- Adjust the atmosphere (page 156) by:
  1. Subtracting music, noise, adult bustling around
  2. Adding music, bouncy play, toys that make more sound and motion
- Add protections like highchairs, walkers, playpens for breaks from the action
- Plan for good play opportunities: When is a not-hungry, not-sleepy time? Who is available for play then? What would be fun to do?

TODDLERS

Parents and teachers can work to develop:
- Respect for Self (page 159):

1. Notice and name the part of social contact a child enjoys or hates; give the message: How you feel counts.
2. Arrange and name some activities especially for a child; give the message: Your style counts.
3. Take control calmly; give the message: So you can't manage everything all the time—that's okay.
- Respect for Others
   1. Notice and name other children and their activities in photos, in the room; give the message: People are interesting.
   2. Stick up for other children's rights (and adults'!) in a matter of fact way. Give the message: Other people have rights, too; they count.
- Respect for Process
   1. Help children get past tough moments; let them stop, recover, and try again.
   2. Take time to explain other people's confusing cues or behavior.
   3. Feed the words needed about wants, likes, needs.
   4. Call attention to important cues: repeat words, notice faces.

PRESCHOOLERS (pages 161–163)

- Describe choices, with play partners and inside play scenes.
- Talk about the groups a child does belong to: the day-care group, the family.
- Comment on a child's lovableness; Send the message: You are *enjoyable*—with extra playtime or loving remarks.
- Explore other groups on weekend time around gymnastics, swimming, church.
- Invite a day-care child over to see if special private time without competition gets a relationship over the first hump.

Social Life: Skills: Finding the Questions

> While Lisa is giving the teacher the morning's news, Billy walks over to little Jodi, who is sitting on the floor trying to diaper a baby doll. Coming up behind her, he wraps both arms around her neck and pulls up tight. Jodi screams and reaches around to claw him.
>
> Too embarrassed to move, Lisa watches the teacher untangle them. Why did he do that! Jodi wasn't doing anything to him. He's not a mean kid. The teacher says, "Billy—were you trying to *hug* Jodi?" Wide eyes, a nod, and a sorrowful slump from Billy. "I don't think Jodi wants a hug right now"—fierce agreeing looks from Jodi—"but you can just say 'Hi! Hi, Jodi!'"

The Right Fork When parents see their children blunder into other children (or blunder away from them), they may just wince: Why does my child have to *do* this! They want a loving circle of friends for their child; they imagine a life of rejections. They may wonder if there's something essentially awkward in their child's natural style or if day care isn't really working or if chaos in their own parenting is producing a selfish, graceless child. Most of the time, none of these Big Picture items needs review: All the impulses and circumstances are fine; it's just that social skills need work.

To many parents, "social skills" for day-care years sounds like a euphemism for "not pounding on your friends." When parents think about "social skills," they mean things like the right framing of invitations or letters of sympathy—what does this have to do with children's play? Or they may focus on the Thanksgiving Dinner side of things: saying "please" and "thank you" and *not* burping as often and loudly as possible. In fact, spending the day with other children presents a lot of real social questions: How do you get other children's attention? What can you do with other children *after* you have their attention? How do you join other children who are playing something you like? When should you stand up for yourself, when negotiate, when give in gracefully, when leave? Young children meet all the challenges their parents might meet at a large party or conference; what to do, even what would feel good, isn't always obvious. If children start by grabbing each other around the neck or hiding behind a parent, it may only be ignorance showing.

Greeting the Guests Children sometimes act *least* skilled at drop-off and pickup times: They may attack a child who dares to come near their own parent ("She's mine, you jerk!") or shrug away a friendly hello ("Hey, I'm busy here"). Rough stuff in front of parents is often experimental. When children are confused by having two rule-givers—parents and teachers—in the same space, they check it out: "I know what the teacher does if I push other kids. What will Dad do?" If your child starts trouble with other children the minute you walk in the door, ask teachers who they think should handle it. Some adult ought to respond. It's always worth asking teachers if what you see is typical of the whole day, too. The lack of social graces you see at both ends of the day may be typical only of those special you-are-there times.

Accepting Apologies Sometimes parents are quicker than teachers to see the good intentions behind awkward social moves—like Billy saying "Hi" with strangling. They want to say *something* to help teachers see it, too, but they know they'll sound prejudiced. If you say things like "I think he just wants to play with her," will teachers think you've lost your mind? Gone over the edge in your Doting Parent-mobile? It's possible but still worth doing. The positive perspective is important to keep fresh. Treating children as though they *mean* well brings out their best. Parents who bring up the sweeter possibilities but move right on to the coaching problem often have greatest success: "Well, I *think* he's just trying to say 'hi,' but maybe he really wants to make her scream. . . . In *any* case, it's clear to me he needs your help knowing what to do about her first thing in the morning. . . ."

Diplomatic Coaches Confronted with rude, crude, or sulky social moves from their children, some parents take all the responsibility: "What am I doing wrong?" Others throw up their hands: "What can *I* do? Teachers have to handle this stuff." Parents shouldn't feel *responsible* for all their children's social graces or lack of same. Children of polite parents behave rudely; children of casual parents may treat other children with kid gloves or with iron fists. Certainly, there's no simple, direct translation from one place to the other. Too much depends on a child's age, on teachers' skills, and on the challenges other children present. Teachers do have to do most of the coaching.

On the other hand, parents are not helpless. Every situation involving other people provides a chance for children to practice social skills. Parents are people, too; time with parents teaches. All children have *ways* of greeting parents, getting parents' attention, joining parents' activities, getting a turn with what parents are using, "suggesting" something to play, moving parents out of the way, and so on. If you have been thinking that your child's approaches to other people could use some work, you might ask yourself: How does my child handle me? What are my child's ways of greeting, getting attention, getting a turn, etc., with me? Do I like them? Would they work well with other children? If you're already wishing your child would say "Hi, Mom!" instead of tackling you or ignoring you, or say "Toast, please" instead of grabbing or crying and pointing, go for it. You can use "It's good practice for day care" as extra motivation to work on these graces.

Since teachers do have to do most of the child-to-child coaching, another answer to "What can I do?" is "Support your local teacher." Teachers have a lot of coaching to do and a lot of children to coach: They can wear down. Many parents never ask about their child's social life—it doesn't impinge on home life the way so many other things do. Even parents who are concerned about a shy or rough child may say little, especially if they're embarrassed or counting big on "outgrowing this." You can offer support just by asking how things are going with other children, by praising any good techniques or results you see, and offering home backup: "Is she doing okay with the other kids? . . . Do you think she needs help? . . . How do you work on that—maybe we could work on it at home, too."

By and large, children are gorgeously forgiving with each other. It's as though they know, even better than adults, that they're all just learning the ropes. When an awkwardly shy or rough child finds a new way of doing things, other children respond: Okay! Let's play! The payoff is well worth the work.

Skills: Developmental Issues

INFANTS

Six-month-old Christopher leans out from his nest in a teacher's lap toward five-month-old Bitsy. He coos at her and waits, watching—no reaction. He tries again: Smiling, he flaps his arms and splutters at her. Bitsy freezes, eyes glued to Christopher. He grins, then flaps and splutters again, and waits. She gets it! Bitsy flaps and splutters back, and waits. He flaps. Bitsy flaps back. Then Bitsy leans forward and growls at Christopher—a deep-throated huff of excitement and pleasure. Teachers burst out laughing; Christopher shrieks with glee; Bitsy beams. Then flapping and spluttering start all over again, and again.

Infants come prepared to find other people exciting. When adults talk and smile to three-month-olds, those baby eyes open up, and soon their hands and feet are wiggling:

"Oh yes! Let's do it!" they seem to say. "More!" Building social skills with infants is largely a matter of channeling this whole-body excitement into successful experiences.

Older infants get into all the basic social fixes: 1) How do you make contact with people? 2) What do you say after you say hello? 3) How can you get what you want when someone else has it? A seven-month-old excited to see a "friend" may wriggle over, walrus-style, and crash his whole head on top of the other baby, or reach out and grab for eyes, or pound a nose. As sheer friendly enthusiasm, it's sweet; as "Hello," it's a failure. Around this same age, infants want only toys other infants are using. Ignoring fourteen thousand other toys in the room, they squirm over from baby-miles away to grab the one toy another infant holds. Other baby hands must work as a special display case, a lighted, dressed-up window for toys. Again, the special attraction seems positive: You make things magic!—but the results aren't so hot.

Christopher knew what to say after he said hello. He invited Bitsy to play copy–me: I flap–you flap. Imitation is one of the easiest games to get going with infants, and one of their favorites. They love to shake heads, pound on the floor, and make funny noises in this I do it–you do it rhythm. Peekaboo and chase-me are also quite popular with the quite young, and also have the back-and-forth act-pause-act pattern, basic to all good social play and conversation.

Some teachers solve the "I'm-so-excited-I-have-to-pound-on-you-and-take-your-toys" issues by keeping infants away from each other as much as possible. Sometimes there's no alternative. Good teachers work on showing infants what *else* to do with their excitement. Teachers can show infants how to touch each other gently: "Here—pat gently like this." They can teach baby games by playing copy-me, peekaboo, and chase-me with infants themselves.

When teachers or parents see face-pounding and toy thefts, the natural reaction may be "No! Stop that!" This often makes things worse: Loud, angry sounds startle infants; they're most likely to cry or pound harder. Using calm, it's-going-to-be-okay tones while legs and toys get untangled soothes the jangled nerves more quickly, *and* it sends the right message: "Yes, people get in each others' hair, but we don't have to panic. We can get sorted out." Adults can take the worry out of getting close. You can

SUPPORT BABY SOCIALIZING

- Notice what teachers do right: "I'm so glad you:
  1. Play games with them."
  2. Teach them how to pat each other."
  3. Stay so calm when they get into trouble."
- Tell teachers what you see or what you're working on at home: "He loves playing peekaboo now" "She's into shaking her head and kind of imitating us" "We're working on 'Nice . . . nice' touching; I think he's getting it."
- Practice at home
  1. Play back-and-forth pattern games like copy-me and peekaboo.
  2. Play goofy games. Other infants are goofy, noisy, physical; if your baby is used to this style from you, it's bound to feel more comfortable.
- Play with soft-touching in mind. Parents sometimes put up with face-poundings and cheek-squeezings that other infants will hate. It's confusing if very rough play is okay with *you* but not others. You can just back off from rough baby pounding or demonstrate soft touching yourself.

TODDLERS

Curled up on the couch with his teacher Ann and a book, twenty-one-month-old Roy looks the picture of peace. He's half-dissolved into Ann; he'll never move again. When twenty-month-old Stephanie approaches, however, Roy springs forward. "No!" he yells—loud, fierce, firm.

Ann smiles. Here's "How to Win Friends and Influence People—Toddler Style." These two! They have so much fun sometimes, but they're always ready for battle. She launches into Social Relations 101: the quick shift of focus to details of the contact, followed by grindingly slow and careful attention to joint satisfaction. "Stephanie, are you coming to the couch? . . . Where would you like to sit? . . . Roy, what do you think? Will that be okay? . . . Will it work if I hold the book?" It takes forever, but they get past the panic point, and, it turns out, they're much more interested in all of this than they were in reading anyway.

Adults hear so much "No!" and "Mine!" from toddlers, it's easy to assume they'd just rather be alone. Most of the time, however, toddlers just want to be in charge. We see their drive (and anxiety) to order the world over food, dressing, and sleep. The cracker, the jacket, the blanket, have to go a certain way or they panic. Two toddlers—each with a plan they feel strongly about but can't really explain—naturally run into trouble. Teachers can get them past the panic—and set good examples of social problem-solving in the meantime—by supplying the words and giving lots of specific, small choices so each child can feel in charge.

Good toddler teachers have to see past toddlers' first reactions to any social situation. Not knowing how to manage each other, toddlers hit upon all sorts of ideas, not all of them great.

TODDLER SOCIAL STRATEGIES

- *Saying Hello:* Stick out stomach and bump into someone; watch shyly from behind a large adult or piece of furniture; shove someone, cock head to side, grin, say "hi!"; scream in an ear; stand next to someone and stare; pull on an arm; knock down whatever is in front of someone.
- *Joining a Group:* Run into the middle of a group making a loud noise; stand four feet away and stare; walk your body up slowly and lean all over someone; find an unoccupied space and start doing what other children are doing; go over

and rip a toy out of someone's hands; pull a teacher's arm over to a group.

* *Playing in Close Quarters:* Leave as soon as things get crowded; elbow the person closest to you; hang in there until someone leaves, yell "Move!"; fall on top of someone; move to the least-crowded space; cry.
* *Dealing with Rude Behavior:* Hit back; grab your toy back; cry where you are; go cry in front of or next to a teacher; bite the rude person; yell "Mine!"—"My turn!"—"No, don't!" at the rude person; go get a teacher.
* *Getting a Turn:* Hit and run; wait for the person to put it down; grab it and fight off the other person; say "Wanna turn!" and wait or grab as you speak; go tell a teacher "My turn!"

Lots of toddler strategies involve undesirable behavior, and you may hear about them from teachers: "He's rough with the other kids." "She just cries when the other kids bump or it gets too crowded for her." If adults concentrate on undesirable behavior without teaching a better strategy, change may come very slowly—and the next strategy idea may not be a big improvement. You can help keep the focus on:

BUILDING SKILLS

* Ask teachers about the *point* of a problematic approach—what was your child trying to do? "So Timothy took her bear and she scratched him . . . she needed some way of getting the bear back?"
* Identify the practical alternatives: "What should she have done right then? How do you want kids to handle that situation?"
* Set up goals and teamwork: "How do you teach children to do that [the practical alternative]? We'd be happy to work on that at home too. . . ."

PRESCHOOLERS

ANNA: "Let's play princess!"
TRUDY: "Okay!"
ANNA: "I'll be the princess."
TRUDY: "No."
ANNA: "We can *both* be princesses!"
TRUDY: "I'll be the baby princess—you be the queen princess!"
ANNA: "Okay."

Amid much self-admiration, skirts, shawls, necklaces, and scarves are shared out happily, Anna halts the one wrong move: "Babies don't wear heels!" Now Queen of the Loft, Anna announces "I'm going shopping!" She shoulders the royal black bag and clonks across to the ladder in high silver heels. Just as she reaches it, Hilary's head pops over the ladder top. "No!" Anna yells. "You can't play here!" Hilary will not be cowed: "Yes, I can! You're not the boss!"

Rusty and Miguel run down the play yard, roaring "Get 'em!"; "Kill 'em!"; and "Pa-Kow!" They are Super Ninja Bionic He-Man Good Guys, once again in fierce pursuit of the eternal Bad Guys. André, half a year younger and twenty feet behind them, keeps stumbling and getting up, chasing again, now and then yelling "Yeah! Shoot 'em!" In his own mind, he's riding with Rusty and Miguel; he's happy. When they suddenly stop and point at him "Pa-kow! Pa-kow!," he is stunned. "André! You're dead!" they say; he bursts into tears.

The world of pretend takes over much of preschoolers' play. They don't just run, they chase monsters and bad guys; they don't just change clothes in dress-up anymore, they change identities. This power to dream up characters and a world for them to act in reflects a great leap in mental complexity. Pretend play offers new ways of exploring ideas: What is it, really, to be a grown-up, a baby, to get married, to be sick? It offers a new safety valve for worries: They can feel, in character, completely competent, mighty, in charge, or charmingly small and well cared for. Pretend play also brings two social troubles: exclusion and "violent" play.

Preschoolers, especially four-year-olds, like to "organize" other people: "I'm sitting *here;* you sit *there.*" Part of "You can't play with us!" undoubtedly comes just from this general urge to take charge and boss around. But the most intense, and most keenly felt, rejections often occur in pretend play.

Pretend play is deeply attractive and difficult to achieve. Toddler pretend play is action-centered: cook and eat, go to sleep—wake up, go to work and come back, get dressed and get undressed. Fragments of the personal show up—in sweet, loving tones for "Here's dinner!" and gentle coverings up of "sleepers" or in stern, commanding tones for "Now eat!" and "Go to bed!"—but roles and plots are thin enough for anyone to join in and do anything, really. Toddlers are mastering action sequences and basic scene-setting; who does what with what takes second place.

Preschoolers, on the other hand, care most about character and its props; they see that character is defined by other characters and actions that must have some consistency. It's tricky work: You have to invent a scene that attracts at least one other child, then negotiate for the roles and props and actions available so that you get what you want but others still want to play. "I'll be Beautiful and Bossy; you be Ugly and Obedient" won't work. All Good Guys and no Bad Guys (or vice versa) doesn't work too well either.

Coordination of roles, props, and actions between just two children often taxes preschoolers' skills to the limit. If a third child wants to join the play, the whole fantasy world will have to shift and reorganize: It's too hard! They protest, "You can't play with us!" The fury or heartbreak this brings makes teachers get involved: What is the right rule? Should children be allowed to exclude other children from play? Should children be forced to play with anyone and everyone who wants to do what they're doing? Neither sounds right. Some teachers choose one or the other anyway; some make compromise rules involving particular spaces or permitted lengths of time for private play.

With a variety of rules, teachers can work on social skills that preserve dignity for all. Teachers can show children how to include others without "ruining" play; for example: "The loft belongs to everyone; Hilary can play here if she wants. . . . How could she play what you're playing? Queen Anna is going shopping, and Trudy is the baby—seems like you could use a baby-sitter or a big princess or a cashier for shopping. . . ." If some private play is protected, teachers can demand kindness in rejection: "I don't want you to say 'Go away!'—that hurts Hilary's feelings; you can tell her 'We want to play by ourselves right now, we'll play with you later.'"

Parents can help teachers help children by bringing to light some key connections between:

ACTIONS AND WISHES

- Find out from teachers: Do they see your child ruining his or her chances of good fun in some way? Preschoolers are given to barging in and demanding things; teachers might help by coaching for a softer approach: "*Ask first*, Joey. You can say 'What are you playing? What can I be?' That usually works much better." What skill could your child use help with?
- Find out from your child (without questions; get talk going and listen closely) what the bottom line looks like. Some social miseries that start with "They won't be my friend" can be cured by small things: a chance to go first tomorrow, ten minutes in the Big Witch role next time, *not* sitting next to Scotty *every* day, some cookies to trade *once* in a while.
- Find out what happens (from teachers or listening to your child) *after* your child tries to make a friendly contact and it doesn't work. Do teachers notice and offer sympathy? Do they help your child see other choices? Is your child able to find other things to do? Teachers can say, "Looks like they're too busy with that game right now. What would you like to do? . . . Let's look all over this room and see what's happening. I bet there's something you'd enjoy. . . ."

Adults cannot make all the social contacts come out right. This age group is too busy and opinionated and talks too much for there to be any hope of that. Your preschooler will probably always have some quite legitimate complaints. Do you need to worry? If the atmosphere in the room is mainly playful, if teachers seem fond, patient, and jokey, then the complaints probably speak of standard growing pains. You can add, "Oh. I'm sorry that happened," to the things you say quite regularly, keep up all the ways you say "I believe in you," and retire in peace.

"Violent" Play. Gun-play rules sometimes consume a lot of day-care energy. Everyone's opinions about real war, cartoons, and sexism pop up, along with immediate worries like children poking each other with whatever is being used as a gun. If your day-care provider has been in operation more than a few months, some rules about gun play have probably already been hammered out.

The specific rules may be less important than a steady emphasis on the basics of play: It's not okay to frighten or upset other children, not okay to poke or push them, not okay to drag them into play they don't want any part of; games that get dangerous get stopped.

No-gun rules probably prevent some painful pokes and falls; they don't erase "violent" play. Children just poison or stab or vaporize each other instead. Children denied toy guns use blocks; children denied blocks for gun use make paper guns; children denied paper guns use fingers or sticks that turn into "rakes" when teachers come near. Apparently, this stuff is just too much fun to let go.

If you or your teachers are concerned about how much your child loves shooting games, ask about the practical effects of these games. What actually happens in the game? After the game? Is it fun, exciting, ultimately satisfying and relaxing? Does it get too intense, a little scary? Is everyone a wound-up mess afterward or just happily exercised? Focus-

ing on real children's faces and moods usually makes the
next step much clearer.

Whatever your child's age, it may feel artificial to work
on social skills. "What was the 'social goal'? Come on! she
wanted to bash him—that's it!" Parents, and teachers, enjoy
the raw, right-out-there sides of children; it's a relief, it's
funny, it's real. You don't have to stop appreciating any of
that or worry that it will go away, buried under gray, polite
maneuvers. Children's "Love me! I love you!" yearning for
other children is just as real, fresh, and basic as their "Go
away!" and "Take that!" Giving children social skills gives
them a choice and lets them balance all their purposes.

Skills: Parent-Teacher Talk

- Julia finds Terry playing alone every day when she comes
  to pick him up. Other children are tearing all over the
  climbing structure, laughing, or snuggled in a pile reading
  with a teacher. Maybe he's fine, but this doesn't look right.
- Little Katherine is dynamic, busy, and bossy. Ted hoped
  that day care would channel that energy and take some of
  its edges off: He adores her, but she's a princess. The plan
  isn't working.
- Rosalind thought everything at day care was going great,
  but last night Karen said, "No one ever plays with me!"
- Mickey tags after his big brother, Joe, and Joe's friends
  until they throw him out or come begging for privacy.
  Mickey's parents thought day-care friends would take the
  pressure off. But Mickey isn't interested in the kids at day
  care; weekends are still horrible.

  One week all these parents ask the teacher, "Why doesn't
  my child have any friends? Couldn't you encourage a friendship?" By the end of the week, the teacher is saying, "Look,
  we can't make friends for them! Children have to do that
  themselves."

Finding Goals Good teachers can foster the kinds of social skills that would save American management billions a year and cut the divorce rate in half, but this doesn't automatically lead to friendship. Teachers can't make friends for children any more than they could force two adults to befriend each other. Teachers also see children's own current goals and limits about relationships at day care: adults-only right now; only if I can be the boss; only if someone else makes the first move. And teachers may have a goal priority list in mind: "First we work on not-hitting and then on talking instead of screaming, *then* we see about friendships." Between "I can't make it happen," "Your child isn't really that interested right now," and "We've got half a year's work to do first," you may not get the reaction you hope for with "friends?" questions. *Of course* you want your child to have friends—for all the joy and comfort of it. Parents want friends as naturally as they want every other pleasure for their children. But "having friends" is an unmanageable goal.

You probably have other, more achievable goals in mind when you think of talking with teachers about friends. When parents *sound* like they're pressuring teachers for friends, sometimes they're looking for reassurance about daily happiness, or satisfying curiosity about social likes and dislikes, finding a way to take pressure off home-time demands for play company, decoding a single remark, getting some information about what to expect at a particular age. Teachers can often address questions and goals like these more easily. If you're not getting satisfying answers to "friends?" questions, let teachers know about your other goals.

Any time your talks with teachers bog down around a particular goal, you might try broadening the focus to include other goals—yours, your child's, and teacher's own.

INCLUDING MORE GOALS

- Collect information. What are all the things you, your child, your child's teachers, are working on right now?
- Consider

1. *Limiting Goals:* Would it be best to work on "using words instead of hitting" before working on finding a friend?
2. *Switching Goals:* Would you like to work on redirecting "Play with me!" demands at home while teachers work on other things?
3. *Combining Goals:* Is there a general goal that addresses your concerns about play and teachers' main concerns now? For example, you might both work on encouraging your child to "take initiative" both in making play contacts *and* in putting on shoes, finding art paper, etc.

Talking with teachers about your *child's* goals may help, too. Sometimes children say, "I want to be So-and-so's friend," but what it boils down to is much easier: five minutes as Mommy in the house corner, five minutes playing kickball with the guys, one apology. If what you hear from your child at home makes it seem that something fairly simple is yearned for, let teachers know. They want your child to feel loved and lovable, too; finding the workable how-to's is the main issue.

Skills: Things to Try
INFANTS

Teachers at day care and parents at home can:

- Practice play, especially back-and-forth pattern games: copy-me (cough-cough, flap hands, pound the pillow, shake heads), peekaboo, chase-me, handing things back and forth, catch, touch-my-nose-touch-yours.
- Keep contact positive.
  1. Provide protection from rough stuff (backpacks, walkers, playpens, high places when adults are busy).
  2. Offer calm, gentle rearranging when babies get tangled up with each other or toys, or pound on each other or adults.
- Add toys or spaces that encourage social play, like big pillows in the middle of the room to gather round and pound on, or peekaboo spots.
- Look at the feeding and nap schedule and any other group busy times to see *when* good play can happen most easily.

TODDLERS

Teachers at day care and parents at home can:

- Practice social strategies, especially:
  1. *How to Say Hello:* words, waves, peeking and smiling, tap on shoulder, jumping up and down . . . anything more noticeable than watching and more comfortable than physical assault
  2. *How to Join a Group:* "What am I doing? Would you like to do that, too?"
  3. *How to Play in Close Quarters:* Model key questions: "Is it too crowded right here?" "Do you need more room?" "Where's a little extra space for you?" "Do you want to wait till it's not so crowded?"
  4. *How to Deal with Rude Behavior:* Use words— "Move!"; get help from a grown-up; express yourself—"I don't like that!"
  5. *Get a Turn:* Use words—"Wanna turn!"; tell a grown-up.
- Slow down all social contacts that promise trouble and ask questions about what each person wants.
- Model: Use words a toddler can use when you say hi, join someone in an activity, and so forth, and give live demonstrations when you're showing a child what to do.
- Coach with words: "Just *tell* him 'I'm using that!'"
- Notice and repeat: "What a nice hello! I like the way you said 'Hi, Tammy!'"

Teachers could:

- Remove toys that only one child at a time can use (most of these cause many more frustrations than they could possibly be worth in play stimulation).
- Add toys that many at a time can use: water and sand tables, blocks and other construction toys, dress-ups, beanbags and balls, huge amounts of Play-Doh, clay, paper, and markers, many identical dolls and dishes, etc.

PRESCHOOLERS

Teachers can help them finish incidents where their feelings get hurt (pages 201–203) by:

- A short, firm complaint to the hurter
- A conversation on the bench between two children
- A group conversation about the incident or problem

Teachers and parents can help hurtful incidents get resolved by:

- attentive listening by grown-up
- nonverbal expressions: pictures, jumping, growling, drama
- extra comforts: special attention, food, snuggles

Check (by asking children) if they understand rules about

- tattling versus appropriate getting of grown-up help
- hurting with words and name-calling
- including other children in play versus private play

COMPETITION AND COOPERATION

Parents and teachers could meet as a group or privately and look at what kinds of:

- toys
- activities
- play spaces

bring out competitive or cooperative feelings among children as things stand, and plan a shift toward those that inspire a more cooperative spirit.

Wanting friends for their children can be one of the most frustrating, even heart-wrenching, experiences for parents. It makes such a difference, and they can't make it happen! When children's hunger for friends goes unsatisfied, parents run up against the real limits of their power to create happiness for their children, maybe for the first time. Friendship struggles raise separation issues with a capital S: Whose life is this? We won't always be able to give them the things they really care about? Oh no . . .

When you need cheering up, you might tell yourself that this *is* only the beginning. Through grade school, high school, and beyond, your child will be working on finding people, and ways to enjoy them, that feel right. You are providing a wonderful head start: Day care offers practice, practice, practice for situations that will keep coming up, the way no other child-care arrangement can. What you are both beginning to learn now has years to achieve perfection and will make each of those years a little easier.

Chemistry Worksheet

Do you think your child feels at home with the day-care group? _____

If your doubt comes from
- the drop-off and pickup scene, have you checked with teachers about whether it's typical of the whole day? _____
- how lopsided the group looks in terms of age, sex, or temperament, can you name the problems you think it's creating or might create? (loneliness, bossy or baby behaviors?) _____

Do teachers see some of this? _____

Would it help for
teachers to try dividing the group part of the day? _
teachers to arrange visits to other groups at day care?
you to join other groups on weekends? _____
- your child's personality, describe what worries you: (too slow, too speedy, too prickly, too agreeable, too devilish . . .) _____

_____

Are teachers worried about the same things? _____

If not, would you like to
- meet with them, explain your concerns, make plans to encourage some change? _____
- meet with them, ask them to describe your child's social style and why they like it? _____
- try out the attitude that your child is terrific as is, or at least there's nothing that age won't cure? _____
If teachers are worried, too, when could you meet with them to think about helping your child enjoy, and be enjoyed by, other children? _____

Skills Worksheet

Describe what happens at home when your child needs

your attention: _____

what you're using: _____

more room or time: _____

you to play a certain way: _____

Do you like these ways of managing you? _____

Are they ways that ought to work with children? _____

If you see one that could use a little work, what could

you try? _____

_____

What do teachers say about the ways your child

approaches other children: _____

gets toys and turns and space: _____

gets help from adults: _____

What could your child do, given his/her age, that would
work better?

Your ideas: _____

_____

Teachers' ideas: _____

_____

What will teachers do to help teach this at day care?

_____

Do you suspect that "unskilled social technique" is a sign of stress? _____

How could you make things more relaxed for a week or two? _____

_____

Did it make a difference? _____

6

Fighting: It's a Jungle in There!

Conversations over cooking:
- "What's that bump on Lila's head?" "That new boy at day care apparently pushed her, and her head knocked into the edge of the cubbies." "What kind of place is that! She came home with bite marks last week. Don't they watch them? What are they doing?! And I've about had it with this new kid."
- "Barry had another bad day at day care. He was hitting again. I don't know what's wrong. I'm so embarrassed—and so sick of hearing about this—I don't even want to talk to the teachers anymore. Not much news to get anyway . . . seems like he spends all day in the Blue Chair getting 'time-out.'"
- "Oh come on . . . so Sam clobbered him, and Rory hit him right back. It's not a big deal. Kids fight!"

PUPPIES NIP, kittens and lion cubs hiss and scratch, baby monkeys chase and wrestle. We know that basic animal spirits must be part of children's fighting, as well as some basic animal instincts like self-defense, defense of territory, making a place in the pecking order. It's understandable. But we want to send our children to day care, not the jungle, thank you. We want teachers to protect our young, and to love and help our "villains" when they go astray. This chapter looks at the victims and the villains, and ways to bring the benefits of civilization to both.

Victims: Finding the Questions

When Mark's mother comes to pick him up, she always brings his baby brother, Eddie. As soon as she puts Eddie down to gather belongings, Mark runs over and pushes him. Eddie cries, Mom yells, Mark hides. This happens three or four times before they get out the door. Mark's teacher Lynn thinks, Well, here's good old sibling rivalry—*and* some 'I hate getting coats on.' Mark pushes other children only one other time of day: when the whole group gets coats on for outside. He cannot handle the chaos.

One day Lynn takes Mark aside for a talk. Lynn: "You know how Eddie cries when your mom comes to get you?" Guilt washes over his face; he nods. Lynn: "Why does he cry?" Mark: "Because I push him." Lynn: "Why do you do that?" Mark: "You know that noise Eddie makes?—anh, anh, anh? (crying sounds) Well, I *like* that noise!"

Cain and Abel Some first-time parents find fighting a little frightening, especially if their children are more victims than victors of the current fighting. They wonder, How can this be normal? The pushing, grabbing, scratching, yelling, looks so out of control—they want to whisk their children away and find a sitter or *something*. Maybe their child is too young to be in a group? It may help to remember that brothers and sisters also push, hit, scream, steal, bite, and fight. Even with home care, if you dare to have a second child, fighting will be part of your picture. Little children have a lot to learn about how to get what they want in civilized ways; on the way to learning it all, they use more primitive approaches, no matter where they are.

But why? Why do children pick on each other? As infants, they all seem so sweet, open, trusting. Fighting is an all-purpose tool. It may serve curiosity, jealousy, frustration, panic, self-defense, defense of territory, defense of resources, a need for attention or excitement, affection, or a fascination with the power to have an effect—to make "that noise." If infants had clearer ideas and better coordination, they'd fight, too.

Teachers try to replace physical fighting with different tools—with talk, negotiating skills, appeals to proper authority, positive exercises in social power. (The real teacher of "Mark" got him interested in making his brother laugh instead; this worked for months.) This coaching builds skills children can use in every group, now and in the future, out in the world and home in the family.

If the amount of fighting in your child's group seems intense or excessive to you, you might ask teachers and other parents how it strikes them: Does it seem typical? If not, what is different?

Garden of Eden Some parents find fighting *sad*. For them, fighting represents the fall from grace as children grow, the loss of a simple world, the beginning of "real" life in the dog-eat-dog world: "I know she has to learn to stand up for herself," they say, "but . . ." *Mainly,* they wish the whole thing would go away: Children shouldn't have to be tough. Why can't teachers keep the peace?

Are bite marks and bruises signs that teachers lack the skills to keep the peace? Not necessarily. The same high-energy life force that bursts out in banging on things and running, in "Mine!" and "Watch me!," just naturally brings children into conflict with each other. Many fights are lightning flashes, over almost before they begin. No one could get there in time. You know how fast chlidren move at home: Turn to another task for one second and dinner is on the floor or the baby off the bed. Even with excellent teachers and wonderful children, some bumps are inevitable.

Teachers do have lots of peace-keeping powers: creating an affectionate and appreciative atmosphere to calm nerves, supplying a resource-rich environment to reduce competition, organizing the activities and transitions between them so that children feel safe and stimulated in the right balance, watching like hawks to intercept and head off trouble, and training, training, training for peaceful approaches. All this, however, works slowly over time. Do teachers seem to be managing the group well most of the time? If so, you probably do not need to reevaluate right away. If not, it may be time to bring in reinforcements: What kind of help are they getting?

Becoming the Snake Good teachers spend as much energy coaching the victims of conflicts to stand up for themselves as they do teaching the "villains" better manners. Teachers do this partly because they cannot always get to children fast enough to prevent trouble and partly because standing up for themselves feels much better to children. Parents sometimes worry about what this will mean. Will their child have to change in unwanted ways to survive in the group? "He's really a gentle person by nature, and we like him that way!" Assertiveness training does not change children fundamentally. Children who are quieter and more reflective by nature than the run-of-the-mill Basic Child usually just add a few good ways of saying "Back *off!*" to their total repertoires; they pull these out on an as-needed basis and return to their own business and their own style. Most "Basic Children" flip roles in the group over time, from victim to bully and vice versa, eventually settling down to neither. You might want to offer as much support to parents of the current fighter-biters as you can; you may well be next. If you are concerned about how teachers are supporting assertiveness, you can ask for examples: "What do you actually say?"

Myth and Meaning When they arrive at day care to a bruise, bump, or bite mark, some parents say, "Well, that's life" (as long as it's not too often); some hit the roof. Finding out how your *child* felt about the incident may help most. Just as children get up and run after falls that would put us in the hospital, they often take a lot of rough stuff from each other in stride; they may be confused, even shamed, by adult upset over "simple" bumps. At other times, they welcome every sigh of sympathy. The *meaning* of each incident in the child's own eyes makes the difference. Your child may treat a bump that horrifies you as an unimportant accident, or a terrible insult, or a scary event, or a fascinating body change. Ask your teacher: "How did s/he take it?" Many things contribute to meaning: how much your child likes the other child involved; how completely the teacher was able to comfort; how the whole thing got "finished." You can ask for a description that includes these clues to meaning, and specifics about your child's reaction: Did your child yell, fight back, get help, cry? How long? How was comfort offered and dignity restored?

The Jungle System Finding out how your child reacts to fighting is important for long-term reasons, too. Although "jungle"—as in "It's a jungle out there"—sounds violent, students of animal communication tell us that physical violence *within* animal groups is actually quite rare, especially among the monkeys and apes we take as ancestors. Signals control aggression. Certain ways of hunching shoulders, baring teeth, lowering eyebrows, and staring, certain barks and growls—settle conflicts without hurt.

Young children use this system. Six-month-olds can manage wily nine-month-olds with a steady glare and a few good huffs at the right moment. Toddlers leaning forward, looking "serious," barking "No!" can keep conflict to a standoff (or turn it into giggles). A preschooler pulling a Very Serious face, stance, and voice can prevent very serious trouble.

Parents and teachers can work together to give children whatever coaching and support they need to get this signal system working for them. If you suspect that your child may need help, ask teachers for their take on your child's way of handling conflict and for ideas about how you can help. When parents see a child pushing theirs around, the first urge—even if they are committed to nonviolence in every other area of life—may be to yell "Hit him! Hit him back!"—but hitting is what we're trying to outgrow here. Your teachers should have a few choice phrases for encouraging assertiveness you can use instead. The next section also describes some approaches appropriate to each age.

Focusing on your child's reactions to fighting is a powerful influence for change all by itself. Aggressive children attract everyone's attention. Teachers and parents can easily spend 100 percent of their energy thinking and talking about the aggressive children—what should we do about *them*?!—but the victims need this energy. Protecting children's basic dignity is one of the most important tasks of the day-care years. Conflict itself does not damage dignity, but losing too many struggles may mean losing confidence, and it doesn't have to happen. With attention to comfort, to finishing fights carefully, and to coaching for clear and assertive ways to handle conflicts, children's dignity can be protected and given stronger roots.

Victims: Developmental Issues

INFANTS

> Charlene slides a wiggling Dennis down to the day-care floor. At home here for months now, he's ready to play as soon as they arrive. As he crawls away, eleven-month-old Taylor spies Dennis and heads over. Charlene tenses: Taylor snatched out a handful of Dennis's hair last week; he only has about fifty, he can't afford to lose any more. It's only happened once; maybe she's overreacting. But when Dennis sees Taylor, he freezes, then scuttles back to Charlene. Does he remember the hair? Is more going on than she knows?

Many infant acts of "aggression" are simple extensions of what they do with everything they see and touch, part of

Nature's program on "How to Know Your World." Infants bang on tables; they bang on each other. Infants squeeze blankets and bears; they squeeze each others' hair and faces. Infants shake rattles to make the noise; they poke each other to make the noise, too. All this bumping and banging often bothers infants very little. They seem to understand that it's not personal. One painful encounter may make them wary for a short while, but "Forgive and forget" is the usual credo.

Much of what looks like infant "aggression" comes from raw social energy—wanting to do *something* with this other baby or to have *some* effect. Good teachers will channel this energy, helping infants play close together (stepping in as needed), encouraging their impulses to hand things to each other, imitate each other, chase each other. Infants who know how to make each other smile and laugh and screech for fun are less likely to make each other cry.

Much of what looks like infant helplessness comes from surprise. Goofy play with you at home may help your baby feel more relaxed around other infants—whose play is pretty goofy. You might even go for a little baby assertiveness training: gentle tugs of war with you over toys (baby wins), letting your baby push you over. Infants usually think this great fun; be prepared for enthusiastic repeats.

If your infant seems wary around other children at drop-off or pickup times, ask teachers what the rest of the day is like. Is your child afraid of other infants or one in particular? Does he or she get upset when another infant comes close? When bumped or hurt, does your child take a long time to calm down? If it sounds like things are not feeling safe to your child, talk with teachers about:

CONFIDENCE PROTECTION

- *Complete Comfort* Speedy and thorough comfort after an up-setting event short-circuits infant distress and makes the event smaller, less disorganizing. You might ask, "What do you do when one of them hurts another one?" and emphasize that you care most about having your own child comforted: "I mainly want him to feel you're all his if he's upset."

- *Practicing Safe Play* Some teachers try to avoid infant "fighting" by keeping them apart, not letting them get close or play with each other at all. This usually just makes situations more tense; infant bopping becomes *more* probable. Confidence comes from safe play, not no play. You might ask, "Do they have a chance to practice playing with each other?" and emphasize that you do want your child to learn how to play with others.

- *Periods of Peace* Short breaks in a high chair, a teacher's arms, or any protected private play space can keep infant spirits up and the next contacts positive. You might ask, "When does she seem to get the most frazzled with other children? Is there somewhere she could take a break right then?"

TODDLERS

Dana's cry sails over the play-yard clamor. Turning to help, her teacher sees little Kevin, standing nose-to-nose with Dana, holding on to the front flaps of her sweater. He's just standing and holding the sweater edges, watching her scream.

Kevin has had a "thing" for Dana for a couple of weeks. He used to steal the dolly she brought from home or launch himself at her from across the room. The sweater holding is refined technique: Now he's really got her number.

Unlike infant "aggression," toddler attacks are sometimes very personal. Exploring personal power is the name of their game with parents this year, and with other toddlers, too. Toddlers study how to get a reaction from each other, and they get good at it. The power to drive someone crazy—by holding sweater flaps, by "scooching" too close, by touching the edge of a blanket, by splashing just a little bit of sink water—is just irresistible. With adults, and with each other, toddlers test and re-test the real meaning of one toe over the line.

Adults are tempted to scold the "victim" when damage seems small: "Come on. She's not *hurting* you." This is ineffective at best; at worst, it undermines children's confidence about protecting themselves. Toddlers ought to react when they feel assaulted; trying to work on what *should* feel like an assault is too confusing. Adults can work, however, on helping them react more *effectively*. Crying and screaming don't work. Too often, these behaviors *interest* other toddles, encouraging them to do "it" again. Controlled and definite reactions work better.

Teaching a toddler to be more assertive—that's an *answer*? Seems like our toddlers just go around asserting themselves right and left, all over our kitchens, living rooms, and bedrooms, most of the morning and too much of the night. The ways our toddlers keep us in line, however—"If you do that I'll throw myself sobbing on the floor"—are not always genuinely assertive, and, again, might be just interesting to another toddler. We *could* coach our toddlers to give us steely glares and tell us "I don't like that!" or "Go away!" These may be the very moves they need at day care. But how many of us really want to hear that kind of stuff? Teaching them new ways to be mad at us doesn't leap to mind as the solution to anything.

Teachers find themselves in the same bind. When they're already very busy catering to toddlers' picky cracker requirements and smoothing invisible wrinkles in nap blankets, coaching for assertiveness hardly seems necessary. If teachers *also* fall into the trap of spending all their energies on the "villains," then toddlers aren't learning good, strong "Back off!" signals at day care either.

Even young toddlers have the language and conceptual skills to learn from coaching in the moment, just *before* things happen—"Oh! She's trying to take your toy! What do *you* say? You can say '*No! My* turn!'" Toddlers' longer memories make it possible, and essential, for teachers to help them *after* attacks, too. Wounded pride often lasts longer than the physical hurt, and does the most damage. Teachers can repair it by coaching for a strong finish to conflicts. Many a miserable toddler recovers dignity and cheer completely by delivering a good loud "I don't *yike dat!*" to the attacker. Seems like things should be much more complicated than this, but quite often, they're not. Best of all, this strong attitude eventually moves back in the time sequence until toddlers are able to say it early, in time to ward off trouble.

If your child seems timid around the other children at arrival and departure times, ask your teacher about the rest of the day: What usually happens when your child comes into conflict with another toddler? If you hear about too much losing, backing off, crying, and sulking on your child's part and lots of dealing with the aggressor on the teacher's part, you can work on:

ASSERTIVENESS PROTECTION

- *Ask teachers, "What do you think my child should do when someone . . . [pushes, steals, holds sweater flaps] . . . How do you teach that?"* If teachers have a stock phrase, you can look for opportunities to use it at home, too.
- *Emphasize your priorities to the teacher:* Complete comfort first, coach for a strong finish next, deal with the culprit last.
- *Ask teachers about special supports:* How could some extra protection be added to hard-to-supervise times, like diapering? Could your child use reminders to take some quiet book-looking time, as a break from things? Is there one type of play they could help make a real success with a little special attention?
- *Keep teachers conscious of your goals.* Ask regularly how your child is handling upsets with other children. Any signs of progress? Seize on them and thank the teacher for his or her efforts. Nothing works better than thanks. No progress? Tell what you're trying at home.

Here are some things you might try at home:

- *Tell the Story:* When you know the story of some bad event at day care, tell it at home. Leave room for your child to tell about his or her feelings and describe your own, especially your hopes about "next time": "I heard that Helene knocked you right down in the yard today! . . . I bet that was scary (or "That doesn't seem fair" or "That would make me mad!") . . . I hope next time you tell her 'I don't like that!' with your *big* voice."
- *Praise Assertiveness You See or Hear About:* "I like the way you told me 'I don't want to.' You didn't scream, and you used your words. Good for you."
- *Demonstrate Assertiveness in Play Situations or in Playful Ways:* If your child falls on the sidewalk, you could say, "Oh you terrible sidewalk! You stop that!" Your toddler may get the giggles but still get the message.
- *Set a Good Example:* Remember you're a behavior coach even when you don't want to be. If you find yourself whimpering to your child, "Oh, honey . . . come *on* . . . *please*" in pitiful tones, try getting something more assertive out: "We're not doing that right now. Now we're going to . . ." When you don't have the energy to win a struggle, try to avoid outright sulking or miserable martyrdom; demonstrate giving-in-with-dignity: "Okay, five more minutes to play— have fun."
- *Coach in the Moment:* When your child is sulking or whining, suggest a more assertive response: "You can tell me, 'I don't want that!' or 'That makes me mad!' It's all right." You don't have to change the rule you just laid down one bit; just offer the chance to finish strong. (This is not every parent's favorite educational activity. Often we'd rather have silent sulks, frankly. Try it and see what happens. Think of it as insurance: What if assertiveness, like charity, begins at home? You'll have covered all the angles.)

Toddlers usually like learning to say "No!," "You stop!," and "I don't like that!" to each other and to us. Standing up for themselves in a dignified way just feels good. If your toddler isn't interested at the moment, however, don't push it. If you get frustrated, you can't offer real support. Being on their side emotionally—"No wonder you're mad!"—starts the chain of change. The rest usually comes with time. One toddler teacher used word-magic to emphasize her support: When one toddler came to her with a complaint about another, she'd straighten up, let a look of horror and disgust fall across her face, and pronounce, "Well, *isn't* he *just* being ri*dic*ulous!" By midyear, half the class could freeze each other with "You! You be-*dick!*-lee-us!" Usually, they then broke up laughing and went on to play some more.

PRESCHOOLERS

PARENT: "You look kind of sad, honey . . . something sad happen today?"

CHILD: "I wanted to play witches with Sue Ann and Marla, and they said I couldn't be a witch—I could only be a baby witch! And I didn't *want* to be a baby witch! And Marla said I was a dummy! *I'm not a dummy!*"

Many preschoolers still need steady work on the basics: Use your words, not your fists; ask first, don't just grab; talk, don't scream; wait, don't shove. Because they have mastered so much language now, they can come out of the jungle . . . but the jungle is never very far away. Language mastery doesn't solve it all. (For example: Teacher to Edgar, whose fist is raised to hit Chris: "Use your words!" Edgar to Chris: "F—— off!") Words become devastating weapons themselves: "Dummy!" or "You're not my friend!" or "You can't come to my birthday party!" hurt more than a slap in the face.

Standard toddler teachings still apply to preschool jungle behavior: Stop action, calm down, insist on the words (acceptable ones), stick to the rules. Standard no-hitting rules should apply to verbal slaps in the face: It's not okay to hurt-and-run with hands, feet, *or* words. Teachers still ask, "What should you do instead?" Teachers still say, "If you can't play without hurting people, you're benched."

What's new for this age group is their capacity to mull over hurts. Expanded memory and language abilities mean that they can capture bad moments on mental tape and play them back over and over. One bad moment can set up a hundred others, because an already injured mood makes flare-ups much more likely.

Preschoolers mainly brood over unfinished business: wrongs not righted, feelings unattended. "I had the big shovel, and Ronny got it, and I got it back. But then the teacher gave it to Ronny, and she said I had to wait. And then we had to go in! I didn't get my turn! I *hate* Ronny!" "Amy called me 'stupid-face'!" 'Did the teacher help you?" "She said I had to id-nore Amy!" When adults hear stories like these, we tend to ask, "How did it start?"—but "How did it *end*?" may be more to the point.

Preschoolers study fairness with an eye for detail that defeats normal teachers. The thousands of large and small intrusions a group of three-to-five-year-olds make on each other aren't all going to work out perfectly; teachers can't always see who had what first or who started it. We can't prevent all injustice and insult in a preschooler's life. We *can* help preschoolers feel more finished with the troubles, so that wounded spirits don't last too long and poison a day or a relationship.

The following things seem to help preschoolers finish emotional business with other children:

FINISHING UP

- *Making a Firm, Loud Complaint to the Other Child Involved:* "That's not fair!" or "You shouldn't do that!" often does the trick. It restores dignity, often the most important issue.

- *Talking to a Grown-up* "Just complaining" to a grown-up who pays attention and takes *his* or *her* side helps a child much more than you'd expect. Teachers besieged by their preschoolers' complaints once decided to try "just listening" for two weeks. When a child "tattled," they said, "Oh no! That's terrible!" and waited quietly, letting the "tattler" make the next move. Ninety percent of the time, children returned to play right away, completely cheered up.
- *Child-to-Child Conversation* Teachers ask two children to sit out and talk to each other until they "work it out." Older children often have real discussions. They make a new play plan that settles the fight-starting issue. Younger children often ignore (forget?) whatever started the trouble and—after a little solemn silence—start getting silly together and feel finished that way. A good laugh heals.
- *Group Conversations* Teachers bring up an incident at circle time and let any child chime in; they keep talk going until children involved feel better. This has even worked with toddlers: Once when a teacher brought up one child's biting at music time, seven different toddlers piped up with, "She bited me one time, too"; each child pointed out the exact location of the old bite. At the end of this, one child toddled over to the biter and hugged her. Soon everyone was hugging, and a tense mood of several weeks lightened up for everyone.
- *Expressing Their Feelings Without Words:* Teachers suggest drawing a picture (usually one involving angry monsters or some big black marker slashes), or jumping up and down and yelling or growling outside or playing out a drama where they win.
- *Getting a Little Extra Attention* Teachers say, "Well, that was tough! Let's go to the kitchen and get an extra drink of juice" or "Would you like to relax with me and look at a book for a while?"

Almost any way of paying attention to the hurt feelings can help preschoolers feel more finished. Since they can remember much of what went wrong even when they get home, you can try most of these methods yourself. If your child seems to have lots of unfinished business every day, let teachers know. Let them know you don't expect them to prevent all trouble but would appreciate some extra help for your child finishing rough incidents.

Being the victim of too much force is awful. Losing the battle is bad enough; the heightened sense of vulnerability is worse. The experience of helplessness destroys dignity, at least for the moment, and it disorients: If I lack the strength to defend my claims, do I have the right to make them?

Children need and deserve our protection against all such experiences. When adults help children master ways to stand up for themselves *as well as* supplying physical protection, we give them the very best. Adult physical protection only *stops* helplessness experiences in the moment; teaching them clear ways of saying "Look out for me! I count!" *reverses* the impact of helplessness. You can watch it happen: Children stand taller, give bold, proud looks, find clear, strong voices, take up more space—they bloom.

Victims: Parent-Teacher Talk

PARENT: "Something really has to be done about Jerry. Winnie has been saying she doesn't want to come in the morning; when I ask her "Why?," she says, "Jerry." Now that's pretty bad—and I've *seen* him hit kids. Does he have some kind of problem? Do his parents know how bad things are? Maybe this just isn't the right group for him."

TEACHER: "I'm sorry, we really can't talk about the other children. We are working on this."

The Other Child If one child in particular seems to be the source of most fighting, parents often want to know more about that child. Some parents hope for information that will help them stay patient or forgiving; others look for ways to tell how long the problem is likely to last: if something specific just happened, like a parent's hospitalization, the child can be expected to calm down fairly soon.

Should teachers explain the other child to you? If an outburst of aggression comes from pretty simple, unembarrassing sources, they probably will: "Well, the new baby is keeping everyone up all night at his house," "They're moving, and she's really hating it." About everything else, however, teachers ought to be silent. You'd want that for your family, too.

Most of the time, respecting family privacy creates no problems. Most of the time, your own child is the best focus of all talks with teachers. And if your child is losing most battles now, you still want to help focus energy there, on *your* child: How did your child react? How did teachers comfort and coach? When one other child keeps presenting an overwhelming challenge, beyond the reach of normal assertiveness, however, many parents feel it is no longer enough to stay focused on their own. How can you help things change without gossiping?

Parents have sometimes been very effective agents of change in situations of this sort by making their concerns clear and by questioning: Do teachers have all the help they need?

Making your concern clear may be as simple as saying "I'm worried about this." The teaching world is intense enough to become closed, or to feel like a world apart to teachers. Knowing that you are aware of trouble may help them refocus, take a new look at what is going on. If you believe you cannot be asked to wait out a situation with an aggressive child much longer, that is worth saying as well. Children should not be expelled from groups on parent demand, but you have final responsibility for your own child: If you believe you must consider leaving in order to protect your child, let teachers and the director know. You may want to ask questions about time: How long do they expect the current situation to last? What will happen if nothing improves in the next few weeks? And after that? Then you are free to decide if you can live with that time period. Don't be embarrassed to ask these questions. The questions might help teachers get clearer about the whole situation; you do have the right to more than general assurances.

Asking teachers "Do you have all the help you need?" not only offers teachers support but can serve to remind them that extra help should be an option. Extra help might come in any number of forms: more director assistance and supervision, hiring extra classroom aides for a while, calling in a staff consultant for observation and advice, or seeking a more thorough developmental evaluation for the child. Some teachers reach for extra help quickly and easily; others struggle too long to manage difficult situations alone—they may even forget that help can be available.

Whenever you believe a situation calls for more help, you can ask about other resources: "Have you thought about getting some extra help? How about. . . ?" Resources vary from town to town, but the following are possibilities in many places:

EXTRA HELP

- The director or educational coordinator for your place
- Other teachers in the same room, or last year's teachers
- Other teachers in the same center
- The staff consultant or consulting resource teacher
- A special-needs consultant
- The pediatric consultant
- The local Early Childhood Association (for speakers or consultants)
- Local pediatricians or hospitals (for consultants)
- Local resources and referral agencies (for speakers or consultants)

Victims: Things to Try

Most of the things both parents and teachers can try with children who are losing battles at the moment fall into the broad categories of reducing stress and coaching for success.

INFANTS (See CONFIDENCE PROTECTION, page 195)

REDUCE STRESS:

Teachers:

- Turn to victim first, giving complete comfort.
- Arrange for periods of quiet as breaks from play.
- Arrange for physical protection (high chair, playpen) during hard-to-supervise times.

Parents and teachers:

- Work on organizing sleep and eating schedules so infant has plenty of energy during play.

COACH FOR SUCCESS:

Teachers:

- Arrange some "safe play" periods for infants together, closely supervised.
- Help infants discover peaceful baby games (peekaboo, all clap hands or shake heads together, happy chase).

Parents:

- Include some goofy, push-pull kinds of games in play at home.

TODDLERS

REDUCE STRESS:

Teachers: all of the above, plus:

- Arrange a cozy corner where children can get away from it all.

- Plan transition times (between one activity or space and another) so that this child is always in a safe place:
  1. First or last to leave
  2. Standing next to a teacher
  3. In an out-of-the-fray nook or chair
- After conflicts, help child express feelings firmly: "Do you want to say something to Katie? You can tell her 'I don't like that!'"

Parents (As with infants, work on sleep pays off here, too.):

- Slow life down as much as possible nights and weekends.

COACH FOR SUCCESS:

Teachers:

- When conflict threatens, give child the words to stop others: "Tell him 'No! My turn!'"
- After conflict, help child reenact the conflict, saying what might have helped: "Now you try it; say 'Stop that!'"
- Plan types of play this child handles very confidently.
- Praise assertive actions and tones of voice: "I like the way you told her 'That's mine!'"

Parents (see page 199):

- Re-tell the story of conflicts, saying the words you hope your child will use the next time it happens.
- Praise assertiveness you see or hear about.
- Demonstrate assertive reactions in play situations.
- Set a good example.
- Coach your child in using assertive words to you.

PRESCHOOLERS

All of the infant and toddler things to try still apply, and Teachers:

- Help children get back to "attacker" and to object to poor treatment: "That wasn't fair!"

- Offer sympathy without advice when children complain indignantly.
- Sit both children out with instructions to decide how they can play without being unfair or upsetting each other; no one leaves until a teacher has reviewed and approved the plan.
- Bring up conflicts for group discussion; ask for ideas (or stories) from all children about handling such problems.
- Read books to this child and the whole group about characters who stand up for themselves successfully.

Parents:

- Listen without advice to complaints at home.
- After a complaint about something that happened with another child, ask, "What do you wish had happened?" or "What will you do if it happens again?" Allow any answer, but tell teachers about the kind of answers you hear.

Villains: Finding the Questions

Seeing his favorite doggy in little Emily's hands, twenty-month-old Peter marches over, bops her on the head, and takes it "back." Emily bursts out crying, noisily. Peter pushes her down.

Emily sits by the toy shelves, forcing a too-big giraffe into a toy bus. Nearby, Peter is climbing onto a wooden box and leaping onto a big pillow, over and over again. When Peter's next jump lands him close to Emily, he straightens up and pushes her over in one fluid motion. Then he sits on her. Emily screams.

Emily walks over to the wall mirror to admire herself with the large black shoulder bag. Peter, who has been digging through the dress-up bins for this exact item, catches sight of her and grabs for the bag. Emily clutches the straps, and down they go. In the tussle, Emily finds Peter's arm in front of her mouth and bites it. Peter howls. Almost as shocked as Peter is, Emily starts crying, too.

That night Peter's parents and teachers have a long talk about Peter's aggressiveness: This pushing and fighting is getting to be too much. And poor Emily! Peter's parents pray they don't run into *her* parents in the hall. The next morning when Emily arrives, Peter runs over to her, his face alight with excitement. Emily quickly puts her big bear squarely in front of her—a shield?—and then beams back at Peter—after all, they are friends. Parents and teachers watch, amazed. How can she be so forgiving?

Out of Love "Do we have a future delinquent on our hands here or what?" one father joked at a meeting about his child's fighting. Some parents do think teachers take fighting too seriously, but for other parents, this joke would express a quiet fear: "Do I have a bad kid?" When the child of caring and careful parents seems to be hitting, biting, and scratching too much, parents may be confused: *I* am gentle; how could this happen? How can my child be so different?

Is there such a thing as a "bad kid"? Some children, at some phases of life particularly, do seem more difficult to manage than others: They are more impulsive, more easily frustrated, and more disorganized by frustrations. One study of "aggressive children" found that they were also more sociable—and that this fact alone may account for the trouble: When aggressive behaviors were counted as a *percent* of all socially directed actions, children identified by teachers as "aggressive" or "nonaggressive" actually looked the same. Both groups hit, pushed, scratched, grabbed, etc., about 10 percent of the time they interacted with other children. The "aggressive" group was just so much more sociable, period, that 10 percent meant a much bigger number of hits and shoves. Like Peter with Emily, in some ways they were fighting out of love.

Out of Sympathy When their children hurt others, many parents are mainly embarrassed. Up to the first slug, a child's imperfections—not eating, not sleeping, having fussy, cranky days—are mainly private affairs, but hurting other children is a public offense. Day-care parents often nourish each other with praise for the other's child or reassuring reminders that difficult phases will pass. Parents wonder, "If my child starts leaving bite marks and bruises all around, what will happen?" A horrible vision appears: They will stop being "those nice people" and become "that bully's parents."

Teachers may sound unsympathetic as well, especially at the end of the day. If you are concerned about your child's first "offenses," you might talk with teachers and other parents right away: Do other children do this, too? What does it mean? How can adults help? If teachers are feeling guilty about not preventing trouble, or tired from dealing with it, they may not realize that you could use some reassurance. The parent next to you may have been through this already, and much more sympathetic than you expect.

Out of the Picture When teachers report, "He bit two kids today," or "She did a lot of pushing and hitting this afternoon," some parents are mainly *annoyed*. One of the things they wanted from day care was a good social experience for their child; they count on teachers to provide a good social experience. If their child is biting and hitting, teachers are failing at that task, but here they are, acting like this is the child's problem! Or the parents'! They want to know, "Why are you telling *me* this?"

It's not a bad question to ask. Much of the time, teachers don't have a special purpose in reporting news of fighting; it's just the news. They don't really mean to put parents on the spot or upset them; they're not looking for anything; they're putting you in the picture. Sometimes teachers are looking for ideas: Did she get enough sleep last night? Is big brother getting aggressive at home? If you are wondering,

"Why are you telling me this?," ask your teachers. The answer may be reassuring, or at least clarifying for you, and may be thought-provoking for teachers as well.

Out of Control News of fighting makes some parents feel guilty. They have tried hard to be good parents—gentle, understanding, flexible, and firm when necessary; they've set a good example, given good care—it should be enough! Parents may feel accused: "They probably think I never set a single limit at home. It's not true!"

Are you responsible for your child's hitting? *No.* No doubt you could set limits and radiate inner peace more consistently, but children manage quite a lot of imperfection in these areas. Two children raised in the same family, even twins, can be as different as night and day. Context controls, too: One and the same child may be an angel in the toy store, a devil in the grocery store, a saint with younger children, a sinner with olders. Teething, ear infections, frustrations of development, trouble eating and sleeping, provocative peers, grouchy teachers—almost anything that adds tension can add fighting. Parents are not all-powerful.

Parents are also not responsible for preventing a child's fighting. Teachers are there, on the spot; they have to do it. Parents can still help, however. The answer to "What can I do about it?" is not "Nothing."

Parents' hands cannot be there preventing teeth or fists from landing, but your ideas can be there, informing and encouraging teachers' efforts. Parents can brainstorm with teachers about what a child might be needing: Antibiotics? More sleep? Reassuring and explaining talk? Clearer limits? Smaller groups? They can help teachers see what is going on more clearly by asking who-what-where-when questions. Parents' questions can focus teaching strategies. You might ask, "What is my child trying to *do* when fighting breaks out? What *else* could he or she be doing to get that?" When a child's hitting appears to be an awkward way of starting up a little social action, teachers can work on teaching other ways to say "Hi!" and "Let's go!"; when a child hits out at any frustration, teachers can coach a few substitute "curse" words, or how to get adult help faster or how to take a breath and try again. Parents see examples of "Let's play!" and "I'm frustrated!" at home; they have some ideas about when their children get rough.

Time-out: Parents whose children are hitting, biting, and scratching at the moment may hear that teachers are using "time-out" to help control the problem. Very often "time-out" is the day-care equivalent of "Go to your room"; parents who understand that and approve of the technique may feel comfortable about teachers' approach. For some parents, "time-out" sounds awfully mechanical; they may hate the thought of their child sitting all alone in some "technique-y" punishment situation, but already embarrassed by their child's aggressions, they hesitate to ask more about it.

"Time-out" is a term adapted from animal-training studies, in which researchers found that programming periods of time during which animals could *not* peck buttons or press levers for food, to follow mistakes, was more effective than punishment in training: Time-out from playing the food game taught them how to play it right. Other researchers tried this technique in classrooms—using time-out from regular classroom activities as the consequence of hitting, yelling, and other disruptive actions, and found it effective with many children as well.

Does time-out work because a child needs a break anyway? Does it help children *notice* what causes problems? Give them time to think? To calm down? Does it give teachers time to think? "Go to your room" at home sometimes helps most by giving parents time to calm down and focus, and by breaking a cycle of tensions ("You will!"—"I won't!"—"You will!") that keep inspiring more trouble. Time-out in classrooms may function this same way, too.

Whatever the reasons, time-out after hitting, biting, and fighting does seem to help in many cases. Teachers can use it a variety of ways, however; you might want to check how your teachers are using it: In what spirit is a child sent to sit away from the group? Some teachers treat time-out as a punishment: "That's it! Go sit on the couch!"; some present it as a needed break: "You're having a tough time right now—I want you to take a break on the pillows"; some handle time away from the group very neutrally: "If you can't stop yourself from pushing, you'll have to sit out." You might also ask if teachers *talk* to your child about what happened after a calming-down time. What do they say? Children tune out long lectures about their behavior; short explanations and coachings work best. If you can agree with teachers on a few phrases, you can support the effort at home, too.

Long bouts of fighting create a situation in which everyone needs support. Children need our support: fighting, biting children are often feeling overwhelmed from within (tired, confused, trapped) or from without (by demands of other children, noise, expectations they cannot meet and tasks they cannot yet do). Teachers need support: Dealing with fury and tears over and over and over again is wearing by itself, and full of failure. And parents need the support of knowing that their children are still loved and still seen in a whole, full-of-faith way. If the energy to take care of each other grows thin, think about importing some energy from outside: the center director, or some outside consultant help. Widening the circle may keep your inner circle strong.

Villains: Developmental Issues

INFANTS

> Fourteen-month-old Rita throws herself at the wooden gate to the infant room—crash! The gate swings open, and she marches in, making a beeline to William, who is fondling some crackers at the eating table. She sweeps the crackers to the floor. Reaching across William, she bops Jesse on the head, then pivots toward the play area. Freddy stands frozen in her path; Rita pushes him down. Striding into the play area, Rita grabs a doll out of Aliza's hands and pitches it across the room. Ten seconds have passed since Rita walked through the gate; four infants are crying. Rita is here!

The first appearance of hitting-on-purpose dismays first-time parents. How could we have ruined them already?! "Babies are a lot of work," we used to say, "but they're so sweet! It makes up for everything." If the sweetness disappears, what will we do? Hitting-on-purpose seems utterly new—evil creeping into our paradise. It's not evil, of course, and only partly new. We've seen a little hair-pulling, scratching, pounding, and biting at younger ages: Some face or body got too close, too loud, too interfering, even too exciting, and zap—trouble. Kind of accidental all around. Nothing serious, over fast. Little firefly flashes in the great summer dark.

In older infants, hitting just looks different, looks on-purpose. *All* their behavior is getting organized enough to look purposeful now. Newly walking infants are especially likely to be:

- *Feeling Crowded and Cooped Up:* Walking demands more room than lolling around or crawling did.
- *Awake-but-Exhausted:* Walking is such a thrill at first, many children need more rest but do not take it. Sometimes you can

see those little feet going even during naps. Many children are also shifting from two daytime naps to one at this age.

- *Very Interested in Other Infants' Reactions:* Young infants like to bang on shelves, xylophones, Busy Boxes, and each other "to make the noise." Older infants see that *people*, unlike shelves, make an interesting *variety* of noises and movements when you hit them. This discovery often invites quite a lot of retesting.
- *Frustrated:* The downside of being old enough to have goals or big ideas about what to do is that you are wide open to frustration.

If you are a younger infant looking at a beanbag and an empty dump truck, you might "decide" to put the bag in the truck, then take it out, a few times in a row. If you miss the truck with the bag or another child takes the bag out and chews on it for a bit, you don't mind too much—it's all pretty interesting. If you are an older infant seeing the same materials, however, you might get an idea like "put *all* the beanbags in the truck, then drive it to the other side of the room and dump them out, then put them back in, and drive back." A big job. Locating all the bags, replacing bags that bounce out or fall off, getting around all the other toys in your drive across the room—these tasks will stretch your patience. If, on *top* of this, other infants snatch a bag or sit on one that falls off or put a block in your truck or plop down in the only clear driving space . . . well, you just might hit them.

All these new factors can be playing a role in hitting like Rita's. If your infant is hitting a lot at day care, you might help with the:

JUST-WALKING GROUCHIES

- Arrange more elbow room.
  1. *Come earlier.* Earlier means fewer children, less crowding, fewer interferences with toys and teachers' attention. If getting out earlier would make your own morning much

yuckier, you might just try it for a week. See if the benefits outweigh the costs in your case.

2. *Ask teachers about times and places infants can stretch their legs and spirits.* Is it time to start more visits to a gym or the yard or other rooms?

• Check on rest: Has it changed? How could extra sleep or quiet playtime be encouraged at day care? At home?

• Ask teachers if they think the hitting is done for effect. Is your child "saying" "Hey! Wake up! Play with me!"? "Hmmmm. You feel interesting . . . How hard *are* you?" "Will you get out of here!?" "Let's hear some noise from you!"? "Hey, teach! I'm gonna poke the baby—whaddaya think of that?" Plan how you could both teach your baby *other* ways of getting some action.

The on-purposeness of older infants saddens some teachers and parents: It's the end of innocence. This new world, with "Wake up!" and "Back off!" in it, is a richer, more fully human, more interesting world; still, the change can be hard. If you think your teacher is having trouble with the shift, you might take a minute to mourn the change together: "I miss the way she was when she was a real *baby* . . . do you?"

TODDLERS

As soon as he shakes off his jacket this morning, Georgie runs into the toddler room and belly-bumps Joshua to the floor. At cleanup time Georgie hits Daniel. As he sits down for snack, Georgie shoves Emery off her stool. When the toddlers are all getting ready to go outside, he hits Jenny with his jacket. Georgie, his teachers say, has "trouble with transitions."

Many children, especially toddlers, seem to get into trouble mainly during "transitions"—which is day-care-ese for changes from one semiorganized activity to another. Transitions are tough on toddlers. Many toddlers' sense of "me" continually oozes over the borders of their bodies to become attached, like tentacles, to the objects, activities, and people in their immediate vicinity. A change of scene is almost life-threatening: All these arms of self must be ripped up. In between settled scenes, they flail around: Who am I? Where am I?

Good teachers help toddlers through transitions by giving them something to hang on to—a song or step-by-step directions: "Put your cup in the trash, set your lunchbox on the shelf, and go to the rug." If your child fights during transitions, he or she may need a stronger version of something to hang on to: a teacher's hand, a special place to sit, an uncrowded time (first or last) to make the change.

Transition times are certainly not the only occasions for fighting and biting in toddler groups. Any invasion or frustration can send them over the edge. (They seem to be people living constantly on the edge—is it raging hormonal imbalance?) They may react swiftly and violently to small things. "Natalie! Why did you bite Aaron?"—"He touched my *muffin!*" "Robert! No hitting! You can't just grab that truck and hit him!" "But I *want* it!" When we object, they are surprised. Their faces ask us: "What did you *expect* me to do? Did I have a *choice?!*"

These are precisely the questions teachers have to answer for them. Teachers usually want toddlers to try *talking*, saying "Move!" and "Wanna turn!," "Stop that!" and even "Mine!" Using words to get what they want is so new to toddlers, they forget easily in moments of passion. And it takes time for toddlers to realize they can talk to *each other*. They have been understandable mainly by their parents for so long, the idea of talking to each other does not always pop up. The novelty helps make it work, too: The "enemy" often steps swiftly aside or hands over the toy like a hot potato. Toddlers can use all the encouragement you and teachers can supply to use words for any demand situation.

Using words instead of teeth or fists is one kind of choice toddlers can learn to make. Other choices teachers may emphasize: "Bite on *this* [pacifier, teething toy] . . . *not* on people," or "It's too crowded here . . . you need to play somewhere else," or "You've got a problem. You can say, 'Help me, please!'" Good teachers also clarify simple choices for toddlers: "You can wait for a turn with *this* truck *or* you can get a *different* truck."

Using words and making conscious choices are a stretch for toddlers, and the more relaxed they are, the easier it is to be so mature. Subtracting tension becomes a main method of supporting change in toddler fighting. If you or your teachers are concerned about your child's fighting, you might look into

INVESTIGATING TODDLER STRESS

- *Physical Stresses:* Could your child be tired? Teething? Getting sick? Fighting an ear infection? Check for changes in sleep patterns, drooling and gnawing, ear pulling. "Irritability" is a symptom of many discomforts toddlers can't locate or describe for us—headaches, sore throats, stiff necks.
- *Situational Stresses:* Does fighting tend to happen during changes of scene? With one particular child, activity, or space? You might ask teachers to keep short records of the who-when-what-where of your child's fights for two weeks, and look for a pattern to gather ideas on how to ease things. Trying smaller groups or more tightly organized changes of scene may also provide clues.
- *Psychological Stresses:* Are there any changes at day care or home that might cause extra worry or chronic bad mood? New people? Missing people? New schedules? Especially grouchy grown-ups? Just naming the situation out loud often relaxes toddlers: "Well, it sure is crazy around here with . . ." Your talking about "it" in matter-of-fact tones says, "I know all about this and I'm not worried"—and that's just what toddlers needed to know.
- *Social Stresses:* If your child just gets wound up by the ex-

citement of other children and special activities, you might talk with teachers about using "time-outs." Taking toddlers out of play for a while relieves them of the work of coping with other people and tasks; it should provide a time for healing ragged nerves. Adrenaline in the bloodstream can wash out, breathing catch up, brain rest. This "time-out" should be a gift from the Adult Perspective: "You need a rest; take it."

You might also look for ways to:

SUPPORT SOCIAL SUCCESS

- *Praising/Breaking the Cycle:* Fighting can become a self-sustaining cycle: Fighting creates tense situations with peers and teachers, and that tension sparks off more fighting. Praise for what's right can help break the cycle. Let teachers know that you think praise will help; ask for examples you can praise at home: "Jan told me that Brett took your truck in the yard today, and you told him, 'No! My turn!' Good for you—you used your words! I'm proud of you." Noticing what your child handles well may help teachers remember to praise, too.
- *Practice at Home:* Social situations come up at home, too. Toddlers also grab things from parents, push parents out of the way, bite parents. You can find out what teachers say in these situations and use them at home. Toddlers need repetitions.

Throughout our nervous system—in both its wiring and its chemical codes—some parts are "Go!" and some are "Stop!" The "Stop!" parts take longer to get organized; the ability to inhibit an action is a relatively late development. During the time children change from infants to preschoolers, they become able to recognize, label, and control impulses. Toilet training relies on these developments; so does learning to control the impulse to hit. Good teachers will work on recognition and labeling: "That made you mad! You wanted to hit him—but you stopped yourself. Good for you!" Your work with teachers on stress control will help.

Reactions to events seem to be "stacked," with a child's most mature reaction on top. Stress topples the pile; the least mature reactions take over. Decreases in tension let a child operate from the top of the deck. In all this work, though, remember that time is on your side. As the Stop! part of your child's nervous system grows, it will be easier and easier to guide your whole child.

PRESCHOOLERS

TEACHER: "Jason, you are doing a lot of hitting today. What's the matter?"

JASON: (If only he could remember it all)

- "I couldn't have my muffin this morning because there was only one left and Dad said if I had one, Kerry would want one too, so I had to have oatmeal. I *hate* oatmeal and I hate Kerry. . . ."
- "I wanted to wear my Batman sweatshirt, but Mom said it was too cold. I wasn't cold. I had to wear my dumb old jacket, and it was my baby jacket from last year. She never gets me any good clothes. . . ."
- "Barbara [the morning teacher] said I couldn't play with the blocks this morning because I didn't clean up good yesterday. Lewis didn't clean up either, and he got to play. It's not fair. . . ."
- "No one will play with me because Boris is playing with Andrew already, and everyone else is dumb. . . ."
- "I didn't get to do calendar *again* today. Barbara says you have to be quiet to do calendar, and I *am* quiet, but she never sees me when I'm quiet. Ella always gets to do calendar. . . ."
- "Geraldine said her picture was the best 'cause I only used one color, and anyway I only ever draw monsters. . . ."
- "I was playing with the green ball, and Jackie took it. I told the teacher, but she just said to get another ball. I didn't want another ball. I only like the green one. . . ."

Between ages three and five children develop a keen eye for rules and fairness, and a long memory for injustice. They become vulnerable to verbal hurts of all sorts—criticism, comparison, and insult. They get status-conscious about clothing, toys, trips, friends, and facts. They want to be big, to be their own boss, and to be the best. They care about being fair themselves, and try, but some days it seems that they are the only ones who are trying. The whole world looks unfair and mean, full of traps and rules and losing. Adults are no help; they're part of the problem. Aggrieved and alone, angry and abandoned, they blow up.

(Of course, it's totally unfair for them to feel alone and abandoned when they're the ones growing away from us, getting so interested in friends and doing things on their own. And it's unreasonable for them to feel trapped by rules and comparisons when they are the ones arguing about rules all the time instead of just taking our advice, and they are the ones getting competitive. But there it is.)

If your child just has one of these boil-over days every now and then, you don't have to be concerned. Teachers may ask you, "What's up?," but they should be able to allow for a Bad Day. You can both agree just to keep ears open for clues. A preschooler who has lots of boil-over days may need help turning the heat down. Many of the questions and approaches that help toddlers work with preschoolers; check the previous section for ideas.

Preschoolers can be trickier to help than infants and toddlers in two ways: 1) They are so smart now that their pressures include all kinds of factors we can't *see*—confusing ideas, overheard conversations, past wrongs, imagined judgments of friends or teachers; 2) They are so "old" now that simple comforts and straightforward coaching sometimes offends their pride. We can't just wrap them up and rock them and make it all go away like we used to (sigh).

Because preschoolers remember and talk so much more fluently than toddlers, parents have a special power to help now. Researching the pressures important to one child takes time and a not-too-interrupted listening space; parents, however busy, still can arrange one-to-one time more easily than teachers. And of course children will tell parents things they might not tell anyone else.

RESEARCHING PRESCHOOL PRESSURES

You might try:

- *"Asking" Your Child:* You can't say, "Well, dear, I've been thinking about the many pressures preschoolers face today and wondering how you see your own particular situation. . . ."—but when your child complains about anything, clamp your teeth on advice and explanation; express quiet sympathy: "Ooooh" is all you need. The space to talk, uninterrupted by adult ideas, often drags to light a list of complaints. Try just to take it in; think about what it means after your child's bedtime.
- *Asking Teachers:* Sometimes fighting happens mainly in one situation, with one child, or during one time of day. You might ask teachers to look for this kind of clue, or to keep a record of who, when, and where for you for a week or two.
- *Asking Yourself:* Anything new or missing at home? Any discussions, events, strains, or excitements your child could be misinterpreting? Preschoolers are somewhat less directly sensitive to parent mood than toddlers, but they are more sensitive to currents *between* parents and to talk of the *future*.
- *Asking Other Parents:* Any news? Are their children worrying about anything special these days? Preschoolers can catch anxiety from each other. If one child is worried about moving to a new house, a change of schools, parents fighting, or the death of a pet, other children may start thinking about these possibilities in their own lives.

Researching your child's pressures should spark some ideas about how you or teachers can keep things feeling easier and more manageable for your child. When the things your child is worrying about are not concrete ("Are my drawings good?") or changeable (a new baby brother), you can now turn down the heat with words.

Preschoolers' fluency with language and concepts and their sensitivity to parents as *adults* provide new powers of reassurance. Infants barely see parents as separate. Toddlers work on setting up an independent self, use parents mostly as an anchor while they bounce back and forth between independence and "Carry me!" Now they've made it, they know adults are different. Adults and children have different needs, rules, responsibilities, and powers. Preschoolers certainly don't love all these differences, but they will often let us use our special status for their own good. When they need a little magic from us, we can suddenly become Keepers of the Truth, Seers of the Future. Making Bald Statements—statements that go straight for the throat of a large worry—is one way we can use this power to reassure them.

If we were looking for Bald Statements to help Jason in the anecdote opening this preschool section, we might try making one or more of these pronouncements:

- "I love you. I love Kerry too, but you are my Very Special, four-year-old son! and I'm going to love you forever no matter what."
- "You are so cool you don't even *need* clothes. You could go to day care naked and still be cool."
- "It's not fair about Lewis and the blocks. Teachers sometimes make mistakes. Everyone makes mistakes."
- "You love Boris. I think Boris loves you, too. People just don't show their love all the time."
- "Someday the teacher will see how quiet you are. You will get a turn to do calendar, and you will be great."
- "I like your monster pictures. They're scary and fierce. I especially like the way you drew the long claws—your monsters look ready to pounce. Can I put this one on the refrigerator?"
- "The green ball was a real problem. Hitting Jackie got you into trouble. I know you are going to find a way to solve problems without hitting."

A good Bald Statement has no advice and asks for no thinking. Its sole purpose is to reassure. When your goal is to slip in a little advice or get your child thinking practically about problems, ask leading questions instead. Your reassurance may clear the way for this problem-solving work; you can certainly add some practical help, too, like buying more muffins or shopping for Batman underwear, or talking to the teachers about calendar turns—but reassurance from you may be all that's needed.

DEVELOPMENTAL SKILLS AND FIGHTING

Kenny holds on to his feet at circle time to keep himself still—he doesn't want to get in trouble again. The teacher is talking about something—rain? Wednesday?—and moving little numbers around on the big calendar. Kenny's fingers find his new Velcro shoes, bought because he couldn't learn to tie laces and teachers got tired of doing it for him. Even the Velcro gives him trouble. Zap! He rips them open. "Kenny!" Oops. On she goes . . . April? Twelfthththth? Kenny's knees start bouncing on their own. "Kenny!" Slowly, the sound of her voice drifts off again. Kenny catches Tony's eye across the circle; Tony makes a face. Kenny clenches his fists to Tony and pulls a tough face. Teacher: "Kenny? We're doing calendar now; leave Tony alone. Do you know what day of the week it is?" "No." "Please pay attention—Mason, do you?" Stupid old Mason always knows. Next to him, Greg starts to fidget; he bumps into Kenny. Kenny pushes Greg back, a little too hard. Greg yells. Kenny pushes him again—the stupid! "That's it, Kenny!" the teacher says, "No pushing! You know that! Leave the circle and go sit out."

When a child's abilities—to sit still, to understand the words used, to make needed hand coordinations—do not match the demands of a day-care program, frustrations become chronic. And chronic frustration very often leads to "aggression." The daily teases, bumps, or disappointments other children can brush off fall on already irritated nerves; children lash out. Teachers see an uncontrollable, unpredictably angry child, whose hitting seems unrelated to what's going on or out of proportion to provocations. Such a child may be just at wit's end—developmentally speaking—in that particular program. In the Boston area, some developmental therapists travel directly to day-care settings; astonished teachers have reported skill improvements *and* amazing changes in fighting.

If you suspect that chronic frustrations of this sort play a part in your child's hitting, you might:

CHECK FOR DEVELOPMENTAL FRUSTRATIONS

- *Get more information about your child's developing skills:*
  1. *Ask teachers to do an official assessment:* Many centers have a standard skills checklist teachers can use; working on an assessment may spark new ideas about your child or the program.
  2. *Arrange for an outside assessment:* Your teacher, director, pediatrician, or local school board may know whom to call in your area. Outside evaluators can usually provide easy access to extra help and consultations for teachers, too.
- *Brainstorm with teachers about ways to cut down some daily frustrations:* Shorter "Everybody sit still" periods? Using more gestures to give directions? Steering your child to more skills-appropriate, success-supporting activities?
- *Arrange for extra help:*
  1. With teachers, plan activities that supply extra skill practice at home or day care or both.
  2. Through your local early intervention programs or school districts, arrange regular visits or regular consultations with developmental specialists at home or day care.
- *Visit other day-care possibilities.* Day-care programs differ in what they demand of children and in how easily they handle children's differing abilities. You might look for a more play-

oriented program in general, or for teachers whose ways of handling frequently frustrated children seem more positive.

Sometimes a child's only alternative to fighting is to avoid people and struggle of all kinds, to go *quietly* crazy with confusions and frustrations too big to handle. Fighting is so much better! It wears everyone out, but it *does* get everyone's attention, and that usually means help will come, eventually.

Villains: Parent-Teacher Talk

TEACHER: "Ricky had a really hard day today. He was fighting and hitting other children quite a lot. I had to send him to time-out three or four times."
PARENT: "Oh . . . well . . . I'm sorry to hear that. . . ."
TEACHER: "I just thought you should know."

Staying on the Case Listening to teachers' Crime Reports after a hard day at the office with dinner still to come is no one's idea of a good time. What are we supposed to say—"Better luck next time"? Do they expect us to blurt out some dreadful secret that accounts for it all—"Actually, I've started plotting to murder my husband/wife; the suspense must be affecting my child . . ."?

Teachers often *don't* have a particular purpose in mind when they report fighting. It's just the news today, what they noticed, like a drippy nose. Or it's a form of Complaining to the Management: "You're in charge; you should know." Teachers may be preparing against a future day. If it's October and they *might* end up calling a conference in February to discuss fighting, they don't want to be accused of never letting us know there was a problem. They may be making sure we know *their* side of a possible child's report like "June was mean. She made me sit out All Day. I didn't get to play At All." They may be testing the waters: How will we react? Can they talk to us about this stuff? If you're stumped about how to respond to Crime Reports, you might let teachers know: "I don't know what to say when you tell me things like this. I don't know why you are telling me this."

The first couple of times we hear about hitting problems at day care, maybe we're just terrific: alert, sympathetic, interested in exploring the roots of the trouble, ready to check in on progress every day. But the tenth time? Twentieth? When fighting phases drag on, it's hard to stay on the case. Hearing about it gets discouraging, boring, and, if it crowds out all good news, frustrating.

Teachers often don't realize when they've been handing out bad news relentlessly. They talk to lots of parents every day; they have lots of contact with our children. They forget what they've said and how often; they forget that we don't automatically know all the good things that are going on, too. The fact that parents tend to be richer, older, and more settled in their lives may also blind teachers to how much worry constant bad news can create. Sometimes teachers are not blind, just desperate. They hope for help.

If fighting has been going on for a while, teachers may be hoping for support in the form of appreciation. Teachers want to spend their days having charming and educational chats with children; fighting forces them to spend their time disciplining children and comforting the wounded. Teachers hope for friendly chats with parents at the end of the day; physical fighting makes them face parents of victims every night, to apologize, explain, and promise again to watch more carefully. Lots of parents are mad at them. Who remains cool under such circumstances? If your child has been doing some damage recently, you might consider saying something like: "This must make a lot of extra work for you; thanks for doing it."

If you hear exasperation in your teachers' voices, "thank you" may not leap to mind. You need to know, and to hear about, all the good stuff, too. Let teachers know: "You sound like you've had it." "I never hear good news anymore; isn't there anything else to report?" "I'm beginning to worry if you still like him." Teachers may sound more negative than they feel, or need help seeing the whole picture.

Teachers want parents to stay in touch about fighting problems; making it easy for parents to listen should be part of the deal. No normal human being can be expected to stay keen for communication about trouble. What would make staying in touch about fighting easier?

3-D NEWS

You might try:

DEALS:

- Ask for news in notes, so you can wait until you're ready.
- Arrange for "a kiss and a kick" deal: "Could you give me one piece of good news for every piece of bad news?"

DIFFERENT DAYS:

- Saying what kind of day it is for your morale: "If it's not major murder, I'd rather not know today. . . ."
- Saying what kind of time for talk you have: "This needs to be a quick-exit day" or "I have some time today, how did it go?"

DEFINED CHECK-INS:

- Asking teachers what they would find helpful from you when they have bad news about fighting—information, sympathy, ideas?
- Planning strategies and check-in times in longer talks, so you can ask, "Is it working?" on a schedule and drop the topic the rest of the time.

A long bout of fighting can be so wearing for parents and teachers you may run out of verbal ways to support each other. You might consider a fourth "D" if this happens—donations. Buy yourself some chocolate or flowers and bring a few in for teachers as well.

Villains: Things to Try

INFANTS

- For trouble at arrival time:
  1. Come when the room is emptier.
  2. Hold your child (or ask the teacher to) until the first excitement of arrival is past and territory established.
- Talk with teachers about providing more elbow room to take care of that crowded feeling and make space to blow off steam.
  1. Can the room be rearranged some way?
  2. Can older infants visit other spaces? Go outside more?
  3. Is there a way more complicated play can be protected?
- Keep working on sleep at home and at day care. Teachers might try long walks in a stroller, even inside.
- Work on "what else?" infants can do, at home and at day care
  1. Other ways of saying "hi"
  2. Other ways of touching, like soft patting
  3. Other ways to produce an effect, like peekaboo and copy-me
  4. Other things to bang on and bite on (When adults supply a substitute during, or just after, a baby attack, the babies seem to get the idea and start turning to substitutes in the middle of social situations.)

TODDLERS

Parents can:

- Check ears, teeth, throat, health news.
- Check side effect of medicine. Some cold and allergy medicines list "irritability" as a side effect. If your child has been on one such medicine for a while, you might check with your

pediatrician: Is there a good substitute available? Would changing the brand help?
- Try having short talks about any possibly puzzling events or changes at home. Watch toddler faces for clues—a worried or angry look may mean "More reassurance here, please."

Teachers can:

- Think about or record the who, what, where, when, and why of a child's fighting and focus on changing something specific:
    1. Guiding children into groups with easier social partners
    2. Organizing children into smaller groups
    3. Buying more of a popular toy
    4. Reorganizing a time of day or staying near during that time
- Provide more anchors during transition time
    1. For the whole group
        a) Songs "It's time to put the toys away, and then we'll play another day. . . ."
        b) Pretend contexts: "Let's all be tigers and crawl to the bathroom."
    2. For one child
        a) Dressing or getting ready to sleep in a separate, quieter place or with a book to help waiting
        b) Holding a teacher's hand until the transition is over
- Arrange as much blow-off-steam time as possible—outside play or dancing, especially after concentrated attention or one-on-one playtimes.
- Use time-outs for calming down. After five or ten minutes, explain briefly how conflicts should be handled; hug and go play.

Parents and teachers can:

- Praise the small steps in waiting for turns, using words, or stopping a hit midstream.
- Redo conflict situations so children can practice: Take whatever was grabbed back, and ask toddler to say, "Can I have a turn?" ("Turn?" counts). Praise all practice efforts.

PRESCHOOLERS

All toddler things to try, plus:
Parents and teachers can:

- Listen, hearing out whatever is not feeling right without advice or explanation.
- Check for the spread of *other* children's worries (Has another child moved, visited kindergarten, lost a parent to serious illness for a while?).
- Reassure children with Bald Statements (see pages 223–224) about:
  1. A child's lovability
  2. A child's lack of special guilt: "Everyone makes mistakes."
  3. Time and effort: "You won't feel so new after we've been here awhile." "Once you couldn't walk and you couldn't talk—now you do both! You'll be able to do this pretty soon."
- Reading fairy tales about problems overcome by clever children
- Remembering out loud some strong moments in a child's past

DEVELOPMENTAL DIFFICULTIES

Parents or teachers can:

- Get more specific information about a child's developmental skills and plan activities that
  1. Provide practice
  2. Minimize confusion and frustration
- Arrange for visits and consultation with developmental specialists.

Teachers can:

- Use simpler words, shorter sentences, and more gestures when explaining things or giving instructions.
- Cut down on the time a child (or the whole group) has to sit still and pay attention to grown-ups.

Parents can visit other day-care possibilities, looking for:

• A play-oriented program
• A smaller group
• Teachers with special patience and creativity

Although it sometimes feels like we are mainly *coping* with children's jungle urges until they outgrow them, in reality, parents' and teachers' work on fighting can do much more. By the way we respond to their conflicts, we can teach them that they and their wishes are important, that respect for other people's rights feels better and works better than railroading, that conflicts can be problems to solve, not relationship-destroyers, that giving yourself a break is sometimes the smartest move to make, and that they are not out there alone in the jungle—there is help of all kinds available.

Worksheet for Parents of "Victims"

Does the amount or intensity of fighting in the group seem normal to you? _____ to teachers? _____ other parents? _____

If not, what is different? _____

_____

Are teachers getting any help with the special issue? _____

Do teachers seem to be managing the group well, outside of the fighting issue? _____ If not, who can help them become better managers? _____

Could you speak about getting extra help
to teachers? _____
to the director or educational coordinator? _____
at a parent meeting? _____

Describe (from teachers' reports) how your child typically responds when another child starts to push, take a toy, or get too close:

_____

_____

Do you think your child could use some more effective ways of getting other children to back off? _____

What are teachers doing to teach your child new ways of reacting to these "threats" from other children? _____

_____

_____

What could you do at home to encourage assertiveness?

1. _____

2. _____

3. _____

Describe (from teachers' reports) what they typically do after a conflict breaks out: _____

_____

_____

Do you wish they would put more emphasis on
comforting your child? _____
coaching your child for next time? _____
coaching the child who started the conflict? _____

How could you let teachers know more about what you
want? Check one:
_____ Come a few minutes early one day next week
and talk
_____ Write a note
_____ Call during naptime
_____ Talk to the director and ask him or her to relay
your thoughts
_____ Ask for a conference

Worksheet for Parents of "Villains"

Does it seem to you that your child is more than usually
aggressive? _____ Do teachers? _____

Do teachers think your child's fighting is different from others' in the group? _____ How? _____

_____

Are you comfortable with teachers' attitudes about your
child in general? _____ around the fighting is-

sue? _____ If not, what is not right? _____

_____

When could you talk with teachers about that? _____

What are your best guesses about why your child is fighting a lot right now? (or what situations spark the fighting?)

1. _____

2. _____

3. _____

What do those ideas suggest as ways to help?

1. _____

2. _____

3. _____

Have you passed these ideas along to teachers? _____

What do your teachers do when your child hits/pushes/ bites? _____

_____

_____

Is there something you would like to change or add? _____ If so, describe it: _____

_____

How could you let teachers know about these ideas? __

_____

7

Feelings: Lions and Tigers and Bears, Oh My!

- "This is really embarrassing, but—the first time she threw a tantrum? We took her to the emergency room. We thought she was having convulsions!"
- "I figured it was our crazy lives, finally getting to him. We're always too busy, *and* we're disorganized. I forgot his favorite teacher just left!"
- "He was so wild; the teachers couldn't manage him. I thought, We've created a monster—they'll kick us out. It turned out he had an ear infection all this time!"
- "She comes home with all this stuff about who is whose *friend*, and who sat next to the girl *she's* trying to be friends with, and who said what about her *picture* . . . I don't know what to say! I wish we were back in the old days when carrying her around took care of everything."

WHAT WITH FLU, phases, discipline, day care, and just daily life, it is difficult to know where children's feelings come from. If we do know, it is not always clear how to help: How can you "fix" a phase? A bad day? A friend? The chapters on arriving, separating, eating, friends, fighting, leaving—all explore children's feelings about those particular situations. This chapter offers ways of sorting out what's going on when you do not know the situation—you just have a stormy mood on your hands; it describes some changes in feelings that come mainly with age; it describes "high-tech" listening and offers some all-purpose ways of reassuring children.

Feelings: Finding the Questions

"Move!" Megan yells at her mother; she reaches around for a cereal box. Sheila says, "Hey! I'm cooking! And I don't want you to eat now." "But I'm *hun-gry!*" The fury in Megan's tone makes Sheila calculate real dinnertime—not soon enough for this mood! "Okay, a *little* snack. Wait! Let me pour that for you!" *"I can do it!"* Megan pours cereal too hard: a big spill. She whirls away from the mess and throws both fists at Sheila's stomach: "I hate you!"

Sheila freezes: That's a bit much for an I'm-hungry bad mood. What's going on? She feels Megan's forehead—not hot. Did something happen at day care today? Megan has been getting hard to handle in general lately . . . maybe she needs a refresher on the rules. . . .

Sheila turns up Megan's chin. What a miserable face! She crouches down: "You don't feel so good right now, do you, honey? . . ." Megan begins to cry hard. Between sobs comes a story about a white dress and her friend Nancy at day care. Sheila tries to get the sense of it, still wondering if she should check in with the doctor or the teacher tomorrow. Megan winds down and snuggles into Sheila: "I love you, Mom—you're the best." Two minutes later, Megan hops out of the kitchen to her room, singing no less. Sheila shakes her head: Kids are amazing.

Stop, Look, Listen If you have an older toddler or preschooler, you might try the shortcut of pure listening before exploring a mood further. "Just listening" may provide an answer to "What brought this on?" and provide a cure all at once. You may not even need to understand the problem, let alone "fix" it. When parents can be lightning rods for feelings, children are relieved.

Most parents aren't prepared for this simplicity. Infancy's bad days mean long hours holding a baby or hours at the doctor's office or complex diet replannings—and toddler moods! Children get more and more complicated; don't parents' responses need to get more complicated? Listening seems too easy. (Effective listening doesn't come completely naturally: See pages 262–265.)

After unusually stormy scenes with their children, some parents feel they must schedule some action quickly: make a doctor's appointment, ask for a teacher conference, make some new family rules, call around about other day-care options. Other parents scold themselves: If only they were wiser, tougher, more patient, better organized, more creative! If you can, save time and pain by trying Stop/Look/Listen first. It should bring you useful information, and it may be the only thing you need to do.

Look Both Ways Often what concerns parents is not one particular emotional storm but a whole shift in their children's range of feeling, a child's becoming more fearful or angry or desperate in general. With these kinds of shifts, it makes sense to touch all the bases: health, developmental stage, important relationships, recent events at home and day care. Few adults do this kind of whole-child review. It seems time-consuming and overcomplicated, and many of us have a favorite kind of explanation that works most of the time. If your favorite explanation fails you, however, remember you have many other options.

Slippery When Wet Some parents (and teachers) are reluctant to consider physical explanations. Looking for a physical cause in diet, sleep, or health seems to deny children the dignity of having *real* feelings. In arguments, they say, "Oh, you *always* think it's food!" or "She has a mind, too, you know." Statements like "You're just tired" certainly *can* be a way of writing off feelings; protecting your child against that *is* important.

Most parents, however, have had this experience at least once: A crabby, cranky, helpless half hour with your child gets you reviewing your entire parenting approach and remembering some aunt or uncle who could have contributed difficult genes to the family stock; just to get some peace, you offer an extra snack. Five minutes later, your child is completely charming again. Aarg! It was only hunger.

Longer-term mood shifts may also reflect mainly physical changes. On the verge of being asked to leave their day-care center, parents of one superactive toddler tried cutting out all his apple-juice bottles; recent hot weather had practically doubled his intake, and they thought so much sugary juice might have been more than his particular chemistry could handle. Result: a much more manageable child. Other parents, in despair over their four-year-old's end-of-day hysterics, suddenly realized that he'd started giving up his midday nap at day care. They couldn't change the exhaustion problem, but they could stop worrying. When a months-old ear infection was discovered and treated, a months-long debate between parents and teachers about behavior management stopped as well.

Moods may have purely physical roots; more commonly, physical disorganization of some kind is only part of a more complicated story. The child of parents who had to leave overnight for a few days had trouble sleeping while they were away and for several nights after they returned; when she was irritable and clingy the following week, was that "exhausted" or "angry and worried"? Probably both. Some toddlers bite other children when they are teething; do they need medicine or social education? Probably both.

If you have a sense that a mood is more than "just physical," hang on to it. Parents (and teachers) who hate physical explanations often fear that equally important parts of a whole situation will be ignored. This doesn't have to happen.

You can ask, "Is something physical *part* of this mood?" without ignoring anything else.

Go Slow—Children You're sick; you're moving; you have a big project due at work; your sister's large family has arrived for the weekend. And right then, when you need your child to keep it together and stay steady, he or she falls apart. Some parents find this so completely understandable they don't give it a second thought: "Oh well, we're all feeling stressed and awful—why should she be different?" Some worry: "Wouldn't a really secure child cope better than this?" Some exasperated parents wonder why they've failed to notice before how spoiled and demanding their child has become: "He's just used to being the center of attention!"

Changes—even some that seem minor to adults—often throw children, even secure, unspoiled children. Because children understand so little of cause and effect, one change can threaten everything: "If this can go, anything can go." Some children develop a general nervousness about what will change next and follow parents from room to room; some develop a desperate urge to take charge of little things—seating arrangements, clothes. Good listening may reveal a specific worry: You'll die; you'll leave me behind; you don't like me anymore; my cousin John will hit me. The common, bottom-line dread seems to be: No one will take care of me; I'll be all alone. Changes at day care can bring up similar fears. If your child seems suddenly insecure or desperate about controlling things, it's always worth asking yourself and teachers: What's new? What has changed?

Some parents hate being asked, "Has anything changed at home?" They feel accused, or overanalyzed, or depressed right away because too many things are always changing in their lives and they do not have control over that. Adults do not, however, have a duty to make sure nothing ever changes in children's lives; our responsibility lies in doing what we can to help children feel safe during changes. Chapter 9 is devoted to ideas for making change easier.

Road Under Construction Children go through periods of having relatively steady or ragged nerves as part of normal development. How can you know when your child's changed mood is mainly just part of growing up? The "Developmental Issues" section details some of the age-related changes in feelings and mood; many parents have found the Frances Ilg and Louise Ames series *Your Two Year Old, Your Three Year Old,* and *Your Four Year Old* very useful. You can also use your day-care network. Teachers see lots of children moving through phases in their age group; they should be able to describe what parts of a new mood come mainly with age and how they adjust for it. Other parents in your group may be able to tell you what they have been going through and what has helped. You can describe what your child is doing that concerns you and ask, "Does this sound familiar?"

Many parents can drink in all the reassurance that "It's a phase" has to offer: The new mood is *not* a symptom that something is wrong with child, parents, or teachers. Some parents hate "It's a phase." They are not worried, they're frustrated. The real question for them is "Can't we make life easier?," and "It's a phase" sounds like "No." You don't need to take no for an answer. Even when a new mood is a natural part of growing up, how you handle it will make a difference. If you want more than "It's normal" from teachers, you might ask directly, "How are *you* handling this?"

Junction Ahead As children grow, the kind of support they need from parents changes—and it is not a simple, straight-line increase toward more independence. In some periods, they need elbow room to work on new skills and ideas; they may suddenly feel crowded, hovered over, and interrupted by our old ways of handling them. At other times, they need us right close behind them or even out front facing the world first; our old ways are feeling much too casual to them.

Many parents report that moods improve when they

catch up to the "get back!" or "take charge!" spirit of a new phase: "It always takes me too long to see when he's in a new place . . . I finally got it! I was treating him like a baby. I needed to let go a little more, let him try more things on his own. Now we're doing great." "Giving her choices always worked before. When she started giving me the silent treatment—or changing her mind ten times—I didn't know what to do! Now I just *tell* her what we're going to do most of the time. I thought she'd throw fits, but she's acting relieved."

Yield Teachers sometimes say "It's a phase" mainly to say "Relax!" This strikes some parents as both impossible and ignorant: No one who really knew what living with this child was like at the moment would consider relaxing.

Adult tensions, however, can feed into children's tensions so that a cycle gets going. Some parents find that relaxing about a new mood or behavior does help: "I decided to carry him whenever he wanted—it's easier on both of us. He's heavy, but at least we're skipping all those minutes when he cried and I stood there not knowing what to do." "I realized I wasn't letting her be mad! By trying so hard to keep her from having tantrums, I was driving us both crazy. Now I tell myself, 'So she's mad. She has a right to be mad sometimes. It's normal; it'll pass'—and it does."

No Passing The power of relaxing about phases reflects a larger truth: Adult moods affect children's moods, just as theirs affect us. Some people see this as a sixth sens: "Children *know*, don't they?" Since feelings show in faces, tones of voice, ways of touching and moving, even infants can pick up moods through normal senses. Any time your child's mood seems completely mysterious, it's worth asking "How am *I* feeling?" You may discover some good clues. Younger children may simply *react* to a parent mood; older children may *worry* about your mood.

This is not to say "Pretend to be happy all the time." Many parents already feel too much pressure to be sweet and cheerful. All those sweet parents in sitcoms, so full of wit and wisdom: *Their* children's troubles dissolve in twenty-two minutes—why not ours? Parents often find that taking care of themselves feeds calm back into the family: "It's hard to leave them, but it always pays off. Just one night away can change the way everything looks." "I learned to make myself have a cup of tea alone, without doing any work, *before* I picked them up. It was hard at first—I always felt like I should rush to day care—but those few quiet moments really made a big difference." Older children can also use simple explanations about adult moods and a little direct reassurance: "I have too many things to do at work right now; if I look grumpy, I'm not mad at *you*, I'm mad at work. *You* are great; *work* is yucky right now."

As you consider health, recent events, phases of development, your child's need for elbow room versus leadership, and your own feelings, something may hit you: "Ah-ha! Of course!" More often, no one thing seems to be "it"; a few different things look worth checking. An analysis of many moods would read like a recipe: a cup of this, a teaspoon of that, a pinch of something else. You might just watch your child for extra clues with those things in mind for a few days, and ask teachers to do the same. Like listening to a particular feeling, just paying attention to a mood shift may have a magical effect: "We finally scheduled the big conference to figure this all out, and this week he's fine! We haven't even talked yet!" You can enlist fresh eyes and ears from the center director or staff consultant, or just try what makes the most sense to you first. An amazing variety of things have helped children in mysterious moods.

Children's happiness is sunshine: It brings light, warmth, color, and fragrance to our lives. And it is a mighty reassurance. When they are happy, we know that we are doing it right, and that we *are* right, fundamentally, in ourselves. Miserable moods rob us of these comforts; we may start to hunt down the causes somewhat desperately. A gentle hunt helps most. We teach every minute, whether we mean to or not, and a gentle spirit gives the message: Feelings are important but not dangerous. It also lets us give the best immediate comfort: the understanding company of a good friend.

Feelings: Developmental Issues

New Skills Some children seem to "decide" that it is time to crawl, walk, talk, or make a friend, and throw themselves at the task with total commitment. They clamber back to their feet after a hundred falls, keep talking and talking through a hundred stutters, chase after that would-be friend despite a hundred rejections. Such hard work may leave a child mainly exhausted; new skill work shakes some children's self-confidence, so they are clingier as well. If your child seems fine in the mornings but comes home unusually cranky or fragile, you might check with teachers: "Does s/he seem to be working on anything special right now?"

Shifting Gears Between Skill Systems Children can get stuck in transit between two systems of communicating, moving, or socializing; they reach a place where nothing works. Older infants can communicate beautifully with raised eyebrows, pointing fingers, head shakings, a few all-purpose "Da!"s; younger toddlers can use a small batch of words and two-word combinations to say a great many things; older toddlers explode with language, adding fifty words a week, saying long and brand-new sentences never heard before. In between these stages, each of which works well, children sometimes find themselves with *no* method of communicating. Young toddlers who can't think of a word they want forget that they could point; they just cry in frustration. Older toddlers who might have yelled "My turn!" automatically a month ago suddenly want the words to explain "I only left it for a minute" or "I've been waiting too long!"; when they cannot think of them, they don't yell "My turn!"—they hit or cry.

These bouts of helpless, "babyish" behavior may puzzle and frustrate adults, too: "I *know* she could tell me if she wanted to!" "He knows what to say, he just won't." These are prime times for adult suspicions: Maybe younger children at home or day care are bad influences; maybe parents or teachers are "spoiling." Collapses between systems may create terrible moods for everyone until the new system plugs in. Adults can help by:

FILLING IN THE GAPS

- *Avoid test pressure:* "Now what's this?" "What do you say? Come on, you know. . . ."
- *Step in with needed support:* Do this only to get past the immediate obstacle, *if a child is giving up.* When adults try to help in the *middle* of a child's effort, the interruption makes things worse. If a child seems to be giving up, supply the missing words, movements, or social skills: "Do you want this? . . . this?" or "I can carry you," or "Were you trying to get a turn?"
- *Protect the patience supply:* Remind yourself or teachers, Development goes three steps forward, two steps back. Remind children, "Sometimes, you just can't do it! Then, later, you can! Let's do something else for now."

Cycles of Organization Children do not get steadily more mature in every way, month by month. "Three steps forward, two steps back" happens not only with particular skills, but also in general: A child may look organized for a while, then act very disorganized for several months. A friendly, relaxed, predictable, everything-works phase will be followed by a nervous, grouchy, off-schedule phase. Some psychologists believe that organized-disorganized periods follow a six-month schedule, with the first six months of every year running fairly smoothly and the second not. Others see fewer periods of collapse. One friend said, "I do see an organized-disorganized cycle in every year, but it's not a six-month thing. With my kids, the organized phase lasts about four weeks; all the rest is rough."

You have to judge for yourself. If your child suddenly seems much *less* mature than he or she did the month before, you may well be headed for a disorganized phase. That's the bad news. The good news is that these cycles are normal and natural, not your fault or anyone else's, and that an easier phase is bound to follow.

INFANTS—THE PRE-WALKING BLUES

> Thirteen-month-old Daniel has been cruising confidently around the infant room, sidestepping more smoothly every day. To great applause, he has even ventured some steps alone. His parents and teachers have been telling each other "He'll be walking any day now" for two weeks. At the moment, they can't believe their old confidence. Daniel has stopped cruising *and* stepping. When his teacher Susan or his mother at home moves away from him even briefly now, Daniel panics, crying and reaching, but not moving. Has he even forgotten how to crawl?

Chapter 2 discusses infancy's most famous phase—separation anxiety. Pure separation can begin any time an infant's mental powers develop to the prediction point: When they are able to make the connection between activities like getting belongings and heading for doors with parent departure. When infants who have never cried at good-byes suddenly start, you know this new power has just plugged in. Infants who were and are very happy at day care still go through it; for many children, nine to fifteen months is a peak time.

Pre-walking blues usually overlap separation anxiety in time and look similar in that any adult bustling around may produce tears and reaching. With pure separation anxiety, however, infants often try to follow the adult around crawling or toddling a few steps behind; during the pre-walking blues, infants don't try to follow. They cry.

The sudden appearance of helplessness in a baby who has been cruising around happily may worry the adults: "Why is she so insecure right now?"—or frustrate them. Older infants are too heavy to carry around for long, and when you know they can move—in several different ways, for heaven's sake—the "Carry me!" business seems very demanding. Teachers and parents may begin to suspect each other of "spoiling" or "carrying him around too much."

If your baby's urgent demands to be held and carried come just at the brink of walking, you can take these:

PRE-WALKING BLUES STEPS

- Reassure yourself and teachers that this is a normal phase and usually does not last too long (3–4 weeks).
- Let teachers know you think it is fine to "give in" and carry your child (or stay put as much as possible); you are not worried about spoiling.
- Tell teachers things you find useful at home. Some possibilities:
  1. Keeping voice contact by calm talk when you have to move away
  2. Giving all the extra comforts when you have to move: favorite blanket, toys, pacifier
  3. Using a stroller to move your baby around with you
  4. Organizing the adults so one can sit still nearby while the other does the work that requires moving around

TODDLERS: "IT'S NOT RIGHT!" TANTRUMS

> Twenty-one-month-old Nate is putting the room's entire small plastic car collection in an exact lineup on the top of the bookshelf. He arranges and rearranges them carefully, lovingly, sighting down the line to make sure it's pure and straight. When little Darrel brushes by and knocks the front car off, Nate screams at him and bursts into tears. A teacher comes over, pats him, and replaces the car, putting it at the *end* of the line, facing *backward*. Nate stares at this disaster and flaps his hands wildly. The teacher says, "*Tell* me what's wrong, Nate!" "C-c-car!" he sputters. "I put it back!" she says. Nate grabs the car and throws it across the room; he collapses, sobbing, on the floor.

The ability to plan—to have a vision and make it come true—is an amazing thing. Toddlers, still new to planning and a little shaky about it, often invest so much energy in making things come out according to plan that their universe seems to collapse if the plan collapses. "Getting it right" assumes a terrible, magic importance; they become desperate when failure threatens. Adults, desperate to ward off a tantrum, sometimes try too hard, talk too much and too fast, and end up making things worse.

Toddlers suffer from a difficult mix of skills. They can form complex, invisible goals but cannot achieve all their goals alone; often they lack the words they need to get the right kind of help, yet they understand enough to know when we are bound to do exactly the wrong thing. If toddlers were less competent or more competent, they would have fewer causes for despair.

Toddlers' superstitions about what *must* be done just so tend to be very individual. They need different amounts of time to calm down before adult help can be used and find different things calming. Busy as you are, you are more likely to have this in-depth information about your child and the time to try things one-on-one. Let teachers know what you see and what works at home. Here are some possibilities:

IDEAS FOR "IT'S NOT RIGHT!" TANTRUMS

When a child has not actually collapsed yet, you might:

- *Wait Quietly, Close at Hand:* Three slow breaths for yourself
- *Empathize:* "These cars are making a big problem!"
- *Give Hope:* "Maybe you can fix it. . . ."

When a child is calm enough to talk, you can:

- *Ask:* "Can you *show* me how to help?"
- *Offer Your Three Best Guesses:* "Do you want it this way? or that way?" Simple choices, with gestures to reduce word frustrations, often work best.
- *Redirect Attention:* "I wish I could understand how to help, but I can't. Let's go do something else." When a few guesses get nowhere, adults may have to help children move on.

When you understand the plan, but it requires ice cream before dinner or wearing socks on your ears *all* day, you can still:

- *Wait Quietly:* Say, "I'm sorry, I can't do that right now" and wait, a patient friend in a troubled time. A tantrum may come, but the accepting spirit helps.
- *Empathize:* "We can't do it now—what a shame! You really wanted that ice cream!"
- *Give Hope:* "We can have ice cream/be silly again *after* dinner."

Tone of voice communicates most. A newscaster tone can become a signal: You understand the feelings; you have done what you can do; it's over now. You will be ready for a finish-up hug when your child is ready.

TODDLERS: "GET OUT OF MY FACE!" TANTRUMS

"Marilee, just take one crayon at a time."

"Marilee, we use the crayons for drawing, not throwing. . . ."

"Marilee, I think you're *done* with drawing now. You need to find something else to play."

Marilee looks the teacher in the eye, picks up the box of crayons, and pours them all over the table. When the teacher insists, "Now you need to pick those up!" she turns to run. Captured, she hits the teacher and screams, "Nononononononoonoooo!"

Some days, from the toddler point of view, *they* just keep having great, interesting, lots-of-fun ideas, and *adults* keep interfering for no reason. It is infuriating; the interference issue becomes personal—they go for us. Imagine trying to take a walk on a fine day and the same person keeps popping out of the bushes, planting himself squarely in your path, and ordering you to turn off this way or that way or to stop altogether. At first you might ask why or just cooperate for the sake of peace, but eventually you would take up the main matter: Whose walk *is* this? Get out of my face! When children get old enough to begin having plans and ideas of their own, they have this experience all the time.

Many conflicts with toddlers are unavoidable: Their own ideas involve dangerous, inconvenient, or impossible feats. We have no choice but to oppose them, but this builds tension like a chemical in the bloodstream. Tantrums seem designed to release that tension. What other forms of release are open to toddlers, after all? They can't run smoothly enough to jog off stress; they can't blob out with a beer. Tantrums frequently leave a more relaxed and capable child.

Toddlers seem to appreciate the freedom to blow off steam this way. Many toddler rooms have a special place for throwing tantrums—the couch or a corner full of pillows.

When teachers ask, "Do you need the pillows?," toddlers often take *themselves* over, *quietly,* and then throw themselves down and scream. After a few minutes, they pick themselves up and return to the group, announcing, "I'm done!"—satisfied, some need met. Lines may form on rainy days.

Many toddler teachers have great sympathy and a healthy sense of humor about tantrums that helps these fairly inevitable storms stay simple. Even great teachers may need your support from time to time. Tantrums are show-stoppers. Right when your child needs some tantrum time to blow off steam, other children may want the show—the trip outside, the singing at circle—to go on, and feel just as desperate about it. High-voltage conflicts between children's needs wear teachers out. Your sympathy counts. Remarks like "I could never do what you do all day!" or "I really appreciate how patient you are" make more difference than you might expect.

If you think the teacher has lost sympathy with your child, is provoking tantrums unnecessarily, or is intimidated by your child, plan a longer conversation. Children need just as much sympathy when they're angry as they do when they're sad or frightened; if either teacher or child comes to see tantrums as weapons, tantrums become more frequent and complicated.

You might also try one or more of these tactics and let teachers know what helps your child most:

IDEAS FOR "GET OUT OF MY FACE!" TANTRUMS

- *Give Warnings About Adults' Plans:* "In two minutes we're going to get jackets on."
- *Give Choices:* "You can use *one* crayon; do you want the red one or the blue one?" "You can *draw* with the crayons or you could *throw* the beanbags; do you want to draw or throw?"
- *Sympathize:* "I know you're busy with the blocks now, but . . ."
- *Slow Down the Pace of Adult-Dictated Changes:* Larger blocks of toddler-controlled time may soothe nerves.

TODDLERS AND YOUNG PRESCHOOLERS: IRRATIONAL FEARS

Recognize any of these?

Vacuum Cleaners	Garbage trucks
Bees	Radiator noises
Dogs	Birthday candles
Drains	Toilet flushes

Children between two and three are vulnerable to specific "irrational" fears—fears that have no basis in experience. Children who've had *no* violent encounters with vacuum cleaners may still, suddenly, become terrified of the machine.

Children's thinking tends to be "magical" in general at this age, operating more on fairy-tale rules than on adult logic. Nothing is just what it is; almost anything is possible. A special pair of shoes can win your prince, dance you to death, or save you from the wicked witch and take you home. Pumpkins, apples, and grandmothers can be coaches, poison, wolves.

This system of thinking has its own rules and timing, like language. Adults influence it very little. You can tell toddlers many, many times that squirrels—or cows—are not "doggies," and you still hear "See the doggie!" for those and most other animals until a new system of categories is ready for the more precise information. When a vacuum cleaner becomes the Great Growling Intruder in the universe, you're likely to be just as helpless. You can say "The vacuum cleaner won't hurt you" until you're blue in the face and only damage your credibility.

Tell your teacher about your child's special fears as soon as you suspect them. If your child hates and fears garbage trucks, for example, and the city garbage truck always comes during yard time, your child may be pulling out all the stops in an effort to avoid the yard: refusing to put on outdoor clothing or to go anywhere near the outside door—mystifying teachers completely. Teachers may or may not be able to rearrange things around a special fear, but your information saves confusion and supports patience.

These special fears seem to come from nowhere and disappear into the dust with time. Adults have little power over this coming and going, but they can offer comfort freely in the meantime and work to keep one fear from making a child feel fearful in general. You might try, or suggest to teachers, some of these ways of

CONFINING SPECIAL FEARS

- *Give advance notice and offer support ahead of time:* "We are going outside in five minutes; I don't think there are any bees there, but I'll be right with you anyway."
- *Make an advance plan with the child, with room for child choices:* "We have to vacuum now; do you want to sit on the couch and put your hands over your ears or put on a tape *really loud.* . . . What do you think would help?" Children sometimes invent helps we would never think of, from their own magical-thinking world: "I know! I'll bring this Bee Stick [a bare twig fragment to the ordinary adult] and spray them!" If it works for you . . . ?
- *Remind the child (any time) that he or she is not frightened by everything:* "Those bees scare you, but you're *not* scared of . . ." (clouds, trucks, the blender—something a *little* scary might feel like a bigger compliment).

PRESCHOOLERS: THREE AND A HALF

> When he turned three, Willy shed good-bye scenes, dia-
> pers, tantrums, and the baseball cap he *had* to wear to day
> care every day. He swaggered into the center, waved good-
> bye, and rushed to play with good friends. Everything
> seemed easy for him. His parents slowly drew a deep breath
> of relief—we're out of the woods!
>
> This month, Willy has fallen apart. He's stuttering; he
> says he "can't" get his pants on in the morning; barely a
> breakfast goes by without a big spill or a scattering mess. He
> has to have his baseball cap again. Teachers say they are hav-
> ing a very hard time getting through to him—maybe his
> hearing should be checked? He sulks at good-byes; he's rude
> at pickup time. What happened?

The organized-disorganized cycle of early development
becomes dramatically visible at three and a half. It catches
most of us by surprise. We are prepared for two to be terrible; the three-and-a-half collapse is underadvertised. In con-
trast to the often charming and confident average three year
old, the average three-and-a-half-year-old stumbles and falls
more, stutters more, whines, and says "I can't" more, draws
with thin, wavery lines (instead of a three's clear, bold
strokes), has trouble building with blocks (marked hand
tremors are common), has pitched battles with parents over
simple events, sets up "nothing pleases me" situations, is
insecure and self-willed, anxious and demanding, emotionally extreme and inconsistent. Tense eye blinking is also
common. (This summary is taken from Frances Ilg and Louise Ames's *Your Three Year Old*.)

Tell your teachers about this phase; they may be victims of
the same underadvertising. If your relatively calm, cheerful,
cooperative three-year-old starts acting helpless *and* stubborn
at day care, they will be puzzled and frustrated, too.

The tough side of three and a half may not show up as

strongly at day care as at home. Peer relationships take a definite upturn at three and a half, and teachers may be much more tuned in to this. Three-and-a-half-year-olds co-operate with each other much more easily; they have fewer squabbles over materials, can defer to each others' wishes, even show admiration for each other. Their imaginations take off. Their shakier eyes, hands, and mouths do not interfere with high jumping, smooth running, real hopping; real ball play appears. This age loves to play with words, make up words, find silly rhymes. To the extent that day-care life is busy with these things, teachers may report that your child is just charming there; remember not to take that as a *sign* of parenting problems. This may be an especially good time to:

USE YOUR DAY-CARE NETWORK

You might:

- Talk to other parents informally about home struggles: "What do you do about. . . ?"
- Let teachers know you would like to have a room meeting or potluck to talk about the age, and breakfast, and dinner, and sleep, and TV, and weekends. . . .
- Check in with teachers about reasonable expectations for things that concern you. Many preschoolers say they "can't" dress themselves or help clean up toys at home but do some of this at day care. You may still decide not to push these things at home, but you can have the comfort of knowing the skills are getting practice *somewhere*.
- Ask teachers how they handle specific pieces of unreasonable behavior: "What do you do when they just won't listen? I've asked him four hundred times not to jump on the couch, but . . ." Teachers may have a few good tricks of the trade, geared specifically for this age group, one of which you could use: turning off lights a minute to focus attention, stickers, etc.

PRESCHOOLERS: FAMILY FEARS

> Two-year-old Blake has been playing in the wading pools outside. In the period between having his waterlogged diaper removed and a fresh one installed, he looks down at his penis, fondles it wistfully, looks up at the teacher, and says, "Cut it off?" His teacher sputters, "Cut it off! Did you say 'Cut it off?' Oh no, no, absolutely not. No, no. No one is going to cut it off, it's just fine like it is, you're fine. . . . Um, let's see, what do you have in your lunchbox today?"
>
> She reports Blake's question to his parents, hoping for a clue, and they have it: Although he has seen his mother naked before, last night for the first time Blake really noticed her. When he sees her getting out of the bath, he points in the significant direction and asks, "What happened to Mommy?" Despite his parents' careful answers to the question that night, Blake made up his own answer: cut it off.

This precocious toddler may have mainly wondered about the mechanics of sex differences; three-to-five-year-olds mull over the whole context of sex, marriage, power, and love. Preschoolers wonder about sex differences; they wonder about their place in the family and want the best one. We hear things like, "When I grow up, I'm going to marry *you*, Daddy. . . ." Daddy: "What about Mom?" Child: "Oh, she'll be dead by then." "I'm stronger than Dad, Mom." "We're girls, right, Mom? Dad, you can't sing this song—this is a *girls'* song." "*Who do you love the best?*"

At least three special developments contribute to preschoolers' family concerns: the ability to compare, the idea of relationships, and the amazing revelation that people's bodies come in two varieties, not one.

Before three, things are themselves—unique, alone, here, and mine. Three-year-olds begin to compare things. A block is no longer just this block; now they see that one block is bigger or longer or heavier than another one. By three and a half, they are very interested in what is "biggest" and "longest" and "best" in any way.

Before three, relationship words are used, if at all, as names for single objects: "Mommy" and "Daddy" are names of *people*, not names of relationships: "My Mommy" is "Daddy's Mommy," not his wife. Toddlers hear the words "husband" and "wife" but do not use them; relationship words make no sense yet. Before three, children use the word "friend," but mainly as "familiar person." (Joyous friendships exist among toddlers, but they don't need the word; a name says it all.) Preschoolers do see "friend" as a relationship—a relationship that can be won, lost, earned, or betrayed, and *compared* to others.

Toddlers use "boy" and "girl" occasionally but not very often or very well, and they don't care much about it. Beginning around three, the notion that people are either boys *or* girls but not both hits children like a ton of bricks. Some just reject the ridiculous facts: A younger sister of three brothers says, "Well, I'm going to be a boy *next* year!" A loving son says, "I'm a boy, and I have a penis, but I have breasts, too! Look!" Young preschoolers work hard to make sense of sex differences. They try out rules: "Girls can't do this, only boys." "Boys can't play here." They try claiming whatever biological equipment attracts them, in all combinations. Adults try to clear things up and make it all seem okay by saying "Mommy is a girl; Daddy's a boy"—but *this* is the worst news yet. How can your very own body be like one of your parents' but not the other? What could it possibly mean?

All these new notions about "best," about earning and betraying special relationships, and about boys and girls, create questions about the family for preschoolers. They notice that Mommy and Daddy have a special relationship to each other—is it a better one? What do you have to do to be the best? Be a boy? Or a girl? Be bigger? Stronger? Get rid of the competition? Some children go straight for the mark: They notice that Mommy and Daddy's special relationship involves sleeping in the same bed—that's what they want, too. The "extra" person can sleep alone, and it's not going to be him (or her) anymore.

When this interest in competition, relationships, and sex differences is rumbling around at low levels, it's often lighthearted and funny, even for the children themselves. At peak intensity, however, family fears generate tremendous anxiety. Children seem to worry about both parents more. Day-care separations become more difficult. It's not clear whether children think parents are getting together while they're at day care or if it's even more complicated.

Young children are confused about the power of wishes—can wishing make it so? If they are wishing—just for today maybe—that one parent would disappear so they could enjoy a special relationship with the other one, they're not *certain* the wish won't make it happen. They do want to have one parent to themselves, but they don't really want to lose the other parent, and they certainly don't want to feel responsible for breaking up the family. Too scary altogether. At home they can see proof of the other parent's health and safety. When they're at day care, there's room for doubt. If your preschooler seems sensitive about family relationships and suddenly starts looking very anxious at day-care good-byes, try making a special point of saying that the "endangered" parent is safe—"Daddy [or Mommy] will be fine at work. It's very safe there." Strange as this may seem, it often helps when nothing else does.

How can you handle preschoolers' "Who do you love best?" "I love you both the same" rarely satisfies. You can stress that this is an apples-and-oranges situation; people are different, full of different things to love: "Daddy is my favorite *man; you* are my favorite *boy* . . . [It never hurts to go on a bit about your child's fine qualities at this point.] And I really love you! You are handsome, you build amazing things, you make me laugh. . . ."

If your child's concern with differences and competition

seems too intense to you, you might work with teachers to bring differences into a warmer circle. Children too easily see differences as having only one dimension: better-worse. They can sink into seeing themselves in light of only one salient difference: "I am a girl; I wear only girls' clothes [yes, tights in July if necessary]; I do only girl things; I am the best girl in the house." Increasing a child's awareness of the many simple, interesting, and useful ways people differ can pull a little of the tension out of the idea of difference. Parents and teachers can help:

BRING DIFFERENCES INTO A WARM CIRCLE

- *Call attention to a wide variety of differences in an appreciative way.* Two apples, two leaves, two drawings, two children, and two family members all differ in interesting, noncompetitive, lovable ways. Adults can treat their comments as perceptual-enrichment exercises: "Look—this one has different patches of color over here, and this color is all the same; this one is long that way but shorter here; this is squiggly here, this one is straight . . ."
- *Emphasize the flexibility and interest value of different groupings.* Having children re-sort any material—shells, rocks, leaves, blocks—can help get the basic idea across, but ways of sorting people are the most important. Teachers can make a practice of re-sorting children for everyday transitions: "I want the people with striped shirts at this table and one-color shirts at that table. . . ." or "If you have curly hair, go get your coat now . . ." At home, too, you can play around with in-family differences: "Bedtime for short people!"
- *Notice and create situations in which differences work together for a common good:* "You need short people for getting out low things and tall people for reaching the high things—together we can get out the cooking stuff fastest and best!" "Hugh, you help Dan with his shoes, and Dan, you tell Hugh those freeze-tag rules—then we can get playing fast!"

The urge to feel big, strong, lovable, and best will stay strong in preschoolers no matter what we do. In their own eyes, they are on the brink of adulthood—a very exciting, and very scary, time. They need to feel terrific about their chances out there in the big world: They're up to it, right? Warming up the idea of differences won't change this, but it can help them give themselves, and others, a little room to be whoever they are right now.

When these developmental storms hit, you have to let children plead "temporary insanity" and not worry too much about teaching them to be courageous, relaxed, or reasonable right then. You have your whole life to convey these qualities. You do not have to see your patience as a passive surrender or a detached distance. It is a great gift. When you make room for your child's emotional storms, they can stay simple and free to move on. When you comfort without panic and reassure without scorn, you make the world within them—the one world they keep forever—safe, and full of your love.

Feelings: Parent-Teacher Talk

> TEACHER: ("Oh, shoot. Here's Sean's mom, and he had *another* bad day. She looks so tired. I don't want to tell her he was miserable and fighting with his friends all day. It must be something *we're* doing anyway—she never says anything but 'He's fine' at home.) "Hi, Gwen. Sean had an okay day. His jacket got a little wet at outside time, but it should be dry by now."
>
> PARENT: ("Why is he always fine at day care? He's such a mess at home these days. I don't know what we're doing wrong.) "Okay, thanks. Sean! Let's go!"

Go for the Max When children are happy, adults can relax: We must be doing things right. When children are *un*happy, we are oppressed: *Somebody* is doing it wrong. The bad-mood news options all look bad: Confess or accuse. Teachers and parents sometimes forget that *not* telling the bad-mood news also leaves a lot to be desired: Adults suffer guiltily in silence, and children don't get both sides working for them. Maximizing information *ought* to get help to both adults and children. Why don't we all believe this and act on it?

Sometimes parents and teachers hesitate to tell each other the bad-mood news because they don't want to lay themselves open to the other's theories about this bad mood. Raising a child with someone—teacher or mate—brings out differences of opinion about psychology, even in little things: When a child falls down, should you say "Oh, poor you!" Or "Hey! You're okay!"? Does sympathy help or weaken and mislead? People discover beliefs about what makes people tick they didn't even know they had. Parents disagree with each other about what all kinds of things *mean* for children, about whether adults should try to *change* or just *survive* bad feelings or unpleasant behavior, and *how* to go about either one.

You and your day-care teacher are likely to have differences of opinion, too, especially around mysterious moods. You may find your teacher too "soft" or too "psychological," too prone to overlook the possible ear infection. You wonder if that so-sympathetic approach to every mood change is creating a moody child. Or you may find your teacher too hard-nosed, brisk, or impatient, stuffed to the gills with behavior-management ideas but completely lost to the memory of what it's like to be a small child. You wonder if that unsympathetic teacher is creating a moody child by failing to provide enough emotional support during the day.

Is silence the only option? If you decide to open up a topic anyway—despite differences of view you dread—you might:

MAKE WAY FOR MORE IDEAS

- *Find out what an idea "boils down to" in action:* "If that was the reason, what does it mean we would be *doing*?" Sometimes perfectly reasonable things to do or try out come attached to unattractive general ideas.

- *Focus on a discovery process:* "Well, I guess that could be it. How would we find out?" The process of checking out an idea might be harmless at least, quite worthwhile at best.
- *Ask about other possibilities:* "That's an interesting idea. . . . Have you ever seen children like this for *other* reasons? I'm trying to think of *everything* this could possibly *be.*"
- *Place ideas on a priority list:* "That sounds like it's worth checking out. But I think I'll take her to the doctor first, just to make sure nothing physical is wrong."

With any of these approaches, you don't have to reject a teacher's idea completely or accept an idea you don't like. You can simply increase the number of things you can both be looking out for, trying out, or keeping in mind. You might use one of these tactics to free your own mind as well—sometimes a child's rough mood makes parents feel too guilty even to consider all of their *own* ideas.

Getting free to pool *all* the news with teachers also gives you the best chance of knowing when the answer to "Where does this mood come from?" is "It's a phase." The worlds of day care and home are so different in so many ways that identical behavior in both places is always a good sign of a phase. You may still want to brainstorm with teachers about ways to make surviving the phase easier on everyone, but at least you can stop wondering "Who's doing it wrong?"

Listening

Listening helps adults unlock the mysteries of children's moods while we love and calm them. With infants and young toddlers, we "listen" best by focusing on their immediate moments; usually that's where all the action is. This next section applies mainly to late toddlers and preschoolers, whose slippery hold on language and ideas makes a lot of trouble but also opens up the chance to help through talk.

Rebecca, who will be three next Sunday, is collapsing for the third time this morning. Adam took a piece of her Play-Doh. Normally, she would simply swipe it back, or yell and tell if he persisted. Lately, however, any minor setback undoes her. Her teacher Janelle has been puzzled, and checked for news of any sort with her parents. They report she is unusually "fragile" at home, too, but they haven't a clue why. They are expecting a new baby, but they've been talking about that on and off for months. It's old news.

With a sobbing Rebecca in her lap, Janelle tries the open-ended fishing expedition: "Something is making you very sad. . . ." Rebecca cries harder, snuggles deeper, then suddenly lifts up her head to wail, "But I can't *find* an apartment!"

When our infants and young toddlers cried, we thought, It will be so much easier when they can *talk*, and tell us what's wrong! We forgot that as children get more complicated, the things that make them cry or yell get more complicated, too. We still have to be detectives.

Why did Rebecca think she had to find an apartment? Rebecca's view, slowly unraveled by Janelle and her parents: The baby was coming. Families have two parents and *one* child (not two children). Obviously, she would have to move out. Next week was her birthday. She would be three, a big girl, old enough to live alone. Probably she was supposed to leave her old home right after the birthday party. But she didn't know how to find an apartment!

When we have figured out that a child's mood is not a phase but a reaction to some recent or upcoming event—and talked about this with our children—we hope to be all done. We know that big stresses for adults like new babies, housing moves, or marital trouble affect children. We know that preparing children ahead of time usually helps; having the facts often makes things feel less frightening. We hope that discussing these events openly will lay their worries to rest. Sometimes this approach works perfectly. A couple of good chats, some steadfast patience, and a general readiness to answer questions as they arise defang the monsters of change completely.

Children lack so much information about the world, and apply such unique logic to the information they have, that it's virtually impossible to anticipate all the troubles events can stir up. Rebecca had lots of information about the coming baby, but she made up some terrible "information" of her own that no one could have prepared her against ahead of time.

If your child seems mysteriously upset, you want to go looking for more clues. One of the best ways to get clues from children who can talk is to do some "high-tech" listening. Listening sounds simple enough—and will look simple here. It is surprisingly hard to do. Good listening goes against too many ingrained communication habits.

Regular old everyday listening finds us putting away the socks, picking up the toys, or trying to make dinner at the same time. High-tech listening means stopping all action, sitting quietly, and giving your full attention to a child. In everyday listening, we might:

- *Interrupt with challenging questions:* "Why did you do that?" or "What do you mean?"
- *Deny or correct the child's view:* "Oh, I'm sure Jared didn't *mean* to hurt your feelings," "You don't *really* hate Michelle."
- *Find fault:* "Well, if you hit him first, what did you expect?" "You shouldn't have been making that noise in the first place."
- *Give advice:* "Maybe you just shouldn't play with him if he's going to be rough." "Did you tell a teacher about this?"
- *Get into the act:* "That's terrible! That makes me mad, too," or "When I was a little kid . . ."
- *Take over:* "I'll talk to your teacher/her parents about this." "I'm sure you'll feel better after you've had something to eat."

- *Explain:* "But it's too late to do that now." "That's just because she's younger, honey."

Explaining, taking over, coaching for new behavior, and asking questions are all things we need to do with young children from time to time, but *not* when we want them to talk to us. When you want children to talk:

TRY HIGH-TECH LISTENING

- Describe what you see, naming a feeling: "You look kind of worried about this. . . ." "Something is making you sad right now." "You sound pretty angry about that!"
- Wait. Stop yourself from advising, explaining, correcting, etc.
- After the first burst of talk:
  1. Say: "I see . . ."; "Ohhhh . . ."; "Yes . . ."; or
  2. Repeat a phrase they've used: "And you hated that." "It wasn't fair."
  3. Wait for more talk.

(See *How to Talk So Kids Will Listen and Listen So Kids Will Talk* by Adele Faber and Elaine Mazlish for a full description of this approach.)

When the Iron Is Hot If you can start this kind of listening in the middle of a child's display of feeling and stick with it, you may get all the clues you need in the next three minutes. Even if children *start* talking about a very *specific* grievance, if they have the listening space, they often get around to everything that's bothering them. Rebecca's complaint, for example, might well have begun with protests about Adam's swiping her Play-Doh, but proceeded rapidly to the whole apartment problem when it became clear that a good supply of time and sympathy were available. Have you ever noticed that children who are discussing today's scratch will often also give you a list of similar events? "And yesterday [three months ago] I hurted my knee at my house, and I remember one time, I fell down outside, and—see *this* boo-boo?" Children remember things most easily in "feeling packages." Once children get started talking about one thing that made them sad, or angry, a long list of events that made them feel the same way often emerges. Using emotion words triggers the whole stack.

If your child stays very specific but you suspect that you haven't got the whole story yet, you can fish for it by naming the feeling again, but in a slightly broader context:

- "So you've been feeling pretty worried *today*. . . ."
- "I wonder if something *else* is making you sad, too. . . ."
- "I think you have a *lot* of things you're mad about. . . ."

Starting Cold Children's outbursts of feeling may be miserably timed; you can't always listen when feelings are hot, but you can get back to them. Striking up a conversation cold is usually more difficult, but still worth the try. Be prepared for the mood to heat up again if you're successful.
Openers are the same: Describe something concrete, naming a feeling:

- "Eileen told me that you were sad at naptime when I was on my trip."
- "Mom and I were fighting at dinner. You were very quiet. I wondered if you were worried. . . ."
- "You didn't like it when I had to feed Claire and you couldn't sit on my lap. You looked mad *and* sad. . . ."

Display extra support very clearly:

- "That must have been tough for you. . . ."
- "You didn't like that at all. . . ."
- "I bet that didn't feel so safe. . . ."

Once you've got the clues and the news, it should be much clearer what comes next. Sometimes there's a misunderstanding you can clear up, a problem you can relieve with new arrangements or strategies, or a need for extra re-assurance about their place in your sun. Always consider the possibility that you don't need to *do* anything. The developments or events responsible for the basic feelings may lie outside your control, *and* your show of attention, sympathy, and respect for their own struggles may provide everything they need right there.

If you can, tell teachers the stories you hear. Such stories may not only spark good ideas, but will remind teachers that moody, demanding children can be struggling with big issues; the extra patience required is a contribution to a worthy cause.

Extra Reassurances

REASSURANCE ABOUT THE FUTURE

Three-and-a-half-year-old Bert is sitting alone, fiddling around with scraps of collage paper, trying to make them fit together neatly. He's busy and quiet, but his teacher Margaret is worried. Bert's parents have begun intensive preparation for the baby girl due next month. He's seen the room they've organized, been drilled in who will take care of him while they're at the hospital, and what the baby will be like. Bert, "a born worrier," usually thrives on advance information, but this time it seems to have driven him underground. He's barely said a word all week.

Margaret decides to try drawing him out a little. She sits down next to him silently for a few minutes, then says, "I like the way you're matching those papers. . . . You know, I was thinking about your baby coming—she's going to be born in the hospital, right?" Bert bolts upright. "*No!*" he yells, anger and panic on his face, "she's going to be born in *July!*"

Whatever sense the words "in July" and "in the hospital" made to Bert, clearly they did not have the adult sense. Bert may not have the foggiest idea of what a hospital is and may hate thinking of his mother going to a mystery place, or he may know only the scariest things—that accident victims go to the hospital in wailing ambulances. We just can't count on children sharing our meaning for words. In the first example, Rebecca's own definition of "family" spelled disaster. Unfamiliar *and* familiar words can be equally slippery.

Bert may have reacted more to "July" than to "hospital." Three-year-olds are usually just grasping the idea that "yesterday" and "tomorrow" are not the same thing; their take on the meaning of other time words like "July" is anybody's guess. What we do know is that Bert had a lot of emotion packed behind his shaky hold on the facts he'd been given. Any time you think your child is struggling over information about the future, you have at least two options:

CHANGING THE CONTEXT FOR FACTS

- *Make the key facts more concrete:* Bert's parents could take him to *see* the hospital, or give him a calendar and mark off days as they pass.
- *Deemphasize facts, focus on direct reassurance:* "You don't have to know any of this stuff about the baby. What you *really* need to know is: We love you, and we're taking care of everything so that we'll all be fine when the baby comes. Mom's going to be fine, and you're going to be fine."

You can try both approaches, giving information first and then placing it in a generally reassuring context, or letting children know that they don't *have* to hear about what's going to happen, but if they'd *like* to, you can tell them some more things.

A teacher reported this exchange with a three-and-a-half-year-old:

"*My* family's having a baby in October."

"Oh, *how* can that *be*!?"
"Well, I wanted one, so now one's coming up."
"Coming up? Like on the escalator?"
(Fit of giggling). "No, silly."
"The elevator?"
(More giggles). "No! It's like this. The baby comes out here. . . ."

There followed a confident description of how it's done, and a much more relaxed child.

Playing "dumb" about words or events, making the child the expert, sometimes relaxes children. Taking the role of expert can reawaken lost confidence and remind them what a lot they know about what is coming up.

REASSURANCE ABOUT THE PAST

TEACHER: "You are so angry this morning, Bart. You're fighting with everyone. Why are you fighting so much?"
BART: "I just fight. I'm bad. That's what I do!"
T: "I don't think you're bad. I like you. . . ."
B: "I'm bad. I fight . . . My mom and dad fighted."
T: "I know. . . . Your mom's not in your house now, is she?"
B: "They're getting a divorce."
T: "Why do you think they're getting a divorce?"
B: "'Cause I fight with my sister too much."

Guilt Young children's guilt feelings surprise many of us. Guilt seems like such an *adult* business. And so often when we think they ought to feel guilty, they get silly or run away. Young children do feel guilt, but not always where we expect it. Just as they don't understand the limits of any one change the way adults do, they don't understand the limits of responsibility. They may not feel guilty about leaving toys on the stairs or waking a baby up or any adult rules but still take on responsibility for parents' fighting, absences, or grumpy moods. With any really important event, they can't imagine that they have nothing to do with it.

The me-centered thinking that creates extended responsibility is so much a part of their age that explanations about where real responsibility lies don't always sink in. "Me-centered" messages have a better chance of getting through. Parents can say, "I love *you*." "*You* are a *good* part of my life." "There's nothing *you* can do right now except be your regular self; adults have to fix this."

When they are feeling guilty, children may act like they're "asking for it." One logic behind this goes: "I've done this terrible thing, so they've got to be mad at me; sometimes they stop being mad after they punish me; let's get them mad, get punished, and get it over with." Telling children that things will be getting better "in a few more weeks" or "after this next trip" may help. It lets them off the hook (even if they don't understand time words): They don't have to try to change things; change is coming anyway.

If listening to a child, or watching angry behavior, turns up "guilt" as a problem, you might try

EASING THE GUILT

- *Make a "Bald Statement" (see page 223) like:* "We're having a tough time right now, but things are going to get easier." "I love you no matter what! Even if we fight a lot—even if we fought all day, every day—I would still really love you."
- *Tell stories about wonderful things a child has done in the past:* "One time we were all tired and grouchy from driving on this long trip, and you just started singing in your car seat—'Da da-da da-da.' Everybody laughed and cheered right up."
- *Emphasize the no-effort ways a child can make life better in the present:* "When I see your little face there on the pillow, I always feel warm inside."

REASSURANCE ABOUT THE PRESENT

Young children's active sense of magic opens some special ways of reassuring them about the present. Here are a few:

MAGIC MEASURES

Write It Out You can suggest making a "worry" list or an "I hate it" list. Children know that parents write down important messages, numbers, and events—being the subject of a list boosts morale by itself. Writing belongs to the powerful adult world; it makes no visual sense to them; it has magic. The act of writing down tames mental beasts. Writing gets worries *down* in black-and-white and wraps them up in visible packages. Big, vague, scary troubles now look important but safe, like the grocery list.

Use a Calendar Many worries intensify over time confusions. Children don't really "get" time until they are in first or second grade, and even then it can be very wobbly. Children may get upset because they can't tell the difference (ahead of time) between a three-day parent absence and a hundred-day trip, or because they can't tell if they will be moving "tomorrow" or months later, or because they can't keep track of who will be picking them up in a real tomorrow. Marking special days in different colors or counting days until something happens or crossing off days becomes magic actions that hog-tie worries. The big, huge worry shrinks into the tidy calendar squares, and children feel in charge: "I mark it off, I count it, so I'm the boss of it."

Use Books Many children's books, especially fairy tales, convey very reassuring messages to children. In these tales, the little clever child—with courage, determination, and some aid from unexpected forces—wins out in the end. The mistreated conquer; the unappreciated triumph; members of the stupid older generation are rescued or vanquished by the fabulous young. What could be better? The romance of myth and magic packs an extra wallop that invites them to believe in themselves, too, and eases the pressure to be on top of everything right now.

Tell Tales from Their Own Past You can make reassuring fairy tales from your child's own past. Even the funny moments of family life may have good you-can-make-it-in-the-tight-spots messages: "Once when you were two and Gerald was teasing you, you got so mad. But you had your hands full of crackers; you couldn't hit him. So you roared at him, 'Aaaaaarrgggh!'—like that—and he was so surprised he fell down. You laughed and laughed. So then you roared again, and he fell down again. He fell down on purpose so many times the floor almost cracked. You were Really Smart that time!"

Use Heroic Labels to Make a New Mirror Older toddlers and preschoolers can "see" themselves a little bit. They can compare themselves to others, and they have big ears for adult talk about children. During a difficult time, they may begin to see themselves as people who have "tempers" or "trouble at day care," and feel alone or discouraged. Adults can give children more hopeful ideas about themselves by calling attention to good moments with heroic labels: "That was really frustrating, but you used your brains to get through it. You're a Super-Duper Problem-Solver!" "Sounds like you wanted to smack him, but you used your words instead. That took Real Power Control. Good for you!" "So you got the help you needed! You're a great Team Leader!"

Not every child in a terrible mood is harboring a terrible misunderstanding. Besides being hungry, tired, sick, developmentally stuck, or in a tough phase, children may be plain furious or nervous; they don't *like* what's happening, and it shows. And they have a right to be irritated and worried, just like the rest of us. A little careful listening is worth doing, however, just to make sure. A good listening session delivers the message: You are important to me—in a very direct way. This reassurance, and the chance to air fears and grievances, is the closest thing to a general cure we know.

Feelings: Things to Try

IN THE MOMENT (BESIDES FOOD):

- Full-attention listening

IN GENERAL:

Checking with relevant experts (including yourself) on:

- Body news: sleeping, eating, ears, teeth, throat, sickness at day care, work, or older child's school
- Developmental news: particular skills, phases
- Special events at day care: new children or teachers or rules
- Special events at home: new people, people missing, new moods

DEVELOPMENTAL DIFFICULTIES: FILLING IN THE GAPS (page 245)

- Avoid test pressure.
- Step in with help if a child is giving up.
- Protect the patience supply; remind self and child this will pass.

INFANTS

THE PRE-WALKING BLUES (page 246):

- Reassure yourself and teachers: It's a normal, short phase.
- Give teachers permission to carry or sit with your child without fear of spoiling.
- Tell teachers what you find useful at home:
  1. Voice contact

2. Extra comforts: favorite blankets, toys, pacifier
3. A stroller
4. Adults organized so one sits, the other moves around

TODDLERS

"IT'S NOT RIGHT!" TANTRUMS (page 248):

- Wait quietly close by.
- Sympathize: "What a problem!"
- Give hope: "Maybe you can fix it."
- Ask: "Can you *show* me?"
- Try your three best guesses: "This way, or that way?"
- Redirect attention: "Let's go do something else."

"GET OUT OF MY FACE!" TANTRUMS (page 250):

- Warn about adult interruptions: "In two minutes . . ."
- Give choices: "Come! You can crawl or you can jump. . . ."
- Sympathize: "I know you're busy with that now, but . . ."
- Slow down the pace of adult-dictated changes: more no-errands time?

TODDLERS AND PRESCHOOLERS

IRRATIONAL FEARS (page 252):

- Give advance notice and offer support.
- Make a plan together.
- Remind child of things s/he is not afraid of.

THREE AND A HALF

USE YOUR DAY-CARE NETWORK (page 255):

- Talk to other parents.
- Suggest a meeting or meeting topics to teachers.
- Ask about teachers' expectations for independence.
- Ask about teachers' tricks for handling three-and-a-half-year-olds.

FAMILY FEARS

- Reassure child that *parents* are fine during day-care time.
- Talk about the *unique* things you love about family members, not the better-best dimensions.
- Warm up differences (page 259):
  1. Call appreciative attention to a variety of differences.
  2. Re-sort people in many kinds of groupings.
  3. Notice and create situations in which differences help.

LISTENING (page 262):

- Stop what you're doing, sit down, look at your child.
- Describe what you see, naming a feeling.
- Wait.
- Say, "I see," "Ohhh," "Yes," or repeat a phrase from child's talk.
- Wait for more talk.
- If you have to start cold, give extra show of support: "That must have been really scary. . . ."

REASSURANCE ABOUT THE FUTURE (page 267):

- Talk about what's coming up in child-oriented words.
- Change the Context for Facts (page 268).
- If child stays tense:
  1. Make key facts more concrete.
     a) Show the places or people involved.
     b) Use a calendar to make time real.
  2. Deemphasize facts; emphasize adult responsibility and hopes.
- Ask "dumb" questions; make child the expert.

REASSURANCE ABOUT THE PAST (SEE EASING THE GUILT, page 269):

- Make Bald Statements proclaiming love and hope.
- Tell stories about wonderful acts in the past.
- Emphasize no-effort ways a child makes present better.

REASSURANCE ABOUT THE PRESENT (SEE MAGIC
MEASURES, page 271):

- Make a "worry" list or an "I hate it" list.
- Mark off calendar days.
- Read fairy tales.
- Tell past tales of a child's heroic moments.
- Give a child's current struggles heroic labels.

Worksheet for Feelings

Have you tried full-attention listening? _____ pure sympathy? _____ food? _____ doing something to cheer
yourself up? _____ Were you able to try these long
enough to feel there was a chance of success? _____ If
not, when could you grab the time you need? _____

How do teachers describe your child's mood at day care?

_____

_____

_____

What do teachers think
you could do to help? _____

_____

_____

they could do to help? _____

_____

_____

Do you think you need more information about
physical health? _____
the skills your child is working on? _____
developmental stages? _____
relationships at day care? _____
special events at day care? _____

(Just pick one or two for starters) How could you get the

information you need? _____

_____

_____

How are you feeling these days? _____

_____

_____

Do you think this affects your child's mood? _____ If so, how could you explain your mood to your child? _____

_____

_____

How could you give yourself a break? _____

_____

_____

What would you do differently if you knew that this mood would

go away completely next week? _____

_____

_____

last for the next six months? _____

_____

_____

8

Picking Up: Oh Mommy, One Last Book

"Mom Mom Mom Mom! Look what we're making!" Teddy calls to Amanda when she arrives to pick him up. Amanda smiles: It's nice to be noticed; he doesn't always. She comes over, ready to admire all the wonders of the "fort" they've built, which sprawls over the entire block corner. Teddy's teacher Henry appears and addresses the group of boys: "You guys have to clean up now. It's getting late, and Teddy has to go." A howl of protest; Henry is unmoved. "Come on," he says to Teddy, "you have to help before you go."

Amanda stacks the blocks and helps pack them away. It's not her idea of how to finish a long work day, but she tells Teddy, "Rules are rules." By the time they are finished, Teddy is blaming her for ruining the game and won't talk or look at her. It's going to be a rough ride home. Amanda catches Henry's eye on her way out. Raising a hand and an eyebrow, she asks for news. "He was fine," Henry says. "He had a good day."

WE WOULDN'T REALLY WANT our children to be sitting quietly, doing nothing, just waiting for us at the end of the day. It is good that they are still playing, or being read to, that teachers are still busy caring for them and keeping things organized. That means, however, that we are always walking into the middle of things when we come to pick children up. And in the middle of things, great greetings, abundant news, and easy exits are hard to come by. This chapter offers ideas to make leaving for the day and getting news easier.

Exit Scenes: Finding the Questions

Movie Script 1: Parent and child run toward each other, arms outstretched, through a field of flowers. As the orchestra swells to a crescendo, they meet and embrace, twirling around. Beaming, parent sets child down in tall grass; holding hands, they stroll off together into the setting sun.

Movie Script 2: Parent arrives and threads way through many day-care children to greet child: "Hey!" Gets ignored. Parent gathers belongings, asks, "Ready to go?" Gets ignored. Parent talks to teacher for a while, approaches child in pleading tones: "Come on, honey—time to go!" Gets ignored. Parent hangs around watching other children; tells child firmly, "It's time to go *now.*" Threatening to leave without child, parent heads for door. Child races to parent, whines for special food or clothing favor. Arguing, parent and child head out the door.

The Music Young children draw deep feelings from parents. The first moment of seeing a child after a day apart really should have an orchestral backup—or a brass band: "Ta-da! Here you are! Here I am!" But here you both are, in public, with noisy play for backup. And most children use script 2.

Every child begins a dance when a parent arrives, but each plays private music. The importance of a parent's arrival shows: Some children look down and away as though overwhelmed, full of sudden shyness; in some, the excitement inspires a wild running around, or a spurt of talk and orders: "Watch this!" Little children may laugh and run away; older children brazen it out, too cool, suddenly very busy, hard to interrupt.

Parents interpret these reactions in many ways: "She wants to stay." "This is crazy! She made a big fuss when I left this morning, and now she doesn't want to leave." "I guess he's mad at me for leaving, now he's gertting back at me—it's *my* turn to wait for *him*." It's difficult to know what goes on in those new minds, but their behavior seems to say this at least: This is an awkward social situation for them. It may help to imagine an adult parallel: You are on your own at a gathering of personal friends. Your partner, who knows these people only slightly, has just arrived to pick you up. Your partner appears at your elbow; what do you do? If you were having a terrible time, you might greet the sudden appearance with relief and an instant readiness to leave. If you've been enjoying yourself . . . ? You can see your child's reluctance to leave as a positive sign: It was a good party.

The Stars What is it that children want at pickup time? Do they really want to stay? For some children, the instant answer would be yes—*with* their parents. Once parents have arrived at day care, they finally have everything they like all together in one space: Mom or Dad and all their other friends. They want to show things to parents and play there together. Other children just want a chance to stay and finish whatever they're in the middle of—the picture, the puzzle, the game. They may panic irritably: "No! I'm not done!" Some children want *time:* a few minutes to reorient themselves, to get used to the idea of changing places. They may wander around, start playing with something entirely new. None of this means they aren't glad to see parents again.

Truly satisfying, "thrilled-to-see you" greetings are rare, but certainly some reunions are more relaxed than others. How do you get one of those? Some of it's luck. Some children find changes of scene relatively easy; their parents know that getting out won't be too hard or take too long; the family schedule permits whatever time is needed; the teachers don't mind a certain amount of disorganized hanging around at the end of the day: Everybody can stay relaxed. If you are missing some of this luck and find the end-of-day scene tense, you may want to organize the end of the day more self-consciously.

The Sequence A very small amount of organization may make a difference. One mother who always gave her child time to finish up whatever he was doing was still regularly greeted with "No! Wait! I'm not done!" She began reassuring him immediately on her arrival, getting the words out quickly "Hi-honey-I'm-here-you-can-have-five-more-minutes- to- play." A week or so of this routine finally broke down the automatic panic. A father whose daughter completely ignored his first greeting usually stayed a moment, then left the room to gather up her things from the hall cubbies; she regularly ran after him in tears but then still refused to leave. He tried gathering her things together before he said hello and sitting down next to her until the last minute; reunions became much more relaxed.

Some reunions go well until the last minute. You've gathered the stuff, talked with teachers, allowed your child some finishing-up time, and still your child refuses to go. Now what?

The Critics Most parents have developed ways of extracting their children from parks, toy stores, and friends' playrooms, but they just don't feel *free* to do at day care what they'd do anywhere else. Some parents feel that day care really belongs to teachers and children, and they don't want to be bad guests. They dread making a scene in front of teachers. Parents who would ordinarily just pick up a protesting child and leave a park, howls or no howls, are too embarrassed to do this at day care. Parents who would ordinarily wait out their children's protests, ignoring disapproving looks from righteous strangers, may feel more pressure at day care. What will the teacher think?

If dread of teachers' judgments adds tension to your exit, consider bringing it up for discussion. One parent who felt helpless and ineffective found out that teachers saw her as patient, gentle, and understanding. Another helpless-feeling parent discovered that teachers approved of lifting children up and carrying them out when needed; just knowing she had that backup changed the whole tone of departure. If you are comfortable but think teachers aren't, you can make that clear: "I don't mind our usual scenes when I come, but I worry that you do." If they are comfortable, you can relax more; if they are not, you might find a compromise. Teachers might feel more relaxed if your fuss happened in the hall instead of the room, or at 5:30 instead of 5:45. Either way you can clear the air and make things better. Teachers appreciate being asked.

The Directors Ask yourself, Am *I* comfortable with the end-of-day scene? Children often pick up and act out adult tensions. Anything you can do to make yourself more comfortable should relax your child as well. You may have ideas about ways your teacher could help, like reminding your child shortly before you usually come, or planning a quieter activity at pickup time, or coralling your child for you. You might raise the issue by describing how you feel: "I feel like an idiot at pickup time—I can't get her to do anything!" Or you could describe what you want: "I wish there was a way to get out of here faster, without fighting." You could ask, "How could we make pickup time easier?" to make room for ideas you haven't thought of, or have forgotten.

Don't be embarrassed to bring up end-of-day scenes. The end of the day-care day *is* a murky time between worlds, confusing for adults as well as for children. Finding ways to help children detach all their energies from day care and point them home is neither a trivial nor an obvious task.

Your comfort counts. You must be the bridge between worlds again, the captain for this New York–Paris flight, the director for this film; you should have everything you need.

Exit Scenes: Developmental Issues

INFANTS

Pickup time used to be easy. June would arrive and give Millie a big hello kiss; she chatted about the day with the teacher Martha while she collected the bottles, clothes, food containers. Millie played on the floor happily or watched her, smiling and cooing.

Now Millie grabs for her when she bends down for the hello kiss. If June tries to put Millie down, she cries; Millie cries even if Martha holds her while June gets things ready. Collecting things has turned into mad dashing around with no talk while Millie cries, reaching for her, the whole time. What happened?

Before infants develop the ability to use adult activities as cues, they can be very relaxed about comings and goings. Young infants live in a very immediate world. You disappear? Well, if the service is good where they are, it's okay. You reappear? Great! What a nice surprise! They don't react to the sight of coats or baby bags; they don't see the significance. But older infants do.

When older infants see parents collecting things at day care at the end of the day, they may panic: Are you leaving? In the morning, your baby sees you putting your hands in and out of bags, bins, and refrigerators in the room—and then you leave for the day. When you get busy with bags, bins, and the fridge at pickup time, they can't believe it: You're going to work again? You just got here! They cannot tell time; this visual cue is confusing.

You may see this same predicting power at home in feeding situations. During this phase, infants act *more* desperately hungry once you put on a bib or start mixing the cereal. Your activities signal food; seeing you, they know: Food—yes, that's what I want, and *now!*

In some infants, this phase is very short and mild. If your infant has the longer, more intense version, you may want to spare everyone grief by collecting things another way. You might:

AVOID PACKING-UP PANIC BY

- Asking teachers to gather your baby's belongings for you while you concentrate on hello, or to collect things before you come.
- Looking around the room (with teachers and other parents) to see if cubbies, bins, refrigerators, etc., could be relocated in an out-of-sight space.
- Asking teachers if infants could play in another space at pickup time—the toddler room, a gym space, the nap room?

If none of these ways of collecting things out of sight proves possible, you may be best off with the old standby: holding your baby the whole time, *while* you collect. Parenthood builds many special strengths; the ability to do almost anything with only one hand is one of them. It's a pain, but it's better than the panics, and this phase doesn't last forever.

TODDLERS

Susan wants Howie to get off the trike, say good-bye to the teacher, leave the room, get his coat, put it on, walk down the hall to the front door, cross the parking lot, and get into his car seat. A train of thought, a chain of events, linking present and future. Howie, well, Howie loves the trike: "Watch me!" After Susan's third plea, he gets off and approaches his teacher. Does he say good-bye? He says, "I hurt my finger! See?" Proudly, he shows off a two-day-old Band-Aid. Susan says good-bye for Howie, and leads him into the hall, where he bolts for the older preschool room. She recaptures him and walks him to his cubby. While she puts his coat on, Howie removes objects from a nearby shelf for comment and admiration. After one traditional drink at the hall water fountain and a few other unscheduled stops, Howie and Susan make it to the parking lot. It has great gravel. Howie tries a squishy step, a clattery kick, a dragging slide on the gravel; he shares the wonder of a single piece with Susan: "Look!" No train of thought, no chain of events for Howie. Just lots of interesting life and one frustrated parent.

Toddlers tend to see the world in unconnected snap-shots, and to be filled to the brim with the immediate moment. When parents' goals—like getting home—require them to ignore the present, it goes against the grain. You can make it easier by working with this snapshot view. Pick a picture of one step on the way out that your child likes and use the vision to lure your traveler that far: "Let's get a drink at the water fountain." With older toddlers and pre-schoolers, one picture might get you most of the way out; if Howie were old enough, Susan might use "Let's go to the parking lot and find some gravel" to get most of the way out. Food treats or special music "waiting for you in the car" work this way. For younger toddlers, shorter steps, offered one at a time, work better: "Let's show the teacher your finger." "Let's go see what's on the shelf." "Let's get a drink at the fountain." One father said, "If I could leave a little trail of raisins down the hall, we'd be out of here in no time!" The basic trick is right; just think of other short steps to replace those raisins.

Older toddlers can pretend. Pretend worlds have the great advantage of being *movable*—you can use them to distract your child from immediate delights while you make progress out the door. If your toddler is playing kitty or truck driver, you might have to invent imaginary cat food in the cubby or gassing-up at the drinking fountain to keep things going—all at a time of day when you're not feeling especially creative—but once you dream up something that works, you can use it over and over again.

Toddlers' sensitivity to control issues may rear up fiercely at pickup time. Parents' arrival at the end of the day is almost always sudden and unexpected from a toddler's point of view, and usually signals a big chunk of no-choice time coming up: They have to leave, have to put on outside clothes, have to get strapped in the car. They may throw themselves on the floor in protest. Perhaps they are also protesting the whole thing: You get to come and go when you want to; they don't. Some toddlers react to the shift from teacher-in-charge to parent-in-charge as well: The minute a parent shows up, they try something teachers would not allow—standing on a table, poking another child, eating a cracker on the rug.

Sometimes just sitting with your child awhile before you start a leaving routine helps things stay relaxed. It's as though parents are natural magnets and toddler energies are iron filings spread out over many people, spaces, and things at day care. While you sit there, the energies gather together slowly into a compact, movable form—it just takes time.

Parents sometimes take the edge off that bossed-around feeling by offering simple choices or finding ways to let the toddler be in charge of leaving; "Let's see . . . we need some things! You want to get your lunchbox or your coat?" "Want to open the door for me?" "Shall we go out the front door or the back?" "You can walk or I can carry you; what would you like?" Special objects or routines work well for some toddlers: "Let's go get your bear and your home blanket." "We'll say good-bye to Nancy and blow a kiss to the fish." Older toddlers revere routine and doing things "just so"; for some reason it's all right to let a routine be the boss.

Tired, upset toddlers get beyond the reach of words at times. Sometimes there is little to do but shoulder your bags and your baby, go home, and start being together freshly there. A confident, firm carrying out ultimately sends a comforting message: What must happen will happen, because I can take care of it. You can relax.

TODDLER TAKE-HOME TIME AND SPACE

You can work with your toddler's time sense:

- Give more time to get used to the idea of going home; play with your child at day care for a while, or allow independent play while you talk with teachers and other parents.
- Give clear time limits to the leaving process: "You can have two more minutes to play, then we have to go."
- Give a snapshot of the next step on the way out: "Let's get your cars from your cubby." "Let's go peek over the gate."
- Allow less time for the leaving process so it is short enough and regular enough to form a pattern in your child's mind.

You can also work with your toddler's "I need space," bossed-around feelings by offering choices and sympathy:

- Invite your toddler to "take charge" by helping with packing up or choosing an exit route.
- Define a few choices: "Want to wave good-bye or just go?" "Should we *sneak* out or skip?"
- Wait out protest calmly, or shoulder your child and leave with: "You're mad, I know; I'm sorry, we have to go."

You might ask your teachers what they think would help, too. They may have some good ideas they aren't offering for fear of sounding critical. Teachers have smoothed exits by arranging a quieter activity for a child at the end of the day, reminding a child that a parent is coming ten minutes beforehand, or singing special good-bye songs. Teachers see the whole pattern of pickup time. They know whether your coming ten minutes earlier or later would make a difference; they know which tricks for transitions work best with your child during the day. Most teachers are relieved to be able to help with sticky good-byes; they want to send you both home smiling.

PRESCHOOLERS

"Mom, wait! I have to finish this picture—it's for Dad." Naomi and Louisa usually pick him up on their way home; Louisa won't have another chance to finish her picture, it's true—"Okay, a few minutes." Naomi chats with a teacher a while and collects Louisa's coat. "Sweetheart, that's fine now, just the way it is. He'll love it. Let's go." Louisa protests, "But you haven't read me a story yet!" Reading one book before they go is an old routine from toddler days; Naomi knows it's important to foster a love for books—"Okay." Louisa jumps up. "I want to read *The Tough Princess*! We just got it!" They search for the book, finally finding it in another child's hands. "Looks like Marissa's using it, honey. Let's go now. We can read it tomorrow." "No! Wait! I need to fix my shoes." Louisa drops to the floor and slowly, carefully takes apart and rethreads and readjusts the straps on her red leather buckle shoes. By the time she has finished, the book is free. "Look, Mom! Now we can read!" The note of surprise in Louisa's voice gets a small smile from Naomi. "O-kay," she says, but when she opens the book—"Louisa! This book is twenty pages long *with* little letters! Dad is waiting! We can't read this!" And Louisa says, "But *you promised!*"

Wonderfully verbal, creative, independent, logical preschoolers sometimes bring all these talents to making departures impossible. They hate to leave a good party; they hate being bossed around; they want everything to be "fair." Parents try to understand and to be fair. They want to be civilized about departures, and preschoolers are getting a bit big to be tossed over a shoulder and carted off. Letting preschoolers make *some* decisions about when and how they leave usually helps, but you often have to say "No Deal" at some point; children this age are so interested in negotiations, they can keep you at it forever.

Fortunately, many other special interests can come to your aid at pickup time. Prechoolers like to do things with friends, to listen to and tell stories, to make plans and solve problems; they love Being Big and Best; they appreciate praise. If your preschooler makes leaving more difficult than you'd like, you might try:

THE BIG FINISH

- Leave with friends: "Reggie and Marla are ready to go; let's walk out with them."
- Plan something to do together on the way out: a parent-child race down a safe stretch of hall (parent loses by a hair every time).
- Tell a story together, well-known or invented: "Let's see, Dorothy was just coming to the forest . . ."
- Bring up "How to Leave the Center" at home; make a plan with your child: "What do you think would make it easier to leave when I come? . . . What could we do? (Be prepared for a few wild suggestions at the beginning of the talk.)
- Invite your child to take a Big Helper role: carry a room trash bag or your briefcase out of the building.
- Praise any part of the leaving process that works well: "Yesterday you flipped your coat on like a champ . . . would you show me that again?"

Time tactics are still important at this age; with preschoolers you can use larger sections of time:

- Allow a ten-minute finish: "You can have ten minutes to finish up what you're doing, but *then* we have to go home."

- Offer something to look forward to in the near future: "Let's go see the big building trucks on the corner."

Children of every age can be confused about the end of the day. What are parents doing? What are *they* supposed to be doing? Who decides what happens next? Parents don't always feel completely clear about all that themselves. Many end-of-day reunions are disorganized and a little crabby. As long as you don't really mind it, your child is probably fine, too. If the scene is getting to you, though, you might take a little time when your brain is fresher—a weekend morning?—to look at what usually happens. Or make a date for a short talk or phone call with your teacher. The energy you spend deciding on something new to try may be returned to you a hundred times over in sweeter reunions.

Exit Scenes: Parent-Teacher Talk

Jim finds Beth's shoes lined up neatly in her cubby—she must be playing dress-up with the famous silver heels again. Only one shoe has a sock tucked in the top—a bad sign. This has happened before, and usually means the other sock is gone for good. He checks their extra clothes bag—no socks. Will Beth put her shoes on without two matching socks? No way. Jim thinks, Terrific. I'm beat, we have to hit the grocery store before we can eat, and now I have to search this place for a sock! If keeping track of the *clothing* around here is too hard for these guys, what's easy? He walks over to Beth's teacher George and shows him the half-empty shoes in silence.

George thinks, Give me a break! Don't tell me you never lose a sock at home, and we've got *sixteen* children to dress here! I don't know where the stupid sock is. Do you want a teacher or a maid? George doesn't say any of this out loud either. He starts pawing roughly through the dress-up clothes, sort of looking for the sock.

> Beth thinks, Here's Daddy! My king! My horse! Come
> see your stunning and beautiful Silver Heels Princess! She
> waits for his notice. The king says, "Where did you put your
> other sock?" Beth kicks off the shoes and runs out of the
> room.

Sometimes *adults* make the scenes at the end of the day.
When tired parents arrive to dirty laundry, missing essentials, and sticky children—and find teachers indifferent to
these troubles—it's too much. When tired teachers scrape
up their last ounces of patience and talent to keep a group
of frazzled-but-still-energetic children on an even keel—and
find parents frantic about a stray sock—it's too much. Children's own end-of-day needs get lost in the shuffle.

But what can you do? Parents and teachers must provide
for the life support, the mental and emotional guidance, and
the passing on of civilization to young spirits; they must also
keep track of the baa-baas, binkies, bears, blankets, and
socks. That's life. The "Things to Try" section lists ways to
tackle the practical side of belongings problems.

Belongings problems, and all the daily specifics of life
with children, have another side—their power to poison morale between parents and teachers. Morale in a marriage
may falter over the cap on the toothpaste, the mail on the
kitchen table, or the hair in the bathroom sink when these
things come to stand for a Generally Uncaring Attitude.
Teachers and parents can reach this same point.

A cartoon shows a marriage counselor's door with this
sign:

OUT TO LUNCH

Listen to each other.
Plan some fun.
Try a little tenderness.

If the end-of-day time feels tense with teachers, you might try day-care versions of these. Parents and teachers have so many common experiences, it's easy for them to *expect* each other to understand their separate points of view without much talk or listening. Teachers think we must know what it's like to guide sixteen three-year-olds through clothes-on-clothes-off changes for dress-up, yard play, bathroom, and nap; we think teachers must know what it's like to ride home with a child who can't stop feeling awful about a lost bear or sock. It's just not always true. Giving and getting a more vivid picture of how the other half lives helps patience all around. When their heads are still buzzing with work but turning toward home chores, parents can fall into fast, all-business talk, too short on friendliness, even politeness.

OUT TO LUNCH

- *Listening to each other.* You might try asking your teacher:
  1. About the day in general before bringing up practical problems. Feeling recognized as a teacher *first* makes helping with the "maid" part of child care simpler.
  2. For the inside view of the practical problem: "I can't imagine what it's like to keep track of so many different children's things all day . . . how do you manage it usually?" "What usually happens at lunchtime? How can you keep track of what children are eating?"
  3. To listen to your point of view: "I know it's hard to keep track of everything, but when I come and can't find his hat, it means . . ."
- *Plan a little fun.* Try including some good news in your end-of-day talks:
  1. A story about something fabulous, adorable, or goofy your child has said or done at home.
  2. A comment on something you like about the teacher or group.
  3. Neighbor-style comment on the world outside day care you share as adults—weather, basketball, the day's headlines.

- *Try a little tenderness.* If the intensity and busyness of your life tend to rob your speech of gentle phrasing, try to replace it—it makes a difference. Check for "Where's her sock?" versus "Could you help me find . . ."; "Would you mind . . ."; "I know you try, but . . ."; or "Help! Please!"

Exit Scenes: Things to Try

IN GENERAL:

You might think of the things you usually have to do at pickup time and look for the simplest order. For instance:

- Collect belongings *first*.
- Say hi to your child and give a few minutes' "warning."
- Talk with teachers and relax awhile.
- Call "Time!" and go.

An alternative would be:

- Talk to teachers first.
- Sit and play with your child.
- Let child help you pack up.
- Go.

INFANTS

AVOIDING PACKING-UP PANIC (page 285)
If your infant seems to panic when you arrive, you can:

- Join your infant on the floor or hold your baby right away, talking with teachers and packing while you hold your child or asking them for help with belongings.
- Work with teachers to change storage for belongings to an out-of-sight place.
- Ask teachers if infants could play out of the room at pickup time.
- Hold your child while you gather things.

TODDLERS

WORKING WITH TODDLER TAKE-HOME TIME AND
SPACE (page 288):

- Guide your toddler through changes of scene by giving your
  child a "snapshot" of the next place you need to get to on
  the way out.
- Use pretend play to occupy your child's mind on the way
  past all the chances to dawdle.
- Build up a leaving routine for everyday use.
- Plan an emergency backup: "You can walk or I can carry you."
  If no decision is given, then: "I'll have to carry you today."

PRESCHOOLERS

THE BIG FINISH (page 290)
You could:

- Plan a joint activity on the way out, a walking race down
  a safe stretch of sidewalk, a story to remember or invent:
  "Yesterday, the space invaders landed . . ."
- Invite your child to take a Big Helper role on the way out,
  like carrying out a room trash bag, or your work bag or keys.
- Praise any part of leaving that goes well: "You give your
  teacher the greatest good-byes!" "You're a Super-Duper Coat-
  Flipper." "I think you know exactly how to find the bus now."
- Declare a ten-minute finish: "I can stay for ten minutes, but
  then we have to go."
- Use something to look forward to as a magnetic pullout:
  "Let's go see the big building trucks on the corner." "I have
  a bag of chips waiting for you." "Would you like to see if you
  can unlock the car with my keys again?"

You might ask teachers to:

- Use a predictable order of activities at the end of the day. If
  your child has cleanup, then music, then storytime every day

right before you come, it should be easier to get set for you.

- Remind your child, "Your mom/dad usually comes about five minutes from now."
- Plan end-of-day activities that are easy to interrupt and don't involve big cleanup problems.
- Help develop leaving routines, like singing a good-bye song, coming to the door and hugging the children good-bye, keeping a supply of *short* books for parents to read to children as a "last thing."
- Bring your child out of group for you so you don't have to be the villain-interrupter.

BELONGINGS PROBLEMS: ALL AGES

Teachers could:

- Use belongings bins wherever things tend to get lost—by the changing table, in the nap room, in the yard.
- Arrange easy collection *times*. Teachers might gather all shoes before nap, all bottles before yard play.
- Divide children into small groups for dressing sessions.
- Schedule at least one teacher room-lookover for stray items when children are out of the room or gathered in one part of the room for a story.
- Build a central supply of bottle caps, socks, pants, etc., for emergencies from lost items and donations.
- Design rules to cut down on belongings problems:

  Infants: Physical "rules": pacifiers on short strings tied to shoulder straps, or using hard-to-remove socks and shoes for busy times. (Pulling off socks and flinging them across rooms is a fundamental infant joy; *sometimes* you want easy-off socks.)
  Toddlers: Rules about *when* and *where* clothes can come off or cuddlies cuddled or bottles drunk.
  Preschoolers: Dress-up rule—put your own clothes in cubby first.

Parents could:

- Buy at least two of every essential blanket, bear, doll, and keep scads of extra socks, etc., at center.

- Keep irreplaceable objects at home, in the car, or with your work things; make rules about what comes to day care that reflect the risks of destruction and loss.
- Initial clothing tags and every item that goes to day care with permanent markers.
- Enlist your child's help finding things at day care. A team spirit may unveil good information or just ease the pain.

Not all parents feel the need to change an end-of-day fuss. A parent once said, "Really, I don't mind it. The morning *has* to operate on adult time; I like to let the afternoon operate on child time. It helps to blow off steam a little before the trek home." If you do mind your exit scene, let your teacher know. Daily things wear us down more than anything else. Your child will benefit, too. Just because children seem unable to stop themselves from being irritable or uncooperative doesn't mean they like it. If you can turn things around, your child will be relieved as well.

Getting the News: Finding the Questions

Parent to director: "I'm not getting anything from them! I come to pick Evan up, I haven't seen him for eight hours, and they tell me 'He was fine.' That's *not* enough. Is there some big problem they don't want to talk to me about? Do they have a problem with *me*? Or aren't they paying attention?"

Teacher to director: "But I don't know what to say! How was his day? Well, he played for a while and then got in a fight and was mad, but they made up and we ate snack and he was happy again. He played, he got tired and cranky, but then he was fine after nap. So: He was fine and mad and happy and tired and fine—he just had a day!"

Videotapes For a variety of reasons, many teachers do not give parents really satisfying news of a child's play. Some parents don't mind this too much; they have to hurry, things seem fine, they trust teachers to call attention to anything new and important. Many parents find short or casual news distressing: A whole day's worth of their child's life has gone by, they missed it, they want to *know* about it. Videotapes would be perfect. They understand that teachers cannot describe every single moment, but "she had a good day" does not even feel like news. Very brief news leaves some parents feeling not only deprived but worried: Is my child lost in the shuffle? Doesn't anyone *notice* what happens?

Rewind Good reports to parents require real skill. Teachers must flip back in memory through hours of time with many children who have been in every conceivable mood, for every possible reason, doing and saying something different every two minutes. Finding something *clear* to say about all this life—separately and sensitively for each child's parents—is a power that's not always there at the end of the day. If you ask "How was the day?" and teachers stand mute for a minute or talk in generalities, they may be rewinding the day just this way.

Editing With so much life to sort through, the main problem is editing. Very short or vague news often reflects a teacher's despair: too much to tell, no place to start, nothing sticks out. Parents can help themselves get better news by helping teachers with the editing job. One parent struggling with bare news explained: "Look—all I really need is *one word*—'puzzles,' 'football,' 'painting'—anything!—just something to start a conversation with on the way home." The teacher felt so liberated by this simple, doable task that she began to find many words to offer at pickup time.

Some parents set up the editing job by asking specific questions about their present concerns: "How did he do on the potty today?" or "What was the project this morning?"

Specific questions, regularly asked, help focus daytime attention as well as evening memory. A teacher once confessed, "Ruthie's mother used to drive me crazy. Every day she asked the same questions: 'How was lunch? How was nap? Whom did she play with? What did she do that she really enjoyed?' I thought, Sheesh! I can't remember all that stuff! But now I think she taught me how to be a good day-care parent for my own daughter. I knew she was going to ask me those questions every day; it made me pay more attention to that stuff. After a couple of weeks, I just always *knew* what Ruthie did, without even trying. She trained me!"

If the news you get doesn't satisfy you, you might ask yourself, "What do I really want to know about?" Try to get past "Everything!" as an answer and pick one or two things for special focus. If you can cut down the editing task a little, your teacher may discover a whole new way of talking with you.

The Film Crew Some parents hate the idea and the job of asking specific questions: "I don't want to come in and give a pop quiz every day. I'd feel like a pest—and besides, *you're* the experts. I want *you* to tell *me* what I ought to know. I don't know all the right questions to ask." This kind of conversation has helped parents get better news, too. Some teachers assume they should just answer questions; if parents want to know, they'll ask. Teachers can take a more active role if parents let them know: "Just tell me what you think we should know." "If I could get one good story every day, about anything—you pick!—I'd be happy."

The Ratings The tone of your news may bother you more than its quantity. Consistently good news is not automatically reassuring. Parents know their children: Whole days contain some trouble. When teachers fail to mention anything negative, they wonder: Are teachers hiding something? or—horrible thought—is my child perfect at day care? Are teachers so skillful they actually don't have any trouble? Some parents joke, "Okay, so what did he do wrong today?" Others are more direct: "I'm glad if things are going well, but I wish you'd tell me some bad news every now and then—I'd feel more in touch."

Consistently bad news is not automatically cause for worry. Sometimes teachers unload frustrations without thinking about the picture this creates. Naptime troubles, tantrums, fighting and biting, "not listening" to teachers—all the ordinary daily struggles take a toll; your child's part of them may come pouring out of a tired teacher day after day without really representing the teacher's true view about your child. Brave parents have checked their impressions with "Do you still like my kid?" or "Didn't anything good happen today?" Shocked teachers replied, "But I *love* your kid!" "Actually, we had a *great* day!" You should feel free to ask for good news if you're not getting enough. Teachers might be just editing out what's going right when you could be enjoying it, or they may have lost some perspective—and your request can help restore it.

Consistently bad news may mean that teachers are stuck: They haven't quite decided to call for your help directly, but they have run out of ideas or patience. It's frustrating for parents: "If this is a real problem, let's sit down and solve it; if it's not a real problem, let's talk about something else!" Many teachers hesitate to ask parents for problem-solving time, for the same reasons parents often wait to ask for teachers' help—everyone's busy; it's not always clear what the problem is; maybe it's all their fault anyway, and that will be embarrassing; can anyone outside the situation really have good ideas about how to handle it? When parents have volunteered problem-solving time—"Should we schedule a conference about this?"—they help teachers decide. Sometimes the answer has been a relieved "Yes!" and sometimes a surprised "Oh, no!"; either way the daily news improves.

Split Screen Practical problems interfere with both quantity and quality in teachers' news-giving. If teachers are trying to supervise children, tidy up the room, and talk to several parents at once, if parents, too, are juggling multiple tasks—collecting things, talking to children—then the whole exchange can get lost in the shuffle. If many parents arrive at once, if teachers schedule group singing or reading for the end of the day, parents may end up feeling like part of the shuffle and that teachers don't care about talking with them at all.

Usually, this is not true. Given half a chance, most teachers enjoy telling stories and having the feeling of working *with* parents. It's just that no one has made news-giving a priority and figured out ways around the practical problems.

On an individual basis, parents can sometimes arrange a better climate for news by arriving earlier or later. More general solutions may be needed: scheduling a second teacher to stay late so one is free to talk, paying for cleaning time *after* children have left, reorganizing the type of activities planned for pickup time so adults can talk around them more easily.

Improving the end-of-day news may take some work, and time to think and talk, and courage to bring up the issues. Parents and teachers who work on end-of-day news habits usually report a big payoff: They feel more relaxed, more connected to the children's lives and to each other; difficulties get better attention; everybody hears more good stories; everyone laughs more. That is not only nice for the grownups, but nourishing for children. Seeing their team of experts talk happily together knits up their worlds more cozily.

Getting the News: Developmental Issues

INFANTS

Six-month-old Ariel is fussing steadily in her car seat. Jack steers with one hand while he digs out a pacifier for her. She spits it out; he can't reach it without risking a wreck. It's probably not the answer anyway! he thinks. What's up? Is she just tired? Hungry? Damn! He forgot to ask the teacher about her last feeding time, and about naps—and the teacher forgot to say. He doesn't want to pull over and feed her if she's only restless or a *little* hungry, but he doesn't want to starve the lady either!

Infants depend on their grown-ups to keep them from real hunger or exhaustion and to help them get a bit organized about food and sleep. This usually means we have to keep an eye on a lot of intimate details—feeding ounces, sleep minutes, diaper contents—all kinds of things we've never spent much mental energy on before. Teachers with several babies' details to keep track of can forget quite easily, too. If your teachers don't write the details down, you might suggest it. Sleep and/or food news can be written right on an attendance sheet or a sheet of paper taped to the wall, right as it happens: no memory work. If parents form the habit of checking the written news, information flows, and they can spend talking time on other matters.

In a rush at the end of the day, some parents (and teachers) zero in on body details exclusively: When did she sleep? How did he eat?—and miss everything else. Infants also need teachers' talk, their offering of interesting toys, their willingness to play baby games. Talking about these things with teachers gives an important message: You value this work. Parents often get this talk going by saying what they see at home at playtimes: "I think she's holding things much better now." "He does this fake cough now when he wants to play." "I've noticed she really likes silky things." Some parents just ask, "How was his playtime today?" or "What toys does she like here?—I'd like to get some more for home."

The end of the day offers another way of getting news: watching. When parents don't have to beat the clock to work, they can sometimes sit down and see for themselves. You have to take some tiredness all around into account, but seeing for yourself how teachers work with infants, how comfortable your infants and other infants look, may provide the best news of all.

WAYS TO GET NEWS OF THE NONVERBAL

- Read notes for sleep or food details.
- Talk with teachers about playtime.
- Watch teachers and infants.

TODDLERS

Daily Report for Toddler Tina: Tina was

Delighted With	*Furious About*	*Worried By*
• own shirt	• Penny standing in front of her	• paint on fingers
• dumping out a whole box of blocks	• having to clean up	• Danny pushing John
• long turn with the beaded black bag	• diaper changing	• vacuum-cleaner noise next door
• snack	• tuna at lunch	• peanut butter on fingers
• *Tommy Goes to the Doctor* book	• waiting for a turn with play phone	• Lisa going on break
• falling-down game	• Mark knocking over her tower	• missing button on her overall strap
• pretending to cook	• not singing ABC first this time	• getting splashed at water table
• jumping up and down		• ants outside
• ants outside		

Toddler days almost defy summary. Toddlers seem to do more things per minute, and to feel more passionately about them, than any other age group. What part of all this should teachers report or parents ask about—what they did, what they felt, what they ate?

In most cases, toddlers don't need adults to talk about food and sleep. They eat and sleep on a group schedule;

they have been introduced to all the food groups, have most of their teeth, walk, talk; they are, biologically, mostly out of the woods. With this freedom, and such a variety of life to choose from, parents can be a little more selfish about the news: What would help *you* through the evening, the weekend?

For some parents, the answer is good news: "What a day! Please tell me something nice he did, something he loved. . . ." Any Basic Toddler has eating and sleeping off-days—teething, fighting, biting, stealing, pushing, and tantrums—to contend with as it grows up. The drama of these events may crowd out the good news. Let your teacher know when you'd especially like to hear about the happier side of life. This is *not* entirely selfish: Toddlers need parent patience, and good news can give it a boost.

Getting help from the news means getting ideas for some parents: "I can never get her to nap on the weekends—how do you do it?" or "If we invite a friend over on the weekend, he has fits when the other child tries to play with his toys—how do you get them to share here?" or "He's still not talking very much. Do you think we should be worried?"

For some parents, the best help would be help understanding the age. They mastered infancy, and they expect to understand what's going on when their toddler finally turns into "a real kid" somewhere around three years old. But toddlerhood makes no sense to them; they feel like saying "Why are you doing that!" a thousand times a day. End-of-day news time offers some special opportunities to answer some of those whys. When teachers tell stories about their children, parents can follow through: "Now why would she do that? Where does *that* come from?" or watch the whole group and talk with teachers about what they see. Watching by itself can at least add the relief of "It's a phase" to your private questions.

Toddler teachers sometimes report mainly the group news: "We did painting today." "We had the water table out." "We went to the park." Some parents like this kind of news best: It reassures them that teachers are providing interesting activities, and it gives them something to talk with their child about on the way home. Other parents don't like it; they don't care what the group did. If you need a more individual report, you can follow group news with specific questions: "And did she like it?" "What did he do there?"

NEWS OF TOO-BUSY TODDLERS

You can help teachers select news and use the time in ways that help you by asking for:

- Upbeat stories
- Ideas about trouble spots
- Interpretations of mysterious actions and attitudes
- Clearer pictures of your own child's ways in the group

PRESCHOOLERS

Willie and Ken returned from a weeklong camping trip with their two dads in good spirits. Both families and teachers had been a little nervous: How would the boys handle a whole week away from their mothers? Fathers reported a fabulous time: campfires and marshmallow roasts, fishing—with success!—a trip to a cave for which the boys got to wear child-sized miner hats with real lights on them. When a teacher asked Ken, "How was your trip?" he said, "You know what happened?! Willie and me both got ice-cream cones, and the top of Willie's fell off!" End of trip report.

The language and memory achievements of preschoolers mean that children can at last give parents some news of the day on their own. Preschoolers do not, however, summarize, categorize, and evaluate a day the way adults would. Their headlines are unpredictable. You may hear in mind-numbing detail about one turn with a necklace, one worm on the ground, one ice-cream scoop; or your child may hit you with a question about death, sex, war, marriage, physics, friendship, biology, world hunger: "Are you going to die?" "Do you love Daddy more than me?" "Where does food go?" When preschoolers scoop into their minds' oceans for things to talk about, you never know what will come up in the net.

Preschoolers' parents often use end-of-day time to decode *yesterday*'s news: "Maria said Harold hit her," "José says he never gets a turn to do calendar." The teacher you talk to may not recall or may never have seen a particular incident, but should be able to give some relevant information from the adult view: What sort of relationship Maria and Harold have, how they usually treat each other; what the rules for calendar turns are, when José can next expect one.

In comparison to preschoolers, toddlers are incredibly well rounded and flexible about activities: They'll try anything; they go along with the group and find some way of enjoying the materials and projects offered. Three- and four-year-olds often specialize: They become fanatics for dress-up or Legos or dinosaurs or drawing and lose interest in—even actively avoid—many other activities. In programs that allow a lot of free choice, end-of-day activity news may get a little monotonous.

Some parents aren't bothered by monotonous play news. Thinking ahead to school days, these parents see day-care years as their children's last chance to do whatever they want during the day. If that means hours and hours of dress-ups or dinosaurs, so be it. Some parents become concerned: Are teachers really providing enough interesting things to do? Is my child afraid to try new things, or falling behind in some skills, missing out? Chapter 4 discusses this specialization and offers some ideas for working with teachers when you are concerned.

If your preschooler seems to be doing the same things every day and this concerns you, you might use news-getting time to get a more complete picture. You might ask more about your child's participation in the structured-in variety of the program: "What does she do at music time?" "Did he do the special project this morning?" "How does she use outdoor time?" Or you might ask teachers more about what happens inside your child's preferred activity. Does your child play alone or with other children? How does the play actually go?

Preschoolers can turn one simple-sounding basic play situation to many purposes: making friends, learning how to plan and organize dramatic scenes, learning how to explain ideas and negotiate through conflicts, exploring alliance and power in action and in imagination. Your teacher may not be able to describe the play in detail when you first ask (teachers watch play that is *not* working most closely), but could get back to you in a few days.

NEWS FOR THE PAST AND THE FUTURE

In addition to regular daily news, you might use news time for:

- Decoding your child's version of yesterday's news
- Getting a clearer picture of play variety:
  1. Outside his or her main interests
  2. Inside the favorite play situations

When you have any important issues to bring up with teachers at the end of the day, remember what big ears preschoolers have. Unless you want your child in on the discussion, seek some privacy in physical distance, written notes, or planned phone calls.

Getting the News: Parent-Teacher Talk

> Quickly stuffing Bobby's lunchbox, a muddy pair of socks, and today's pile of sticks, rocks, and little cars into her big canvas bag, Valerie slips past other parents chatting and finds Bobby. "Hi, sweetie, please get your coat right away. It's a zip-zoom day—we're late." Mercifully, Bobby's in a cooperative mood, and they're nearly out the door when Nell stops her: "He's been acting really tired all day today." Valerie shrugs. "He seemed fine this morning"—and hustles Bobby out to the hall.
>
> On a different day, Valerie would have thought no more about this. Children just have tired days from time to time; we all do. But tonight she tosses and turns: What did "acting tired" mean? Was he really tired, or bored? Or sad? Does Nell think they're sending him in sick? Maybe something is wrong. . . .
>
> On a different day, Nell wouldn't have thought twice about Valerie's remark. So Bobby didn't seem tired this morning—it's just information. But tonight she tosses and turns: "He was fine this morning" . . . hmmmm. Does Valerie think she's making this up, exaggerating? That only what she sees at home counts? Doesn't she care who he is during the day? Valerie's usually quite nice. Maybe something is wrong. . . .

Many end-of-day conversations have to be short, and short conversations can be very ambiguous. When a teacher says, "Johnny seemed a little tired today," a parent might hear: "What are you doing—keeping him up all night?" or "You sent your child in sick," or "He's depressed," or "Anything special going on? Any ideas why he would be tired?" When a parent says, "Last night Johnny said he was bored at day care," a teacher might hear: "What are you going to do about that?" or "You are a lazy slob who couldn't teach her way out of a paper bag" or "What should I say to him?" or "I'm worried about Johnny." When parents and teachers are feeling reasonably good about themselves and each other, they are free to choose the best interpretation from all the possibilities. At the very least, they can put the odd remark on hold until they can check it out the next day. When the sense of "We're all okay" goes missing for any reason, however, simple remarks may cause needless bad feelings.

Everything you do to make your relationships with teachers more comfortable helps prevent this kind of confusion; checking back the next day—"I wasn't sure what you meant yesterday . . ."—keeps discomfort short. Ideally, you can save even a night's worth of wondering by a quick, immediate check on meaning.

One way of checking quickly is to:

REPEAT THE MESSAGE

- *Word for word:* "He seemed tired?" and wait for a clearer description or an explanation, or
- *In the version of meaning that's bothering you:* "Did he just seem tired or do you think he might be getting sick?"

If a teacher reacts in a defensive or puzzled way to one of *your* comments, you can repeat your own message, giving a clearer idea of what you are looking for in an answer: "She said she was bored . . .

- . . . and I wondered what she really meant."
- . . . and so now I'm a little worried."

You may discover you'd like to have a longer conversation another day, and still go home mulling things over, but at least in the meantime everyone's thoughts can be headed in the most useful direction.

Getting the News: Things to Try

Parents can help teachers "edit" the whole day's worth of events by asking:

- For one activity word, one mood rating, one story—whatever counts most this week

- Specific questions: Nap? Potty? Food? Best fun? Worst moment?
- The same questions every day for weeks
- Teachers to take charge of figuring out what you need to know
- For more good news or more bad news when you need it
- If teachers want a conference for longer talk

Parents can work with teachers on practical problems that interfere with news time. Would it help to:

- Change the timing, come a little earlier or later?
- Change teachers' activities at the end of days so that:
  1. Both teachers are not reading or singing.
  2. Big cleanup jobs are mainly over.
  3. Children are doing things they could do independently.
- Pay one teacher to stay late to care for children while another gives the news of the day?
- Encourage a pre-parents quiet time for news-giving teacher to collect thoughts?
- Help parents know about easiest talking times. Can news-giving be spread out? Does everyone arrive at once? Would five minutes one way or the other make a difference?

INFANTS

WAYS TO GET NEWS OF THE NONVERBAL

- Create newsboards or keep notebooks for nitty-gritty details.
- Talk with teachers about *play*time.
- Watch teachers and infants.

TODDLERS

NEWS OF TOO-BUSY TODDLERS

Parents can ask for:

- Upbeat stories
- Ideas about trouble spots

- Interpretations of odd remarks by your child
- Clearer pictures of your child's ways in the group

PRESCHOOLERS

NEWS FOR THE PAST AND THE FUTURE

- Ask for ideas about your child's version of yesterday's news.
- Ask often about play variety:
  1. Inside your child's current favorite scene or materials
  2. Outside regular interests
- Use notes for news that needs privacy.
- Plan conferences for bigger topics.

A friend once said, "The best piece of advice I ever read about working and parenting was 'Spend fifteen minutes sitting alone somewhere between work and day care.' It was hard to do—everything in my life then was so rushed, but I was getting crazy. I forced myself to have a cup of tea by myself, *without* doing work while I drank it, every day before I picked up the kids. It made the biggest difference." At the end of the day, we're tired; we just want to get *home*. In some ways, however, thinking like this is a holdover from our childless days, when the time between work and home didn't count for anything, and home was a place you could *rest*. Children change all that. Now between work and home we need to reconnect with our children in body and spirit; we need to use, somehow, this half of our contact time with those who love and teach our children all day long. When we get home, we have to love and teach some more; rest is again postponed. If you yearn for a better end of the day but feel too hurried even to try anything new, think more about that cup of tea.

Exit Scenes Worksheet

Describe what usually happens from the time you arrive to the time you leave day care: _____

_____

_____

_____

_____

Which piece of this would you most like to change? _____

_____

What would you like to try first to improve things? _____

_____

What are teachers' ideas for smoothing out this part of leaving?

_____

_____

Have you tried one of these? _____ Do you think you tried it for a long enough time? _____

If you need some teacher backup for a new plan, what could you say?

_____

Getting News Worksheet

What do teachers usually talk to you about at the end of the day?

_____

_____

_____

Does this satisfy you? _____

Do you wish your talks were
    longer? _____
    more efficient? _____
    more pleasant? _____
    more varied? _____
What stands in the way of this wish? _____

_____

Would you like more news about
    physical patterns (eating, sleeping, etc.)? _____
    activities? _____
    moods? _____
    relations with other children? _____
    one good story? _____

How could you let teachers know about this? _____

_____

9

Changing: New Teachers, New Day Care

"Not that room, this one!" Three-year-old Nia drags her mother toward the Toddler Room. It's September; the older toddlers have just moved into the Stomper Room, a young preschool group. Nia hates this entire idea; it wasn't hers, and it's stupid: she *belongs* in the Toddler Room. Her buddy Roseanne feels pretty much the same way: the Stomper Room was a nice place to visit for a few days, but she doesn't want to *live* there. Roseanne yells, "I already *did* that room!" and, with Nia, marches firmly across the hall to the Toddler Room. Roddy, another ex-toddler, clings and cries to his mom, "Don't go!" The mothers sigh heavily in the hall. They thought morning battles were things of the past. Sure, the Stomper Room teachers and the space itself are new to the children, but all their friends are there, and it's the same basic day-care place. What's all the fuss?

MOST LITTLE CHILDREN HATE big change. They like the same book read every night and the same thing for breakfast every morning; of all their belongings, they treasure most some horrible, chewed-up, filthy thing you are embarrassed to be seen with in public. Knowing this, we aren't totally surprised when they "object" to changing rooms or centers or graduating. Still, we're often unprepared for the strength of their reactions. This chapter looks at what you can do to help children deal with big changes and offers a guide for choosing new day care when that is the change you have to make.

Dealing with Change: Finding the Questions

> Leslie's father, Rick, pops his head around the director's door: "Got a minute?" She says, "Sure, what's up?" "Well, Leslie is really a wreck these days. From Marina's leaving, I guess. It's been awful getting her out of the house this week. She doesn't want to come, and that's never been a problem before. She says she hates the new teacher—Stacey?—that Stacey just bosses them around, and she never gets to play. I'm sure she misses Marina and everything, but this seems pretty intense. She's even waking up at night, with bad dreams." "What do *you* think of Stacey?" the director asks. "I don't know. I don't really know her yet. She *seems* okay. . . ."

New Shoes Pinch When children react strongly to a change in teachers or rooms, parents often wonder, "Is it *just* the change?" They do not want to treat a child's objections as typical adjustment pains if there is a chance something else is wrong. Yes, new shoes need breaking in, but it's hard to be *sure* that's the only problem; those aren't your feet inside. If you are worrying about your child's reaction to a teacher or room change, you might arrange to spend a few hours in the room. You can see for yourself how things are going, and being with you in the new situation may help your child relax. Can it *just* be the change? Absolutely. Changing rooms and teachers uproots important relationships and disturbs a thousand small threads of identity and security.

Protest is in many ways a good sign: Good teachers add

so much pleasure and comfort to a child's life, they are bound to be missed. Some grieving, some pause before leaping into a new relationship, is natural. Sometimes young children also hold a replacement responsible for the loss: In their fairy-tale kind of thinking, new teachers can be the wicked witches who stole the *real* teachers away. Who wants to be friends with the thief?

My Old, Lucky Shirt Their special qualities of mind make change difficult for children in another way. When adults see a boy playing with trucks on a rug next to other truck-loving children, they see a movable feast: This boy could play with other trucks on other rugs next to other people and still be himself, having fun. Young children do not look at life this way. For them, the sensory details are alive—the way a certain truck fits in the hand, the shininess of another, the roughness of the rug, the way the light falls in that corner of the room, the murmur of a particular teacher's voice in the background. And the parts are connected to each other, not really movable; they go together, they are a whole, and they are part of who I am and what I do. Change the trucks, the rug, the light, the background, in any way, and the whole is lost. Sometimes when we pester children—"What's *wrong* with the place?"—they say things like "The rug smells funny." We roll our eyes: "Oh, come on!" What they mean is: My life has a way it goes, and this is *not it*.

But You Picked This Out Last Night Parents may be particularly puzzled over a strong reaction to a change when they have tried to prepare their child: "But we talked about it!" Many parents put a lot of effort into easing the pains of a big change. They talk about what is coming up; they assemble pictures of the old gang or old place; they mark off days on a calendar; they let children pick out special things to bring. All this gives children a chance to take in the idea of change at a pace they can manage and takes the edge off the shock. Most important, preparation spares children the feeling that their parents have betrayed them. Children hold parents responsible for all important events. If parents do not warn them of important events, they are outraged and sometimes frightened as well. "How could you do this!?" vibrates from small shoulders and fists. Preparing your child ahead of time spares both of you this experience. Preparation does help; it just doesn't take care of everything. Losing something familiar still brings grief.

Coming Unzipped Even when they sympathize completely with the pains of changes, parents can find some of children's reactions hard to take. Some children start following parents from room to room, never more than six inches away, lurking and waiting for a lap until the most adoring, patient, and snuggle-loving parent in the universe feels like screaming. Some children try to take over as boss; perhaps they are balancing the loss of control over something big by asserting control over littler things. They act as if adults just lost all claim to fame: "Hey. You guys masterminded this brilliant scheme to rearrange my life, right? Well, just forget the teeth-brushing. You are no longer the managers here—you're fired!" They may spit, swear, hit younger brothers and sisters, refuse food, bath, and bed. Parents wonder, "Do I *have* to put up with this? Does it really *help*?"

Buttoning Up What works to reassure children? Most parents find that bending their usual rules does not work. Extra hugs, extra praise, and stories of past changes survived may all help, but bending the rules does not. It makes sense. In general, children relax more when the fewest possible things change at the same time: a family's rules are part of the familiar world, and sticking to them feels familiar and safe. Most parents find they cannot do much about unconscious reactions (nervous eating, waking up at night, thumb-sucking, sleeve-chewing) but keeping other rules—no hitting, no spitting, no swearing in public—actually relaxes their children. It's as though children, despite their wish to fire the managers, are quietly relieved to find adults still in charge.

Your parent instincts have to guide you through all the balances children need during times of change. To everything there is a moment—a time to explain, a time to listen, a time just to hug, a time for patience, a time to put your foot down, a time to reassure, a time to forget it all and go for ice cream.

Dealing with Change: Developmental Issues
INFANTS

"We've tried everything. If she's not a lot happier soon, we'll have to give up." Will twelve-month-old Kim become the infant room's first failure? Kim's parents don't want her unhappy, but they don't want to give up. "Let's keep trying," they say. "Kim's very stubborn, about *everything*." They can't spend more time getting her used to the new day-care center—they have already used up all their sick time until the year 2000. Finally, Kim's mother has a brainstorm: Try the stroller. At home, Kim likes to climb in her stroller and watch the world from there; the stroller is the most familiar thing in her world next to her parents. It works! From her stroller throne, Kim finishes casing the infant room at her own speed and decides that she likes it after all.

Young infants react most to the general qualities of a place or caretaker; if things are quiet enough or interesting enough, appropriately full of food and sleep—fine. Older infants often react first and most strongly to familiarity. Places and people they already know get good greetings; unfamiliar territory, however beautifully balanced for their needs, is shunned. Without help, it is difficult for them to get past this reaction. Only exploring the new world or new person will make it become familiar; if they are too upset to explore and familiarize themselves, they're stuck.

Parents' physical presence usually breaks the deadlock. When parents can stay in the new situation for a while, radiating their own powerful familiarity over the entire scene, infants can "take it all in" fairly quickly—a day or two of overlap may be all they really need. Older infants might need more time. Just as three-year-olds find most nonsmelly cars basically acceptable while ten-year-olds have opinions about style, color, reputation, and the way the windows work, so a four-month-old and a twelve-month-old tune in to new experiences in very different ways. Young infants' rough blueprints for faces and things make it easier for new examples to feel "familiar." Older infants have more sharply defined images, and familiar *actions* are important to them as well—twirling a certain doll's hair, making certain faces with a particular teacher. Twelve-month-old infants often have the most difficult adjustments, perhaps partly because walking and talking work so much better in familiar territory and leave them feeling a little vulnerable anyway. See the "Things to Try" section for timing ideas with new care.

If your infant is beginning a new day-care arrangement and you cannot spend more time supplying the familiarity, you might ask an aunt, uncle, baby-sitter, or teacher to stand in for you. Familiar blankets, bears, music boxes, and strollers do help; if it's smaller than a breadbox and your baby likes it, it's probably worth a try on the first few days. Keeping things at home as familiar as possible should also help your baby relax. Big changes generally throw off eating and sleeping schedules, but you can keep feeding the same foods, playing the same games, and singing your old songs.

OLD THINGS IN NEW PLACES

You can help your infant relax into new people and places by bringing:

- Yourself or another familiar person
- Special objects from home
- Notes about routines, likes and dislikes, little games

TODDLERS

> One by one, Cassie draws children over to her "sign" during the day and explains that she will be leaving the center for a new job. This Friday will be her last day. The poster holds snapshots of all the toddlers, and five little calendar squares to show the days they have left together. They won't understand it all, but it's a good prop for beginning the tender farewells she must say this week. Most of the children seem a little numb to the news; they mainly point to their pictures: "There's me!" Cassie delays telling Derek until last; he will take her leaving to heart the most. He listens to her for ten seconds, then rips the poster down and stamps on it. Cassie tells herself, "At least I know he understands!" and puts it back. The poster takes a beating all week.

When they hear the news of a change, toddlers frequently act as though they don't have the foggiest idea what you're talking about and wouldn't care to discuss it if they did. They change the subject and invent distractions, or destroy your visual aids and stomp off. You have to keep the faith. Prepared toddlers manage new situations much more calmly than unprepared toddlers.

One of the most important goals in preparing toddlers is sparing them a sense of rejection. The real reasons behind a teacher's departure, or a change of rooms or center—money or career issues, rules about age groups—make no sense to them. All too easily they just feel personally abandoned. One message teachers can give that almost always gets a smile is, "*I* am really going to miss *you*." Feeling sinned against, toddlers may like knowing that the other party will suffer a little; emphasizing teachers' grief may get across the idea that fate, not rejection, is dividing people—and it says very clearly, "I *do* care, no matter how this looks."

Toddlers need visual props to bring abstract future

events into the present where they can be dealt with. Words like "Friday" have no meaning for toddlers, but, with repetition, a little square on the wall can come to mean "When we get here, the teacher leaves." Calendars, posters, good-bye books, cards—all help make the idea real. Toddlers may not get all the facts straight, but the activities of looking at signs, fondling pictures, painting good-bye cards, crossing off calendar days, etc., alerts them that *something* new is afoot. This is worth doing; it lets them relax the rest of the time. They learn that as long as there's no such fuss around, they don't have to worry that people and places will disappear on them. It helps if parents reinforce this kind of preparation work at home. Preschoolers tell each other, "My mommy says," "My dad told me," when they are *clinching* an argument about the absolute truth. Toddlers don't have these words yet but usually feel much the same way: Parents know the real story.

Good teachers generally organize the preparing of a child or a group for departures, but they may falter and need your support as well. Teachers who adore "their" toddlers hate to leave them and hate to see them go; the temptation to downplay departures is strong. When you know of an upcoming change, ask about what is being done. Insisting on honoring the relationships in some way sends a valuable message to both teachers and toddlers.

Parents are often surprised by their toddlers' reactions to losing teachers. Infant teachers spend so much time holding and cooing over children, parents expect that attachment to be strong. Toddler teachers look group-oriented and sound bossy in comparison. Seeing teachers only in the middle of toddlers' more intense good-byes and hellos also makes it difficult to judge the bond. Toddlers who have been with a teacher for several months, however, may see that person as a cornerstone of the universe. The arrival of language brings a new mind, so for toddlers, this year's teachers have been with them forever.

Once in a new situation, toddlers can use all the extra

familiarity you can supply: your own presence or that of another familiar adult, special love objects from home (blankets, bears, etc.), and all the tips you can pass on, just as you would for an infant. Toddlers can be comforted in a new way, too—through your Personal Parent Seal of Approval. Toddlers are tuned in to the personal element of most situations; they watch parents for cues. If you act as though a new adult is okay, worthy of confidence, toddlers relax more quickly. In an ideal transition, an old teacher not only works with the new one before leaving, but uses that time to put on a show: This new teacher is the greatest thing since sliced bread!

TODDLERS AND TEACHER CHANGE

Before a change, you can help your toddler by:

- Finding out how teachers are preparing children, encourage more activity if it seems too slight.
- Using props at home. You might use:
  1. Pictures of teachers or other children in the group, just taped to the fridge or pasted in a homemade book
  2. A one-week calendar for marking off days
  3. A homemade good-bye card
- Talking about feelings:
  1. Teachers': "She is really going to miss you."
  2. Your guesses about your child's feelings, presented as your own: "I hate leaving. I want everything to stay the same."
  3. Your own: "I'm going to miss everybody, but I'm kind of excited about the new place, too."

After a change, you can help by:

- Providing extra familiarity through your own presence, other loved people or objects and tips for teachers about routines, likes and dislikes and favorite games
- Giving your Seal of Approval to the new situation

PRESCHOOLERS

Maisie and Ned are cutting out magazine pictures for a collage with Rob, their teacher. Occasionally, one will say, "Hey! I have this at my house!," but otherwise they are working in silence. What a difference from the fall, Rob thinks; back then they were such motor-mouths you couldn't hear yourself yell. Does this quiet mean something more? These two have been looking a little grim lately. It's May; several children in the group have been talking about leaving the center, going to kindergarten. Rob asks, "So, when are you guys going to kindergarten?" "In a while," Maisie says in her best grown-up voice, "but not very soon." Rob plops his scissors down and puts on a suspicious face. "Come on, you guys. You're leaving *tomorrow*, and you're just not telling me! It's not fair!" Maisie and Ned burst out in grins and giggles. "No, no, *no*, silly! Not till after the *summer!*" Maisie says. Ned climbs up for a hug.

The more preschoolers can feel on top of a change, the easier it is for them. Giving them a manageable amount of information before a change helps them feel in charge, but they may need help remembering what they know. Preschoolers' brains—or at least their stores of information—resemble their toyboxes: lots of interesting stuff in there, but not always organized for easy retrieval. Adults' "dumb" questions work like magnets, pulling out key information. When they recover the facts, preschoolers reassure themselves *and* get to tell a grown-up what's what. Very relaxing.

Preschoolers' attachment to each other makes losing friends an important part of the grief in some changes. Their friendships help when children can move together to a new room or new school, and they help with managing worries ahead of time through play.

Preschoolers generally enjoy playing out the extreme ends of the power spectrum: They like to be babies and pup-

pies and sick, or to be invincible heroes, elegant and domi-
nant ladies, or wonderfully wicked witches. They often play
these roles much more and much more intensely after a big
change is announced. Adults tire of the constant baby talk
and the booming bossy voices, but the extra time and energy
spent in this kind of play makes sense. Preschoolers are sensitive to expectations and competition. New people and
places mean unknown standards, unknown tasks, challenges
they just might not be up to. Kitties and babies are loved
for themselves, not for achievements; heroes and witches
can ignore tasks set by others and the judgments of others;
what a relief. Preschoolers sometimes act out more pointed
fantasies about a change: A pregnant, soon-to-leave teacher,
delighted to see a group of girls building blocks together,
strolled over: "Hey, girls, that's great! What is it?" They said
"We're witches! And this is our altar. We're going to burn
you." Leave *us*, will you!?

Adults can use preschoolers' dramas to understand their
fears or to give them a kind of practice at new situations.
Teachers who have set up pretend "school" have been
astounded to see kindergarten teachers portrayed as vicious
suppressors, barking "Sit down! Be quiet!!" every five seconds. Some pretend-teachers demand impossible feats of
mind: "What is fourteen and nineteen? Quick! You tell me!"
Children in the pretend-class never tired of raising hands
and shouting "I know!" or falling off their seats just to try
out getting into trouble.

Some preschoolers worry most about what it *is* they will
be walking into—what will really happen. Their imaginations often fly to the worst possibilities. A four-year-old once
argued, complained, and wept during the entire two-hour
drive of the family's first camping trip. When they arrived
at a busy family campground, she shouted with relief: "I
didn't know it would be like this! I thought we were going
alone on a mountain with no people and no food." Parents
have reported that their children seemed relieved after visits
to future rooms or schools, or even by looking at pictures:

"He seemed confused about the idea of the baby—'I'm the baby!' he said. A friend suggested we show him a picture of families with two children, and it actually worked. He's much more relaxed."

Some children worry most about what they are supposed to *do* in the new situation: They won't know what to do; they'll just sit there; it'll be awful. Parents have had success with naming all the familiar things to do in a new situation: "They have blocks and puzzles there, and a slide, just like here—you can do those things there, too." Other parents find that a general reassurance works: "Well, I don't know exactly what you'll be doing, but we'll find out. The teacher will tell you what to do; she knows. And we can tell her what you like to do."

As with toddlers, props—calendars, good-bye books, maps, posters—are needed to ensure children's grasp on news of change. Teachers should arrange much of the preparation for changes of teachers, rooms, and graduations, but your encouragement and personal work at home make a difference. Home work is especially important with children who seem a little depressed.

Preschoolers are more likely than toddlers to lock their worries or furies inside, growing quiet or just a bit extra-grouchy on the outside. Parents should intrude on this lockup; it's too lonely for children. A three-year-old or four-year-old may feel put on the spot by the direct-question approach: "How are you feeling?" "Are you mad about something?" Simple statements like "You look kind of sad today" work more often. A child may start with a specific, thirty-minutes-ago complaint but continue to longer-term trouble if uninterrupted. You might try to guess at your child's thoughts and bring them out in the open that way. Preschoolers usually have lots of feelings packed up in what's "fair"—start there if you don't have other guesses: "Well, it's just not fair, is it? Here we are, all *used* to this place and everything, and we have to *leave!*" Telling your child a little about your own past experiences of change may bring relief, especially if you offer a variety of feelings so your child can recognize his or her own among them: "I remember when I was about to start a new school, I was so worried. . . . I didn't know where the bathroon was or anything. . . . I was mad and I couldn't stay with my old friends, and I missed them."

Even though they fight with parents over who is the boss, preschoolers *know* we know more about life. Parents are still the real heroes, and the Keepers of the Truth. Especially during times of change, you can use this role to reassure. Parents know about the limits of a change: how long that "new" feeling will last and how many things will change at once. Preschoolers don't. It's worth finding a chance to say things like "When you make a big change, things feel kind of funny for a while . . . but pretty soon you get used to them, and it *stops* feeling funny." We take this easing-with-time for granted; preschoolers don't know what to expect. Going over what will stay the same also reassures: "Well, you *will* be in a different group, but every day you'll eat breakfast at *this* table, and we'll go in our same old *red car*, and every night you'll come home to *this* house, and to *me*. . . ." With you as Keeper of the Truth, your expressions of faith can also carry real power: "I know you. I am sure that you will figure out this new place very fast. You're pretty smart!"

HELPING PRESCHOOLERS WITH CHANGE

When your preschooler faces a big change, you can try:

- All the things you would do for a toddler (see page 322)
- Playing dumb. Ask "dumb" questions about what will be happening, when, who, how, etc.
- Playing baby or heroes or school with your child, for the relief and for ideas about what they imagine
- Playing a Keeper of the Truth role, to reassure your child that:

1. Feeling out of place will not last forever.
2. Many important parts of life will be staying the same.
3. You have faith in your child: "You can do it!"

Especially when changing involves losing good teachers, parents feel the full weight of needy children. Sometimes it is nice to be needed, but not always, every second. We can understand it. Adult changes in jobs, housing, access to friends, stress us; we get cranky and sleepless; we get sick. We can imagine how big changes feel to children, to some extent. We know so much more, though, about how the world works, how time heals, how people can leave when they still love you, how new people become old people and new places get to feel like home, that new things can turn out to be even more wonderful than the old things. It is hard to remember what *not* knowing all that does to the experience of change. Some parents feel accused by their children's anxieties: "Why is she so worried! It's not like I'm *always* abandoning her on *doorsteps*!" We have to try not to take it so personally or feel too guilty when we cannot "make it all better" fast. Even doing the best we can, new worlds will take time to make child sense.

Dealing with Change: Parent-Teacher Talk

Ashley's mother Jean arrived at morning snack time with an I'm-sorry smile and a change of clothes for Ashley: "Ashley is supposed to visit a kindergarten class this morning—I completely forgot until an hour ago!" The teachers are stunned. They thought Ashley was going to spend another year in the preschool group, had even reassured her she would stay. Ashley is stunned, too. She refuses to leave, won't change clothes, won't get in her jacket; she screams and kicks when Jean tries to make her. Finally, promising lunch out and ice cream and a quick return to the center, Jean gets her out the door.

When they return to the center, Ashley is almost hysteri-
cal. She refused lunch in order to get back to her friends
quickly but now insists on going home. Jean shrugs help-
lessly to the teacher. "I can't believe this. I didn't realize
until I was driving to get her this morning that I've said *nothing* to Ashley about the whole thing—going to a new school,
leaving day care, nothing. She spent the whole visit under a
table." Ashley's teacher manages to set aside her own frustration for a minute: "This must have been hard for you." Jean's
shoulders drop. "I don't know how this happened. I guess I
was feeling so guilty, I couldn't face it. I mean, all her friends
are here, this is her world, and it's all about to end. . . ."

Guilt about the changes they are foisting on children
sometimes keeps parents—and teachers—from working together to make things easier. Parents may "forget" to relay
news of school visits or long business trips; teachers may
"forget" to warn parents or children of long vacations and
departures. Quite often, it is the parents and teachers who
are usually conscientious about such things who forget.

Picking up the distraught-child pieces of someone else's
mistake is such a pain that many people tend to stay righ-
teously angry when important changes are not handled well.
However natural, this does not get children the help they
need. Upset children may take a "Don't get mad, get even"
approach, and then *everyone* is in trouble. Parents and
teachers need "Don't get mad, get better" for their slogan,
and they can help each other do it.

Parents have helped teachers get back on track by seeing
through to a personal side. A teacher who was handling her
approaching departure poorly turned around when a parent
said, "You know, it really is *all right* for you to leave. It's
important for you, and the kids *will* be okay. But I think you
better talk to them about it. . . ." This approach has helped
with other kinds of issues: A teacher who had been fighting
"curriculum pressure" from parents was freed to try more
adventurous activities after a parent reassured her: "You

really *are* a good teacher. You give the children a *lot*, and you do it in some very beautiful ways. I don't think you need to be scared of this. You can do it; you already know how."

DON'T GET MAD, GET BETTER

When *you* are the one making some mistakes (with helping a child manage a change, or other things), you might help teachers with the situation by letting them know:

- *Why it's hard for you to be perfect right now:* "Packing up our place is going to be horrible; I haven't even found day care for him there yet. . . ."
- *What you will be doing now that you see the problem:* "We're planning to talk about it tonight, and take things a little slower for a few days. . . ."
- *That you know they are affected and appreciate their extra efforts:* "I know today will not be easy for her—or for you! I'm sorry. Good luck . . ."

When *teachers* are the ones making some mistakes, you might try letting them know that:

- *You understand why they can't always be perfect:* "I know there's a lot going on for you right now, but . . ."
- *That their efforts to set things right will make a difference:* "She's been very clingy at home, and she keeps asking who will be at day care. I'm sure she will feel better if *you* explain more about what's happening. . . ."
- *That you believe in their ability to do what's needed:* "She really will miss you, and she'll be upset when you tell her. But you have such a great way of explaining things to kids, I know it will help. And she needs to hear it from you."

Dealing with Change: Things to Try

ALL AGES

- Maximize familiarity.
- Ease into necessary changes.
- Add whatever positive pleasures you can.

INFANTS

- *Maximize familiarity:* Don't throw out the old pacifier or stroller yet; wait a week or so with introducing new foods.
- *Ease into changes:* If you know that a new schedule, new type of diapers or bottles, etc., will be required by your change, start whatever you can a little early, so it is not one more piece of unfamiliarity when the big move comes; visit new people or places ahead of time if you can.

With a new day-care place, you* might try this schedule:

Day 1. No separation. Stay with your baby the whole time. Hang back enough that the new teachers can make friends with your child, begin to get familiar.

Day 2. Trial separation. Stay with your baby most of the time but leave for one or two short periods.

Day 3. Short day. Stay a little in the morning, check in during the day, plan for an early pickup. Getting used to a new person or place is tiring for babies, even if they love the change.

- *Add Pleasures:* Because taking in new faces and places usually tires infants, you might want to set extra time aside mainly for the soothing pleasures: long bouts of holding, rocking, singing, strolling outside, gazing and talking.

TODDLERS

- *Maximize familiarity.* Keep as many of the old routines and beloved objects available as possible. Put pictures of old faces and places on the fridge, or walls, or in a book so your child can check in with them as needed.
- *Ease into changes.*
  1. If you know a new group requires children to rely more

---

*If this extra time is impossible for you, you might see if friends, relatives, or old baby-sitters can be available. With a new teacher in an old place, the old teacher can stand in for you, easing children into new faces. Paying for overlap time between new and old teachers can be expensive; not all places make it a priority. Check in with yours if a change is coming up.

on cups than bottles, you might offer a cup more at home before the change, just to develop the coordination; other things—bed and diapers, etc.—are probably best kept familiar.

2. Talk about change beforehand. (See page 322.)
   a) Find how teachers are preparing children.
   b) Use pictures of teachers or children in the group.
   c) Mark off days on a one-week calendar.
   d) Make a good-bye card or poster with your child.
3. Talk about feelings
   a) "Your teacher is really going to miss you."
   b) "I hate leaving. I want everything to stay the same."
   c) "I'm going to miss everybody, but I'm kind of excited about the new place, too."
4. Visit with the new teacher or place once or twice a week or two before the change if possible.

With a new day-care place, you (or another very familiar person) might try this schedule for a smooth transition:

Day 1. Stay the whole morning, try one or two short separations (about ten minutes); leave with your child before nap.

Day 2. One longish separation (about an hour); leave before nap.

Day 3. Nap day. Stay half an hour in the morning, plan return so you can be there when your child wakes up from nap.

Day 4. Plan regular day-care hours, maybe an early pickup, if things seem to be going well. Remember that "going well" with toddlers doesn't mean no tears and no tantrums but short ones, followed by genuine comfort and real play.

Try the Seal of Approval: look as friendly, relaxed, and confident as you can in the new situation.

• *Add Pleasures:* Changes tire toddlers, too; soothing pleasures may help most: long baths or "goof around in the sink" times, long reading or sing-and-rock sessions all cuddled up, stroller walks for some. Some toddlers may need to blow off steam before they can relax: chasing, splashing, wrestling, banging, yelling, and throwing.

Visits to old teachers or day-care friends in the first week or so of a big change are sometimes more confusing and upsetting than helpful. Visits (or phone calls) a few weeks *after* a change do seem to be relaxing and reassuring for toddlers.

PRESCHOOLERS

When your preschooler faces a big change, you can:

- *Maximize familiarity:* Keep as many home routines the same as possible, including your rules for acceptable behavior. Keep pictures of the old familiar people and places available on the wall or in albums.
- *Ease into new situations:* Visit new teachers or places one or two weeks before. Talk about the change coming up:
  1. Play dumb: Ask "dumb" questions about what will be happening, when, who, how, etc.
  2. Be Keeper of the Truth, and reassure your child that:
     a) Feeling new will not last forever
     b) Many parts of life will be staying the same
     c) You have faith in your child—"You can do it!"
  3. Mark off days on a two-week calendar
  4. Make a memories scrapbook (just three or four plain sheets of paper stapled together works fine, with one of your child's drawings, a two-sentence story about something that happened, maybe a snapshot and "good-bye" in big letters).
  5. Plan to bring a flower or a card on the last day, let your child pick it out, or make a card.
  6. Have patience with, or join, your child's playing baby or heroes or school.

With a new day-care situation, you might try this schedule:
   Day 1. Stay for an hour or so. Plan to return or check in by phone around lunchtime. Children who are completely new to day care are not usually comfortable napping the first day; but children who are "old day-care hands" may be. Plan an early pickup.

Day 2. Plan Day 2 with teachers. "Preschool" covers a large age span. Younger children may need to take things more slowly, more like the toddler suggestions above; older children may need less.

- *Add Pleasures:* Since preschoolers work hard at mastering the new rules and getting to know new children, they get very tired the first few days of a change and may best like situations where they don't bump into people or rules at all. TV is an easy situation for some, or private play—brothers and sisters may feel especially crowding right now; you might buy a new version of an old toy (so frustrations are low) to help inspire quiet play. Simple pleasures—baths, digging around for worms, and being read to—will probably fit the bill best.

As with toddlers, visits to old friends and places may be confusing in the first week or two but very welcome after that.

Deciding to Change: Finding the Questions

"I don't know if I should try to find another place for Lou," Marion tells her sister. "He had such a hard time adjusting when we started—I don't want to put either of us through that again. But he just hasn't been happy lately: He asks if it's a 'stay-home' day all the time now. There are new kids in the group—some of them are aggressive, and they *all* seem young. Maybe it's just the change and he'll get used to it and the new kids will settle down, but *maybe* he really needs a different group. . . ."

Looking for Peace of Mind Whatever circumstances force parents to consider changing day-care arrangements, the decision is rarely easy. Parents are concerned, rightly, about making their children get to know a whole new world. Young children's sense of safety, their sense of who they are and how the world works, has its roots in the predictable reactions of the adults who care for them. Change the adults, and all of those understandings become confused for a while; it is not something to do lightly, or very often. At the same time, if the predictable experiences at day care are not building the right sense of things—"I am safe," and "I am terrific"—then changing *something* becomes very, very important.

All the unhappiness that raises the question "Is this the right place?" robs many parents of sleep or any peace of mind during the day. The first thing you can do to make things easier for yourself is to embrace the process: This will not be wasted time. Reevaluating day care usually leaves parents feeling much clearer about a lot of important things; at the end, whether they decide to stay or go, they are richer. In the process of deciding, parents may talk much more with teachers and directors, spend more time with their child's group, look at their child in new ways, visit other day-care possibilities. These experiences can provide insights that make parenting easier long after the one decision is made.

Looking for Commitment Sometimes parents realize suddenly that while they have been *thinking* about a problem for a long time, they haven't actually *said* anything. They may have sent teachers unhappy looks, or, in the middle of pickup time, said, "I am very unhappy about this," but that's all. The difficulty of really talking with teachers may even be one of the problems. Those who decide to arrange a conference—with teachers, the director, or both—usually come away feeling much better. If the conference fails to satisfy them, they can feel more certain about a decision to leave, knowing that "I gave it my best shot." A long, sit-down-without-distractions talk may make leaving unnecessary. Parents on the brink of leaving have come away from their first long talk with teachers surprised: "I thought no one was paying attention—it turns out they've been thinking about it and trying different things for months! *They* thought *I* didn't care!" If you question whether your day-care center has the resources and the will to solve a problem with you, try scheduling a long conference.

Looking Inside Parents who have a general sense that things are not right rather than a specific problem to solve can sometimes find peace of mind by arranging a visit to their child's group. Joining a field trip or taking a morning off to play has brought relief: "Those teachers are terrific! I'd never really seen them in action before. When I'm here, I'm always talking or leaving." Visits cannot answer the question "What is my child like at day care?"—naturally, your child will react to your presence. You will still be able to see the way teachers work with children in general, and you can see the other children in calmer times than drop-off and pickup. You can get a feel for the everyday atmosphere. If what you see is *not* reassuring, you have the comfort of knowing that your decisions can be based on a more complete picture, not just one or two incidents or vague impressions.

Looking Around The main question for some parents is "Do I have some real options?" Checking out other day-care centers becomes the first order of business. If they see a good place, changing centers suddenly feels completely sensible; if they see the same problems in other places, staying put becomes guilt-free: They know there is no quick fix out there.

Visiting other centers may seem a drastic step if you are not completely sure what feels wrong or how important it is, but visiting often answers those questions for parents: "I'd been worrying about how rowdy this year's group is, and a little bit about ABCs and next year . . . so I looked at a few other places. What an eye-opener! Every place I saw looked small and crowded next to ours. I never appreciated how much space we have here"; "I've been thinking maybe this group is just too large for her. I found this little homey day-care center—it's even *in* a house. I think it will be perfect;

it *felt* perfect for her"; "I didn't see a single teacher really talk with children the way ours do." Whole-program comparisons may dispel all doubts or guide decisions about how hard it would be to work for change where you are.

Looking Ahead Many parents reconsider day-care arrangements mainly because their child is getting older. They hate to think about separating their child from friends, but they wonder if the same place that has provided warm and cozy care will be challenging enough to prepare a child for school. Looking at other programs *and* the program for older children in your current center may help. Parents have returned surprised: "I don't know what I was expecting—some kind of space lab for little learners, I guess—but really, there wouldn't be any point in moving. The kids at the fancy school and the kids in the Older Group were doing the exact same things!" Whatever they find, most parents feel better once they can ground their decision in slices of real life. Using reputation alone is nerve-racking. Parents may feel embarrassed about asking to see an older group's teachers at work, especially if they're feeling disloyal about even considering a change. A visit, however, provides the best information for comparison, and a center worth staying in would *rather* have you make an informed decision.

Looking For Day-care rooms are such busy places, there are always a thousand things to watch. If you are taking time from work to visit your own center or others, it may help to think about what you are looking for before you go.

Some parents focus on the children: Are they reasonably happy? Relaxed? Finding things to do? Getting along with each other most of the time? Other parents focus on teachers: Do they talk with children? Listen? Ask interesting questions? Do they catch trouble brewing before it erupts? Give help and direction in inspiring ways? Still others absorb atmosphere without particular focus: Does this feel like a playful, affectionate, interesing place? Or they use imagination: If I were a child, would I like it here?

Some parents despair of the judgment task: "I'm not an expert at this! I know computers, not education." It may help to remember that you don't have to judge a *whole* program or teachers' skills in *general;* you only have to make your best guess about what will serve your own child. A high-energy teacher might be thrilling for one child but overwhelming for another; a low-key program of activities may give many children just the room to bloom they need but leave others feeling a little at sea. You know your own child's needs best; you are the expert on your own child. If you are not feeling very expert at the moment, you might try giving yourself a little extra time to watch your child—at home, with neighbors, at day care—with your current questions in mind. It may help to talk with other adults who know your child, or to ask a good friend to listen to *you* talk, until something in your own words rings a bell.

REVIEW NOTES FOR CHOOSING NEW DAY CARE

In case your old list of questions is buried in the basement next to the *Names for Your Baby* books, here is a streamlined version of How to Check Out Day-Care Possibilities.

- Call and ask, "Do you have a opening for a —— month/year old?" (Remember asking a jillion questions only to find out there wasn't space for your child anyway?) If the answer is no, you might ask when they expect to have openings and how long the waiting list is. Have a brochure or application sent to your house for future reference in case openings are rare all over.
- Clear space to ask your questions: "Do you have a minute right now? I just have a few questions." The politeness of asking gets you better attention; the reassurance about time encourages immediate attention.

Then ask the questions that, if answered wrong, would make a personal visit pointless. For most families, the go/no-go questions include:

THINGS THAT AFFECT FAMILY LIFE IN GENERAL:

- What hours are you open?
- Are you closed only for major holidays or some whole weeks?
- How much is tuition for _____ (full/part time) for this age?
- Does tuition include lunch? Diapers?
- Where are you from _____? (If you do not know exactly where the place is, name a street or landmark you do know so you get an idea of how tough the commute might be.)

CRITICAL QUALITY CONCERNS:

- What is the teacher-child ratio in this age group? (How many adults care for how many children?)
- What is your staff turnover like? How many teachers left last year? The year before?
- What qualifications do the teachers in that room have? (What educational backgrounds, teaching experience, personal strengths?)

YOU MIGHT ALSO WANT TO ASK:

- How many children are there all together? How many teachers? (The last major national child-care study divided sizes at fifty children; it reported that centers with fifty or fewer children tended to have higher-quality care.)
- When do children move into the next-older group? (so you know if your child might be moved sooner or later than you would like)
- When can you visit? If you have some flexibility, think ahead a bit about what *kind* of time you would especially like to see. If the problems at your old center revolved around certain times (separation, lunch, playing in the yard), you might want to schedule a visit for a similar time.

Visits to a center should include both a chance to see the group and to meet with the director or teacher. If you have a choice, observe the group first. What you see should tell you whether you want to pursue things at all, and then you can pursue in the meeting anything puzzling you see in the room.

OBSERVING:

Parents and teachers often fall into talking with each other during observation times. Silent watching is a little awkward for everyone; some chat feels more natural. If you talk through the entire time, however, you will miss the chance to see the teacher in action with children. You might say, "I promised myself I'd just watch for a while, so I better get to it," if observing time begins to run out.

Some parents prefer to absorb the general feel of a place without a specific focus. If you would like to have some things to look for, here are a few key questions:

- How do teachers spend their time? Are they talking, listening, playing with children? Or tidying, talking to each other, lecturing children in large groups?
- How do teachers *sound*? Do you hear affection, sympathy, and curiosity in their voices? Enthusiasm?
- How are children spending time? Busy playing? Waiting or wandering? If a child seems alone or disconnected, does it take a teacher a long time to notice?
- Where are toys, art materials, and pictures? At child eye-level or up too high to see and touch?

MEETING WITH TEACHERS OR DIRECTORS:

Parents often ask directors and teachers:

- What does a typical day look like? What is the schedule?
- What is your sickness policy? When do you send children home?
- What is your philosophy of education?

- What is your discipline policy?
- How do parents participate?

Answers to these questions may contain important surprises; asking them is a good check against unpleasant ones. Part of the point of meeting with day-care staff, however, is to get a feel for them as people. It would help to know: Are they sympathetic to family needs? Do they seem likely to be good problem-solvers? The standard interview questions sometimes net you very standard answers. If you are still missing a sense of the people, you might:

- Describe a situation that bothered you in your old day-care place and ask, "How would you handle something like that?"
- Ask about a "hot" situation, like "How do you handle biters?" or "How do you handle gun play and doctor play?"
- Ask something personal: "How did you get into day care? What keeps you in the field?"
- Confess something personal—"We let her eat crackers in bed for dinner." "We let him stay up for *Letterman*"—along with its day-care relevance: "So we count on teachers to do table manners." "So we usually come late in the morning." It is too hard to solve problems with people who expect an antiseptic family life; you might as well find out now about basic attitudes.

Physically speaking, human beings are terrific at handling change: Our species is spread all over the globe, in friendly and inhospitable places, because we are smart and adaptable. But change is rarely easy for us emotionally. Even a change to something better at first brings waves of feeling loss, feeling lost, and feeling anxious. And even parents who do everything possible to spare children such feelings can't erase them all—they seem to be part of how people are made. At some point, we have to let it be. Our respect for the process of coming to grips with change and our arms around our chlidren's shoulders while we all get through it—these will often be the best we can give. It's a good best.

Dealing with Changes Worksheet

If your child has just been through a change of teachers, room, centers . . .

Does your child's reaction seem too prolonged or too intense to be just "the adjustment"? _____

If yes, have you had a chance to form your own opinion of the new situation? _____ What would help you feel more informed:

some visiting time in the group? _____

a conference with the teacher? _____

talking with the director? _____

talking with other parents? _____

something else? _____

If not, if your child's reactions seem like a natural grief or anger over a change but living with it is very difficult, do you think it would help to:

take a day off? _____

set clearer rules and time limits at home? _____

ask teachers and other parents for ideas? _____

talk more with your child about old times and new times? _____

Deciding to Change Worksheet

What is making you feel that you ought to change your day-care arrangement?

_____

_____

_____

How much time have you spent talking with teachers or the
director about these issues when your child was not in
the room?

_____

_____

_____

Have you visited your child's group lately? _____
   If you want to form a clearer opinion about the issues
      above, what time of day would be best to visit? _____
Do you have some other day-care options? _____
Have you visited other places? _____
What do you value most about the experience in your cur-
rent day-center center?

1. _____

2. _____

3. _____

4. _____

10

Problem-Solving: An All-Purpose, Three-Step Approach

One-week-old Christy is crying. Debbie looks at Al. "She couldn't be hungry again? I just fed her half an hour ago." Debbie offers milk anyway; Christy isn't interested. Al suggests, "Maybe she's wet. I'll see." The new diaper quiets Christy for two minutes. When she starts crying again, Debbie shoulders her and starts humming, and dancing little shuffling steps with her around the kitchen. This, too, works, on and off. "It's a little hot in here," Al says. "We could try taking her sweater off." He eases Christy out of the tiny sweater and takes a turn dancing. Christy snuggles, fusses, then drops her head and snores.

PARENTS INVENT A GOOD basic problem-solving technique in the first week:

1. Ask, "What could this be?"
2. Ask, "What else could we try?"
3. Try something and see.

This is a good approach to problems, even when children get more complicated. When you can get teachers to *join* you in taking all *three* steps, you have the best chance of getting the best care for your child.

Other chapters offer ideas about what the "this" could be for particular problems and lists of specific things to try. Chapter 10 looks at the process of solving problems with teachers in general.

Step 1: Ask: "What Could This Be?"

- "You have to give Shelley more time to eat."
- "I don't want Dean to play with Steven this week. Just keep them away from each other."
- "Rachel is bored here. Could you please get some new puzzles or something?"

versus

- "Shelley's lunchbox has been coming home almost untouched this week . . . any idea what's up?"
- "Dean is complaining that Steven is mean to him. What do you think is going on with those two?"
- "Rachel says she's 'bored.' I'm not sure what she really means. What do you think?"

Ignition Problems Many small and large difficulties at day care never get good attention because parents and teachers start off on the wrong foot. Adults sink potential teamwork by failing to say anything at all, by waiting to say something until they are colossally upset, or by letting their concerns pop out as demands.

Some parents would die before they marched into their child's classroom with an order: "Do this." Acutely aware that teachers' patience and affection get their children through the day, they hesitate to bring up problems, afraid to jeopardize goodwill by sounding critical. When you feel this way, you might think about what would make you more comfortable: setting up a special time to talk? Checking with other teachers or other parents? Airing the issue with a good friend first? Talking about something you *like* at day care first? Simply phrasing your concern in question form may be all you need to do. If you describe what you see that bothers you and ask "What could this be?" you are consulting a teacher, not criticizing. Raising issues this way is not only "safe" but nourishes parent-teacher relationships. Teachers, like most people, take "What do you think?" questions as showing regard for their judgment and expertise.

Stalling Out Some parents raise issues readily but so roughly that good teamwork is sabotaged from the beginning. Working and parenting stretches many, many parents to the limits of their capacity to cope. They have to try to function at work at the same speed as other adults who got much more sleep the night before and started their days quietly with newspaper and coffee instead of feeding and dressing and dropping off children. They try to function at home as though they were not exhausted by a full day's work. They have to fit into too few hours all the laundry, grocery shopping, bill paying, and house upkeep that working adults without children barely manage, and still make time to feel like good parents. They need to count on day care going smoothly; there is too much else to cope with. When problems do crop up at day care, desperate parents want them fixed *fast*. In the interest of speed, or in exhausted frustration, they try to hand teachers a solution: "Do this." They may mean to be helpful and efficient, but that good intention does not usually come across.

If the teachers on the receiving end of "Do this" have complete confidence in parents' respect for their work, understand the stresses that banish tact from daily talk, and basically agree with the suggestions, then some versions of "Do this" may work. That's a big "if."

Fancy Cars, Plain Cars Most day-care teachers make much less money than parents do; day-care teaching does not repay in prestige and respect what it lacks in financial reward. Many teachers are still looking forward to marriage and children of their own. In the current American system of values, all this adds up to social superiority for parents, and teachers are naturally sensitive to being treated as inferiors. When parents skip right to "Try this," teachers are less likely to feel helped than bossed around.

"Try this," even if politely phrased, implies that your teacher a) has not noticed or thought about the problem at all b) would not have anything interesting to contribute to solving it anyway c) does not have other tasks of such importance or complexity that you need to consult before adding other tasks d) is so bland personally and so blank professionally that he or she would not even *have* an opinion about your solution or not one you care to hear. In short, that your teacher is brainless, lazy, and worthless. Oops! That's not what you *meant* to say!

When parents describe a problem and ask "What could this be?," they send a positive message: "I value your opinion." Even if your teacher is not perfect, and even if all you hope for is cooperation with your original idea, this is the right first message to send. Teachers who are not busy warding off sudden demands, or fighting off irritation at being bossed around, can think *with* you and *for* you much more efficiently. Skipping to "Try this" is not a shortcut.

Raising your issue in this open way may be the only self-conscious move you need to make in problem-solving. Teachers may take things from there in satisfying ways. If they don't, though, stay with it. Often a first reaction is not quite right, but—if you don't let it stop the process—the second or third *is*.

The Fast Fixes When parents first present a problem, teachers may offer specific information, broad reassurance, a reluctant "I'll try," or a surprise suggestion of their own. All four of these first reactions can bring problem-solving to a stop. If you stop because you are *satisfied*, great! If not, here are some ways to get things going again.

Specific Information Sometimes specific information teachers have lays a problem to rest. One of the benefits of describing what you see—like Shelley's untouched lunch, Dean's report of Steven's meanness, or Rachel's "I'm bored"—is that it points teachers to the relevant information right away. They can cut to the chase on the problem parents have described: "Oh, we've been letting children share lunch food this week. Shelley's been eating Mary Jo's cheese sandwiches; no one was interested in her tuna fish—that's why her lunchbox was full!" or "Dean wants to play with Steven so badly. He's crushed when Steven doesn't want to play with him. Steven's usually pretty nice about it, but Dean's feelings get hurt anyway," or "Rachel might really be a little bored. We do need new things. Three of us are going shopping on Wednesday."

If your teacher offers specific information like this, and you feel relieved—"Oh! *That's* it!"—then good, you are done problem-solving for now. If you are not relieved, stay with it, or come back the next day. Sometimes parents do not realize that they have a larger concern until teachers respond to a smaller one: *After this* week's lunch problem is explained, *then* they realize that this week was just the tip of the iceberg—actually breakfast, lunch, and dinner haven't been worth two cents in weeks.

When a small-problem fast fix leaves you in a cloud of dust, still holding your problem, find some way of telling teachers, "Slow down." If you see immediately *what* the whole problem is, you can redescribe it: "I just thought of it, but you know, lunch has been a problem for weeks," or "Really, it isn't just this one child he's having trouble with." If you see mainly that there *is* a larger problem, you can describe your feeling: "Somehow I just don't think that's the whole story. *Something* isn't working with [eating or making friends or finding things to do, etc.]—I'm not sure what. Would you keep an eye on it for a few days and let me know how things look to you?"

You almost always get the best help by asking teachers to look at things for a few days and get back to you. Children give adults so many things to watch and to think about; teachers' first reactions may not be up-to-date on your particular question. Taking a few days to look updates their information and gives them time to consider your view outside the pressure of the moment.

Broad Reassurance Teachers sometimes respond with general reassurance to parent questions: "Shelley is just not a big eater—some children aren't." "Children get over these things. Dean will forget all about it by tonight, I'm sure," "I think Rachel was just tired yesterday," or "Oh, it's the age—they all do it."

Sometimes this is exactly what parents want to know. Their main questions are: "Is this normal? Will it go away by itself? Do I need to worry?" Teachers have a lot of this kind of information. They see a lot of children the same age. Offering reassurance first comes naturally.

If teachers say, "You don't have to worry, it's normal" and you feel relieved, good, you're done. If you don't feel relieved, think more about what you want. You might explain, "Even if it's typical for this age, there have to be better and worse ways of handling it: I need ideas," or "Well, even if she does grow out of it, she is upset right now, and I want to help her out with this."

You might also ask "What do *you* do?" or "What *would* you do?" Teachers work all day with things that children grow out of or get over, they have ideas about the best way to deal with children's troubles, especially the normal ones. Again, asking teachers to watch your child for a few days with your question in mind may generate the most help. Teachers cannot always put in words quickly all the ways they work on typical issues; they may need time to watch themselves as well: "What *do* I do that helps, exactly? Have I been doing this lately? Consistently?" Getting teachers thinking about your problem is the main goal in this phase of problem-solving; the extra days are worth the wait.

Reluctant Agreement If you raise your concerns in "What could this be?" form, you may never encounter this type of trouble in problem-solving. When parents hand teachers a "Try this" suggestion out of the blue, however, or if teachers are working in a highly critical environment, teachers sometimes half agree to a proposal, mainly to keep the peace. They are not agreeing to think with parents about a problem or to take that problem seriously. Shelley's teachers might say, "Well, we really don't have much leeway with lunch. A lot of kids are tired by then and need to start napping pretty soon—*but* we'll do what we can." Parents leave disgruntled. They know that the "try" will not be high quality—but what can they do?

Parents' suggestions do sometimes catch teachers so completely by surprise that the first reaction, if not a brush-off, is at least mystified. If a teacher has spent weeks thinking, How can I get Shelley to nap? and What sets up those days that Shelley and Jenny spend fighting constantly?, then a question about lunch will grind the gears: Food? That's not even on the list! Parents and teachers come to problems from different worlds; they are bound to have different worry lists. Husbands and wives disagree about what to take seriously, and their experiences are more similar than parents' and teachers'.

If you sense that your teacher's reluctant agreement is benign—"Seems a little nutty to me, but it won't hurt to try it"—you might let things stand and see what happens. Sometimes just living with a parent's idea in mind for a while changes a teacher's perspective; sometimes giving something even a halfhearted try actually works. If you sense that your teacher really *disagrees* that there *is* a problem but is not telling you—and you want a high-quality try for your idea—find a way to say "Slow down" and get the disagreement out on the table. You might say, "You look like this doesn't make sense to you—why?" or "Do *you* think I should be worried about this? . . . Why not?"

Parents *don't* always diagnose problems perfectly. We have so much history with our children and so little exposure to other children the same age, it is difficult to know what to worry about and what we can let go. A sickly infancy gets eating on the top of our priority list, and it stays there *forever*. A neighbor's child sits calmly through a hundred-year dinner and reads before it talks; suddenly we're failures. Last night's bedtime battles were so horrible, we're not thinking about developmental patterns, family dynamics, or educational objectives; we're thinking about leaving town until the children are ten. Just being parents doesn't mean we know everything there is to know about children in general, or even about our own child during this slice of time. When you can find out why a teacher disagrees about a problem, you may find a perspective that restores your own perspective.

Teachers don't always diagnose problems perfectly either. What looks like a case for counseling can turn out to be an ear infection or vice versa; what might be a typical two's tantrum for most children may be prevented by slipping a cracker to ours. We know what the doctor said; we know how our children *usually* behave when they're hungry, tired, confused, about to get sick; we know what they said about day care during bath time last night. Just being teachers doesn't mean they know everything there is know about our child.

Teachers know how children of a certain age usually eat, play, fight, and entertain themselves in a group. Parents know how long their Shelleys take to eat at home, how Deans play with brothers and neighbors, what Rachels find fascinating on Saturdays. Getting disagreements about what is a problem on the table helps bring out missing information from both sides. Your teacher's comments may convince you, or point the way to a basic misunderstanding; you have to hear more before you can tell.

The Surprise Suggestion When parents bring up a concern, teachers may supply a "fast fix" in the form of a surprise suggestion. To "Shelley doesn't seem to be eating; she's kind of a dawdler, I know," a teacher might say, "You know, there's plenty of time at lunch, but she gets *started* late—she takes *forever* to wash her hands! We could hurry her a little at the sink—I bet that would help." Shelley's parents may suspect that this alone will not be enough but feel sufficiently "heard" to let things be at this point. Who knows? Maybe it will be enough. If your teachers clearly understand your goal and have a sensible-sounding idea for something to try first, you can be done problem-solving until you see whether this idea works.

The "first step" of asking "What could this be?" may serve as the *whole* problem-solving process if teachers' immediate information or ideas satisfy you. By asking in an open-ended way, you have invited the idea you needed. Relax; see how things go for a while. Wonderfully useful problem-solving may take all of ten seconds. You don't have to nail down the absolutely best idea or absolutely perfect course of action before you rest—or move—on any problem: "Sounds good" is enough. You can always come back.

If nothing in a teacher's first reaction feels useful, then asking "What could this be?" and sticking to it through false stopping places is a real "first step." You aren't finished, but by getting teachers to wonder *with* you, you are well begun. When adults get past their automatic ideas, they can begin to think in a new way about a child. That waking up to a child's situation often works wonders all by itself.

STEP 1. "WHAT COULD THIS BE?"

- Describe what bothers you; ask teachers for ideas: "Jonah bit two kids yesterday! What do you think could be wrong?"
- Notice whether you feel relieved by teachers' first responses:

"He seems to be starting a new tooth," or "Toddlers bite! It's par for the course," or "We'll try to stay closer to him, but . . ." or "We could let him have his pacifier—something *else* to bite on!"

- If you are *not* relieved, reinvite your teacher to think *with* you.
  1. When a specific "answer" shows you that your problem is bigger than you first described, you can:
     a) Describe the bigger situation: "Right, but you know, he bites when he's not teething, too. . . ."
     b) Describe your sense that something larger is at work: "But other children teethe and don't bite. . . ."
  2. When "It's normal" is not your main concern, you can:
     a) Explain your goal: "But I want to help him learn some other way—any other way!—of handling things," or
     b) Ask: "What would *you* do?" "How do *you* handle this?"
  3. When you sense disagreement or a brush-off in "We'll try," you can:
     a) Get disagreement out on the table: "You don't think this is a problem—why?"
     b) Describe more clearly how this issue affects you: "I'm really worried that no one will want to play with him, or you'll end up asking us to leave. . . ."
  4. When the surprise suggestion doesn't make sense to you, go to Step 2

Step 2: Ask, "What Else Could We Try?"

Sometimes even a brief talk produces ideas that make sense to try: "We'll send in some cheese sandwiches for Shelley"—"And we'll try cheerleading lunch a little more"; "We'll try having one of the children over on a Saturday"—"And we'll keep an eye on Dean and Steven and see if we can tell where things break down"; "I'll talk to Rachel some more about how she's feeling"—"We were going to start a doctor's office corner in the dress-up area, maybe Rachel would like to help set that up." When acceptable ideas come quickly, the main task is remembering to check back in a week or two to review how the plan is working.

Sometimes, however, no one can think of anything to try right away—"Who knows? Maybe it's the full moon"—or the answer to "What could this be?" seems to lead nowhere: "It's probably a reaction to the new baby," or the only idea proposed so far is unacceptable to teachers or parents: "Let's hang a pacifier around his neck and tell him to bite on that." Keep the faith; there's *always* another possibility out there. Children's complexity makes pinning down simple answers difficult, but it has this advantage: You can usually get at a problem in several different ways. If you make a commitment to generating a *list* of possibilities and then choosing one to try, you can usually get past blocks at this phase.

You can try brainstorming, working with the words used to label the problem, and focusing in on or out from the problem as described. Two options you might consider first, however, are "Wait and see" and "Try it anyway."

The "Wait and See" Option Not every talk with teachers has to generate active new plans. Often it's too soon to make a special plan; just keeping eyes open for some of the things you've talked about makes more sense than plunging ahead. Sometimes a talk turns up some piece of news you hadn't considered before—the dead fish brought in as part of a special project sparked speculation about death for *all* the children, not just yours, or teachers suggest that moving your ailing mother-in-law into the house might be affecting your child after all. You could go home and plan a talk about these things, but you're not sure you want to just yet, or what to say.

After a talk with teachers, parents sometimes feel finished with a problem for the time being. They may have discovered in the talk that teachers have been thinking hard about the very thing that concerns them, or that teachers see their child wisely and affectionately—and this just takes care of things. Sometimes giving teachers all their information and insights feels like enough to parents; it's fine for teachers to take it from there. If no brilliant or obviously useful idea has emerged from your first talk with teachers, you might pause a minute and ask yourself, "Is this enough for right now? Could we all use some time to live with where we've come so far?"

While you wait and see, your child's talk or behavior may change in a way that makes an issue clearer, or it may just "go away." Children often do get better magically after parents and teachers talk. While you wait, teachers may try out ideas they rejected at first; second thoughts are often more flexible.

Even if your plan is "Wait and see," it's a good idea to say that out loud and make a date to check back with teachers. When no one sums up a discussion, people may leave confused and frustrated, or leave assuming that they have agreed to a plan when no such thing happened. With teachers, pick a time when you will *stop* waiting and make a decision about what, if anything, comes next.

The Try-It-Anyway Option When you have tossed around an idea or two with teachers but haven't found an idea you *like*, you might pick the least difficult idea and try it anyway. Trying out an idea has several things to recommend it:

- It's an excellent method of discovering things. Who knows— it might work, or some unexpected part of putting the idea into practice might help.
- It clears the way for other ideas. If this idea gets a good try and fails, then everyone can see it and put it aside finally.
- It may inspire deeper or more flexible thinking all around. When adults set up a new situation, they watch children in new ways and take in new information; unexpected insights may dawn.

Sometimes you're in for the long haul with children's troubles—some natural shortage of patience and balance in a child or a whole situation requires steady creative effort. Amazingly often, however, one small, unlikely sounding action makes an enormous difference. One serious talk about death, a five-minute-a-day attack on sleep timing, a week of putting on a cheerful face at good-byes, moving lunch up fifteen minutes—the effects of trial changes like these have surprised both parents and teachers. You don't always have to have the "real" problem by the throat or the most efficient scheme when you plan a new action. One change can affect several other things, which in turn improve life—a small pebble making wide circles in the pond. Since nothing works for all children all the time, and you can't tell what will help until you try, it's often worth taking even a half-likely idea and giving it a go.

Coming Up with New Ideas If you're not comfortable with ideas for things to try proposed so far and don't want to have "Wait and see" as your current plan, you might propose to teachers, "Let's both think more about this and get back to each other." You might set up a conference time for you both to think more *together*, or set aside some private thinking time for yourself. Alone, or with teachers, you could try some brainstorming, relabeling the problem or changing your focus on a problem.

BRAINSTORMING

"Christine's ten-thirty bedtime is ruining our lives. . . . Maybe she's just one of these people who doesn't need sleep. . . . We should just accept it. . . . Maybe we could train her to stay in her room. . . . If we got more consistent about bedtime routines? . . . That humidifier noise seems to help; we could run it all the time. . . . We could start bedtime earlier. . . . Does she sleep too late at day care?—maybe they could wake her up earlier. . . . If Harry put her to bed all the time, it would probably work better—I get so sucked in. . . . I wonder if that bedtime cocoa wakes her up a little. . . . What did we do for daylight saving time?"

Brainstorming means turning off the critic within you for a while and writing down every idea that pops into your mind. No censorship. However impractical, irrelevant, or silly an idea might seem, write it down. You can cross off the not-so-hot ones later. You can do this alone or with teachers, taking care not to judge ideas until they've stopped coming altogether.

You may think, If I had the answer already in my brain, I wouldn't be in this fix in the first place! You'd be surprised. Time after time, when parents set up special conferences with teachers, parents have the great ideas. They already know exactly what makes sense to try—they just needed the uninterrupted time to explore the issue. Parents' lives get so pressured they literally can't hear themselves think. Brainstorming is listening time.

Working with Words Looking at the individual words of a problem, and thinking of other words you could use to describe it, sometimes opens up new ways to tackle a problem.

"Honey, I'm home!" Joy wants to arrive home at night to wonderful smells of an almost-ready dinner and an aproned person who will give her a big hug. But no. Arnold won't get home for another hour; she has to start dinner right away, or the children will eat each other. They're low on patience before dinner; they whine and fight, they want her help with everything, they're underfoot. This is not exactly Joy's shining hour either. The workday's weariness, the grating sound of tired children's voices, and the constant dread of tripping over a child with a hot pot or large knife in her hands keeps her nerves raw. She's tried brainstorming: all that comes to mind is yelling louder and lashing them to heavy furniture in separate rooms until dinner's ready. Her children need *dinner* and *attention* at the same time; it just can't be done.

Joy might scare up other options by working with "dinner" or "attention." *Food* has to get into children soon, but does it have to be hot dinner? What else could it be? How about "snack"—enough to last until another adult arrives, or everyone's mood improves, or even to *count* for dinner? A good-sized cold snack might take five minutes to produce; then she could sit down, rest, or play a little.

Or Joy could work with "attention": "What do I mean by 'needing my attention'? What else could it be?" When children act like they need "attention," sometimes they need a twenty-minute snuggle, and sometimes they just need two to three minutes of total listening. She could try the short version. Sometimes "companionship" will do. Joy could try setting that up in a way that would be realistic for her: "I'd like to be with you, but I need you *at* the kitchen table, not walking around. You can draw or use Legos. What'll it be today?" That might work with the oldest, but her toddler? All her little one likes to do is pull all the pans out of the cabinet one by one. Still, that would keep her sitting in one place and not whining; they'd be together—it might be worth it.

Any time you have trouble coming up with things to try, you can pick one of the words you are using to describe the problem and relabel it. Some words are too broad to inspire good ideas; some wave red flags that block ideas. Usually, the closer parents and teachers can get to pure descriptions of what they see or hear, the more ideas arise. If a parent says, "She needs more challenging activities," teachers may feel accused of running a boring program and focus on defending their program or counterattack by accusing parents of "pushing" a child. If a parent says, "She never seems really busy with an activity when I come" or "She looks lost to me, kind of wandering around" or "She *says* she's bored," teachers may be freer to focus directly on that child and to see the parents as *concerned* more than critical.

You probably have good guesses about what words would be red flags for your teachers; these you might think about beforehand. You may discover that some of the words teachers use get in *your* way. Most workplaces have a jargon, some in-house ways of describing things. Try to replace those words, too, so you are freer: "You keep saying he's 'having a hard time'—what do you mean exactly? What does he *do*?"

Perhaps you have heard this saying: "Every fact is already theory." For parents and teachers, every description of children is already theory. One adult seeing a child moving from toy to toy might say, "He's puttering happily"; another might say, "He's not interested in anything." You can't really get rid of all "theory" when you redescribe a problem, but by trying out different words, you can hear the new ideas each word suggests. And among those ideas might come one that rings a bell.

Changing the Focus Brainstorming and word work depend on thinking that's loose and specific at the same time—a tap-dancing frame of mind. If you are upset about a problem, your thoughts may be stomping around in heavy boots instead. More methodical approaches to searching out things to try may work better. You might try sharpening your focus on a particular situation and exploring it from several angles *or* pulling your mental camera back and broadening your focus to include more of aspects of life or more of the things you, your teachers, or your child care about right now.

Focusing In If you want to explore your first idea more deeply, turn it into a question: "Shelley needs more time to eat—or does she? How does Shelley use time when she eats?" Then think about how you could answer the question. The ways of finding out are the first things to try. With Shelley's problem, for example:

- Teachers could *try* starting Shelley eating earlier or letting her stay longer than other children at the table and see what happens.
- Teachers could *watch* more closely—how does Shelley use

time when she eats at day care? Does she eat slowly and steadily, or does she eat 80 percent of her final total in the first five minutes and then pick at her food? Does she take twenty minutes to settle down but then really eat?

• Parents could watch more closely at home: How does Shelley use time when she eats at home? Does she eat a lot at the beginning, the end, some food all through the time? When does Shelley usually say she's done? Ten minutes? Forty? never?

Looking at the best and the worst of a problem provides another way of focusing into a first idea. You can ask who, what, where, and when questions about the best and the worst instances of a problem: When does Shelley eat the most (or the least)? What time of day—snacks or official mealtimes? Who's with her, and what is this person doing right? Is it noisy or quiet? Does she like distraction—TV, music, people? What foods? Both parents and teachers could just watch for a while and collect impressions or pick one thing to change—timing, company, noise level—and see what happens.

If Dean's parents focused *in*, making the problem a question, it becomes: Is Steven mean to Dean? How could we find out?

• Teachers could watch the two boys more closely, see what goes wrong or right when they play.
• Parents could pick a quiet moment and ask Dean about his own ideas: What is it like playing with Steven? What would help?
• Parents and teachers could keep ears open: What else does Dean think about Steven? About the other children? How does Dean use the word "mean" at other times?

Or they could look at best and worst times:

• Teachers could look at when, where, and over what Dean and Steven fight—first thing in the morning? Only when they're tired? Just with the blocks indoors? Just outside with the two blue shovels? And when do they get along best? Teachers could just watch and see, or

- Teachers could try changing one thing: send Dean and Steven to different activity groups in the morning, or hide the stupid shovels in the staff bathroom for a few days—does it make a difference?

Focusing Out You can also generate ideas for tackling a problem by focusing out. Pull back from the specific situation you've been thinking about and consider:

- Other parts of life—biology, psychology, and sociology. Look at what's going on in the whole child, the whole day-care group, or the whole family, *or*
- Other goals. What is your child looking for in the situation you want to change? What are teachers trying to accomplish in those situations? Which part of this problem bothers you the most?

Other Parts of Life If Rachel's father was focusing *out* on her "bored at day-care" problem, he could try these different lenses:

- *Biology:* Clearly, Rachel is feeling low. Is there anything going around? Has she been getting enough sleep lately? He could check health and nap news at day care and keep closer track of her weekend sleep for a while.
- *Development:* What is Rachel working on these days? When she was just learning to walk, she didn't want to do anything but cruise around. She'd just had a birthday and had tons of new toys; she totally ignored them. What could be taking up all her energy now? Rachel is always bored when they go to friends' houses where there are no other children, or the other children just don't interest her. Does she have real friends at day care now?
- *Day-care Group:* What's going on there? Did that teacher she liked who was pregnant leave already? Could missing her be part of the "bored" report? Maybe that teacher used to

do something special with Rachel that she's really missing, and someone else could do it.

- *Family:* What's up at home? Anything different? Could she be too worried about something to enjoy anything else? Zeke might watch Rachel's face more closely for a while, maybe strike up a few general conversations. . . .

If you were focusing out in this way, you could review the possibilities lightly until something rings a bell, or check in with teachers more methodically until you have all the information at hand. You might both agree to "wait and see" with some of the new questions in mind.

Other Goals Your child's own special purposes may have more to do with a problem than any outside circumstance. General concerns that you have, or your teachers have, about your child may be affecting clear thinking about this particular problem. Pulling back for a minute to consider the various goals you all have can throw new light on a problem. If the parents in these working examples reviewed goals that might affect their concerns, they could consider:

- *Children's Goals:* Does Shelley care most about eating, about avoiding the postlunch singing session, about striking up friendship at the lunch table? Does Dean want peace, victory, friendship, just more turns with the blue shovels? Does Rachel want a day off, a good buddy, something new?
- *Teacher's Goals:* Do teachers want Shelley to "get with the program" and eat when everyone else does? Do they see her as *always* wanting more time with everything, a way out of routines? Do teachers want Dean to learn how to play with Steven, how to leave him alone, how to find other play partners, to develop flexibility in general? Do teachers want Rachel to learn how to entertain herself, take more advantage of what is available, take initiative in choosing or suggesting activities?
- *Parents' Goals:* Shelley's parents might care most about lunch-eating itself, her total weight, her general health, or

her general comfort at day care—is not-eating a *sign* of something? Dean's parents might want him to be popular, have a good friend, feel loved in general, come home complaint-free. Rachel's parents might want her to be more pleased with life in general, more ready for school, more independent.

Each of these other lenses on life or goals can suggest a number of things to watch for or try out. List-makers beware. The point of all this is not to explore every question worth asking or every action worth trying, but to create enough choice for action that agreement on a first plan can come more easily.

Pushing Through into Action Some of the ideas that pop up during brainstorming, working with words, or refocusing may be unappealing or apparently useless. If an idea seems important, you can explore it more by asking "What does this mean we would *do*?" Suppose it occurs to you or teachers that *your* tense mood is making your child tense. Especially if you're tense because of something you have no power to change—work pressure, your own parent's health—you might hate this idea: "Even if that *is* true, there's nothing I can do about it—it doesn't help." If exploring this idea *really* just involves a short talk with your child about why you are grouchy right now, then you might see a live option—couldn't hurt, might help, why not? Teachers might hate the idea that their curriculum is inadequate in any way. If exploring the idea that "more structured activities would help" *really* means making a special point of inviting a child to join the art-table group and the dance circle at music time, then okay.

Asking "What does this mean we could *do*?" can also help when talk about a problem brings parents and teachers to a big, unmovable cause: a child's age, a new baby, the approach of kindergarten. When they stay committed to trying *something*, parents and teachers can find ways to help—ways to reassure, to subtract other stresses, to blow off steam in ways adults can accept.

Respect for Appeal After you've created a list of possibilities, how do you decide what to try? Most of the ideas in the air probably have *some* merit; every idea has costs—in time, energy, discomfort, disruption of the usual. With separation pains, for example, you might be choosing between trying a cheerful face, speedy exit, and trying to start the adjustment process from scratch or rescheduling family life so you can arrive earlier and see if a quieter start makes a difference. You have to weigh emotional wear and tear, lost work and sleep hours, and teachers' views of what makes sense. How do you pick?

If any one idea *appeals* to you, pick that to try first. The appeal of an idea often represents the final result of a brain's computing all the difficulty factors of all the plans it has considered. Is it *sure* to be the *best* idea? No, but the best idea will be the one that works, and no one will know what works until it happens. Since you're exploring in the dark anyway, you may as well start with the plan that makes the most overall sense to you. If it works, great; if it doesn't, now you are free to try other ideas without feeling like a chump for ignoring your instincts.

Teachers will probably have an idea that appeals most to them, too. If you hate it, say so and look for a second-best favorite. If it seems at least harmless to you, you might want to support the idea. The chance to try out a favorite idea creates energy and clears mental space to try other ideas later.

STEP 2: ASK, "WHAT ELSE COULD WE TRY?"

- Make a list of possibilities, alone or with teachers:
  1. "Wait and see."
  2. Try out a sort-of-sensible idea.
  3. Brainstorm.

4. Relabel the words you use to describe a problem.
5. Focus *in* on your original idea:
   a) Make it a question: Ask, "How could we know?"
   b) Look at the best and worst times for the behavior; ask when, where, who, what questions about the best and worst times.
6. Focus *out* from your original idea to consider:
   a) More life: What's going on in the whole child, whole day-care group, whole family?
   b) More goals: What is your *child* looking for in the situation you want to change? *Teachers?* What part of it do *you* care most about?

- Keep important options open. Before rejecting an idea, ask, "What does this mean we would *do?*" and consider practical actions.
- Pick the idea that appeals to you or to teachers most right now.
- Go to Step 3.

Step 3: Try Something and See

In the best problem-solving sessions, two aspects of a good plan are understood from the outset: 1) *Both* parents and teachers will do *something,* 2) Plans need a *time* limit, after which people check back with each other: Is this helping? Some great ideas for helping children have fallen by the wayside because they were one-sided or indefinite about time. If you are zeroing in on a "final" plan with teachers, consider these parts of planning before you stop.

Team Effort In any brainstorming session, you and teachers are likely to have lots of ideas for what the other side can do. Seeing first how the *other* person can change seems to be a natural human turn of mind. When no one feels attacked, this seeing what the other side can do may serve to multiply ideas: "I see all these things you can do" times two. Pooling ideas, parents and teachers can compensate for each other's natural blind spots.

Some topics lend themselves to lopsided lists of action options. Teachers might have a hundred ideas for things you could try at bedtime and not see anything they could do to help with sleep; you might have a hundred ideas for teachers to try when your child has a fighting-biting day but not see what you could do. The sense of teamwork is so important to sustaining energy, however, it is worth every effort to find something. Any change, at home or day care, will require special effort; both parents and teachers have plenty to do already. Knowing that you will *both* be struggling to get organized and up for a special effort is motivating: It feels fair, and the sense of teamwork provides a little energy of its own.

Planning for both parents and teachers to do something also helps get thinking past questions of guilt or blame. If a plan calls only for *you* to be doing something different, doesn't that mean the problem is all yours? That if you had been doing this something all along, everything would be fine? No one likes this.

So, before you finish planning, consider finding:

SOMETHING FOR EVERYONE

You and teachers might plan that:

- Neither of you will take a new action, but both of you will watch and think for a while.
- One of you will try something new; the other one will watch for signs of improvement and report back.
- Each of you will try out different ideas in your different worlds.
- One of you will work mainly on reassuring this child and subtracting stress while the other focuses on coaching some new behavior.

Time Limits Setting a definite time limit for trying out a plan usually leaves parents and teachers freer to try each other's favorite ideas, makes it easier for them to change a plan, and keeps energy focused on the plan. One to two weeks usually works well. You want to leave room for the accidents of life—sick children or teachers, rainy days, forgetting—but not leave enough time that the problem sinks back into one of a million things you wish were different and will get to someday.

Suppose you think your child's leaving-the-center tantrums reflect separation issues, day-care scheduling, and family life in complex ways, but teachers want you to try a short, firm exit routine first. This strikes you as quite beside the point, but they're hot for the plan, and you see a little spark of appeal in the notion that something so simple could help. If the new exit routine is the *last word* on your problem, you may not want to try it at all; after all, you do not really believe in it. If you are only agreeing to try it for a week or two, you can relax and see what happens: If it works, great; if it doesn't, you can all get back to other ideas. Teachers who might firmly resist the idea of changing their end-of-day activity schedule for all children for all time might well agree to a *week* of quiet time at five o'clock, just to see.

Time limits make it easier to change a plan. When parents and teachers have spent time and energy coming up with a plan, they both need to feel that it had a chance to work. No one should decide, alone, that something is not working after only one day. On the other hand, some ideas turn out to be more difficult to put into action than expected, like "Wake her up earlier." And some plans, once tried, clearly need a different twist to get good results. Some plans do not work. If you have a date with each other to see how things are going, you can change your approach without sabotaging the teamwork you have done so far *or* getting stuck.

Without a time limit, energy to work on a problem for a child tends to peter out, get swamped in the rest of life. Both parents and teachers juggle complex agendas. Some weeks get so bad we don't even remember to take the trash out; other weeks, getting the trash out seems to be the only thing we do accomplish—everything else is too complicated. If you and teachers know this is a special, short-term effort to find out what works, it's much easier to keep going.

STEP 3: TRY SOMETHING AND SEE

When you are finishing up a plan with teachers, consider planning:

- Something for each of you to do
- An exact date for evaluating this plan: Is it working?

Some problem-solving efforts are short and sweet, others long, hard work, with both teachers and parents struggling to keep open minds, see each other's points of view, and come up with acceptable strategies. Like so many parts of parenting, and teaching, working together can be exhausting and enriching at the very same time.

If yours is long, remember you can keep coming back to:

1. "What could this be?"
2. "What else could we try?"
3. Try something and see.

When we fed and changed and danced our newborns around and they finally stopped crying, at least half the time it wasn't clear exactly what worked in the end. Was it the last thing we tried? The last *two* things we tried, *together*? Did the feeding we tried first just take a while to take effect? Was our angel just fussing on the way to sleep the whole time and nothing we actually did really helped? Then, and always perhaps, we have to be content with *results*. We do our best because there's nothing else to do, and our hopeful, honest efforts are our best and brightest love.

Day-Care Information and Referral Services*

Alaska CCR&R Alliance
P.O. Box 103394
Anchorage. AK 99510
907-279-5024

Alabama Assoc. for CCR&R
  Agencies
309 North 23rd Street
Birmingham, AL 35203
205-252-1991

Arkansas Child Care Resource Center
C/oUALR Downtown, 5 Statehouse
  Plaza
Little Rock, AR 72201
501-375-3690

Tucson Association for Child Care,
  Inc.
1030 N. Alvernon Way
Tucson, AZ 85711
602-881-8940

CA CCR&R Network
111 New Montgomery, 7th Fl.
San Francisco, CA 94105
415-882-0234

CO Office of R&R Agencies
7853 East Arapahoe Road, Suite
  3300
Englewood, CO 80112
303-290-9088

United Way of Connecticut/
  Infoline
900 Asylum Ave.
Hartford, CT 06105
203-249-6850

Wash. Child Development Council
2121 Decatur Place NW
Washington, DC 20008
202-387-0002

*The authors wish to thank the National Association of Child Care Resource and
Referral Agencies for providing this list.

Child Care Connection
3411 Silverside Rd, Baynard #100
Wilmington, DE 19810
302-479-1660

Florida Children's Forum
1282 Paul Russell Road
Tallahassee, FL 32301
904-656-2272

Child Care Solutions/Save the
 Children
1340 Spring St. NW, Suite 200
Atlanta, GA 30306
404-885-1578

Patch
810 A Vineyard Blvd
Honolulu, HI 96734
808-842-3874

IA Commission on Child., Youth &
 Fam.
DHS/Hoover State Office Building
Des Moines, IA 50319
515-281-3974

Polk County Child Care Resource
 Center
1200 University, Suite F
Des Moines, IA 50314
515-286-2004

Child Care Connections
P.O. Box 6756
Boise, ID 83707
208-343-5437

IL CCR&R System
100 W. Randolph, Suite 6-206
Chicago, IL 60601
312-814-5524

Indiana Association for CCR&R
4460 Guion Road
Indianapolis, IN 46254
317-299-2750

Child Care Association of Wichita
1069 Parklane Office Park
Wichita, KS 67218
316-682-1853

Child Care Council of KY
880 Sparta Court, #100
Lexington, KY 40504
606-254-9176

Child Care Information, Inc.
P.O. Box 45212, D.223
Baton Rouge, LA 70895
504-293-8523

Executive Office for Health &
 Human Serv.
1 Ashburton Place, 11th Floor
Boston, MA 02108
617-727-8900

Maryland Child Care Resource
 Network
608 Water Street
Baltimore, MD 21202
301-752-7588

Maine Assocc. of CCR&R Agencies
P.O. Box 280 WHCA
Milbridge, ME 04658
207-546-7544

Michigan 4C Association
2875 Northwind Drive, #200
East Lansing, MI 48823
517-351-4171

NACCRRA
2116 Campus Drive SE
Rochester, MN 55904
507-287-2220

Minnesota CCR&R Network
2116 Campus Drive SE
Rochester, MN 55904
507-287-2497

Heart of America Family Services
3217 Broadway #500
Kansas City, MO 64111
816-753-5280

Office for Children & Youth
421 W. Pascagoula St.
Jackson, MS 39203
601-949-2054

Early Childhood Project
Montana State University
Bozeman, MT 59717
406-994-5005

President, NC R&R Network
P.O. Box 250
Webster, NC 28788
704-586-4039

North Carolina CCR&R Network
700 Kenilworth Avenue
Charlotte, NC 28204
704-376-6697

ND Early Childhood Training
    Center
P.O. Box 5057, ND State Univ.
Fargo, ND 58105
701-237-8289

Midwest Child Care Assoc.
5015 Dodge #2
Omaha, NE 68132
402-551-2379

NH Assoc. of CCR&R Agencies
99 Hanover Street, P.O. Box 448
Manchester, NH 03105
603-668-1920

Statewide Clearinghouse/Div of
    Y&F Services
Capitol Center/50 E. State St./CN
    717
Trenton, NJ 08625
609-292-8408

Las Cruces CCR&R
Box 30001, Dept 3CUR
Las Cruces, NM 88003
505-646-1165

Child Care Resource Council
1090 S. Rock Boulevard
Reno, NV 89502
702-785-4200

NY State Child Care Coordinating
    Council
237 Bradford Street
Albany, NY 12206
518-463-8663

Ohio CCR&R Association
92 Jefferson Avenue
Columbus, OH 43215
614-224-0222

Child Care Resource Center
1430 South Boulder
Tulsa, OK 74119
918-585-5551

CCR&R of Linn & Benton
Counties
6500 SW Pacific Boulevard
Albany, OR 97321
503-967-6501

Child Care Choices Resource &
Referral
1233 Locust Street, 3rd Fl.
Philadelphia, PA 19107
215-985-3355

Options for Working Parents
30 Exchange Terrace, Commerce
Center
Providence, RI 02903
401-272-7510

SC CCR&R Network/Co Yes, Inc.
2129 Santee Avenue
Columbia, SC 29205
803-254-9263

SDSU/DHD, Child & Family
Studies
Box 2218
Brookings, SD 57007
605-688-5730

TN CCR&R Services
TN DHS/Day Care Services
Nashville, TN 37248-9600
615-741-3312

TACCRRA, C/o Austin Families
3307 Northland Drive, #460
Austin, TX 78731
512-440-8555

Office of Child Care
324 S. State Street, #500
Salt Lake City, UT 84111
801-538-8695

VA Child Care Resource & Referral
Network
3701 Pender Drive
Fairfax, VA 22030
703-218-3730

VACCRRA
Early Childhood Prgms/Vermont
College
Montpelier, VT 05602
802-828-8771

WA State CCR&R Network
917 Pacific Ave., #301
Tacoma, WA 98402-4421
206-383-1735

WI C.C. Improvement Project
202 S. Dakota Ave, Box 369
Hayward, WI 54843
715-634-3905

Central Child Care of WV, Inc.
P.O. Box 5340
Charleston, WV 25361
304-340-3667

Care Connections, Inc.
125 College Drive/CC Family Res.
Ctr.
Casper, WY 82601
307-472-5535

INDEX